Handbook
for
Mortals

Handbook
for
Mortals

Guidance for People Facing
Serious Illness

JOANNE LYNN, MD,
JOAN HARROLD, MD,
AND
THE CENTER TO IMPROVE CARE OF THE DYING

OXFORD
UNIVERSITY PRESS

OXFORD
UNIVERSITY PRESS

Oxford   New York

Athens   Auckland   Bangkok   Bogotá   Buenos Aires
Cape Town   Chennai   Dar es Salaam   Delhi   Florence   Hong Kong   Istanbul
Karachi   Kolkata   Kuala Lumpur   Madrid   Melbourne   Mexico City   Mumbai
Nairobi   Paris   São Paulo   Shanghai   Singapore   Taipei   Tokyo   Toronto   Warsaw

and associated companies in

Berlin   Ibadan

Copyright © 1999 by Joanne Lynn

First published by Oxford University Press, Inc., 1999

First issued as an Oxford University Press paperback, 2001
198 Madison Avenue, New York, New York 10016

Oxford is a registered trademark of Oxford University Press

Library of Congress Cataloging-in-Publication Data
Handbook for mortals : guidance for people facing serious illness /
Center to Improve Care of the Dying, George Washington University.
p. cm.
Includes bibliographical references.
ISBN 13   978-0-19-511662-5; 978-0-19-514601-1 (pbk.)
ISBN   0-19-511662-3; 0-19-514601-8 (pbk.)
1. Death. 2. Terminally ill. 3. Terminal care. I. Center to
Improve Care of the Dying.
R726.8.H353   1999
362.1'75—dc21
98-33691

5 7 9 10 8 6
Printed in the United States of America
on acid-free paper

❧ *About this Book* ❧

Proceeds from the sale of this book will support Americans for Better Care of the Dying (ABCD), a national charitable organization dedicated to public education and policy advocacy on behalf of improving care for the last phase of life. Updates and reference information will readily be found on our World Wide Web site: www.abcd-caring.org. In addition, ABCD has a newsletter, *The Exchange,* which is available by subscription or on the Web. We encourage all readers to join ABCD in order to raise a voice in policymaking for good care at the end of life (4125 Albemarle St., NW, Washington, DC 20016).

We are grateful for the opportunity to serve you, the reader who is confronting serious illness in some way. We will appreciate your responses and suggestions, your stories, and the resources you find useful. Please send them by mail (RAND Center to Improve Care of the Dying, 1200 S. Hayes St., Arlington, VA 22202-5050) or on the Web at www.medicaring.org. We will be pleased to hear from you.

This book owes its existence to The Alfred P. Sloan Foundation of New York City, which gave a generous grant to enable us to work on it over two years. In addition, the Retirement Research Foundation of Chicago, Illinois, has supported development of a companion book for health care managers and policymakers, and that simultaneous work has enriched this book. The Oxford University Press and especially our editor, Joan Bossert, have been most supportive, flexible, and efficient. We also note with gratitude the guidance and commitment of James Levine, our literary agent.

Many people have been involved in writing and editing this book. Among us, we have cared for thousands of people who died. And among us also are some well-known scholars in art, literature, and health care research.

This book has resulted from an extraordinary collaboration of professional caregivers, scholars, and ordinary citizens. About two hundred people have provided comments and suggestions. We are grateful for all their help.

THE CORE TEAM

Joanne Lynn, M.D., Center to Improve Care of the Dying

Joan Harrold, M.D., Hospice of Lancaster County (Lancaster, PA)

Sandra Bertman, Ph.D., University of Massachusetts Medical Center (Worcester, MA)

Gwen Glesmann, Pensaré Design Group, Ltd.

Janice Lynch, Americans for Better Care of the Dying

Joel D. Smith, Center to Improve Care of the Dying

Mary Ellen Vehlow, Pensaré Design Group, Ltd.

DRAFTING AND RESEARCH, AT GEORGE WASHINGTON UNIVERSITY

Anne Boling	Brian Green	Katalin Roth
Felicia Cohn	Phil Higgins	Mary Ryan
Rachel Duvack	Jill Joseph	Phyllis Schmitz
Janet Heald Forlini	Nicole Makosky	Lisa Spear
Nancy Freeborne	Kristen McNiff	Anne Wilkinson

DRAFTING AND RESEARCH CONTRIBUTORS

Rev. Timothy Cherry, St. Michaels, MD

Rabbi Kenneth L. Cohen, Bethesda, MD

Rev. Hank Dunn, Hospice of Northern Virginia

Marcia Levetown, M.D., Galveston, TX

Cherri McKenzie, McLean, VA

Casey Milne, Resource Connectors, Ltd., Portland, OR

Debra Nichols, M.D., Pittsburgh, PA

Christina Puchalski, M.D.

LITERARY AND VISUAL IMAGES

Lois LaCivita Nixon, Ph.D., Tampa, FL

Marilyn Field, Ph.D., Washington, DC

Michael Lipson, Ph.D., New York, NY

Ronald Carson, Ph.D., Galveston, TX

Digital CLAY Interactive, Ltd.

FOCUS GROUPS

Barbara Kreling, George Washington University Medical Center

Kyle Anne Kenney, George Washington University Medical Center

Susan W. Morris, Global Exchange, Bethesda, MD

WRITTEN CRITIQUES AND SUGGESTIONS

Janet Abrahm	Harlan Krumholz	Marian Secundy
Robert Arnold	Kristie Martin	Mary Sklencar
Marshall Chin	Kyle Nash	Harold Sox
Ann Armstrong-Dailey	Michael Rich	William Steinberg
Myron Ebersole	Walter Robinson	James Tulsky
Ted Greenwood	Ellen Rooney	Marilyn Webb
Patti Homan	Diane Rule	Doron Weber
Hana Janjigian	Greg Sachs	

❧ Contents ❧

by Rosalynn Carter

Our ancestors were all too familiar with serious illness and death. Few lived to old age, and death often came suddenly from infections or accidents. Today, science and modern medical technology have given us different expectations. Most of us can look forward to being healthy longer and we have hope for defeating some of humankind's most terrible diseases. We are fortunate to live in an age of tremendous advances in medicine, but when the inevitable end of life nears, sadly we usually die of slowly worsening illness, and treatment is complex and intimidating. Often, people who suffer and those who care about them do not know what to expect or how to act.

The time near death can be fruitful and worthwhile, but it is a time when we especially need others. I know from our own family experiences that we can all find meaning by caring for one another, even when illness is severe. I always remember my mother's care of my father and grandfather, memories that have continued to inspire me and my family when we have had to face serious illness and death. And when Jimmy's mother, Miss Lillian, was ill, helping her brought our far-flung family together in ways that still endure.

We often put off what is important in life, and it sometimes takes the shadow of death to make us appreciate that love, family, and faith are things that really matter. The *Handbook for Mortals* will help you explore some deep truths about relationships and values — things we often take for granted until death threatens. If you have not been able to find the words for your anguish, you will find them here. If you feel overwhelmed, you will find support and resources. If you are grieving, you will find comfort. Here too, you will find many moving and insightful stories and poems.

The *Handbook*'s practical information will make you confident in your ability to deal with specific issues like pain management and decision making. It will give you information and strategies that let you control the things you can manage — and help you recognize those things that you just have to endure. The *Handbook* gives you facts. Just as every new parent welcomes a friendly and authoritative book on baby care, everyone facing serious illness and death will welcome this guide to end-of-life care.

Serious illness and dying now occupy many years of the lives of most of us. Unfortunately, these years are often a time of fear and suffering. But they need not be. Here is the help you need to be sure that these years, whether your own or those of someone you love, are full and rewarding. Here, too, is help to make sure that the time near death is peaceful and comforted. This, indeed, is the *Handbook* that all of us mortals need.

"I've always looked to the Bible for stories to guide my life. But no one in the Bible lived like this!"

Eighty-two-year-old blind woman
with heart and lung failure

Just two generations ago, serious illness and death were everyday occurrences, experienced within the family and the community. Most people died quickly after an accident or after the onset of serious disease. Now, most people have little experience of dying, and serious illness commonly lingers for years before causing death. Social arrangements and understandings have not yet caught up. Our health care system, our housing, our family expectations, our newspapers and television stories, and even our language have yet to make sense of our new situation. This book aims to help you as you face serious illness or death, your own or that of someone dear to you.

When Elisabeth Kübler-Ross tried to interview "dying" hospital patients a few decades ago, she was told that there were none. In the time since then, our society has learned to label some people as "dying," but we use the term mainly for those who are clearly in their last weeks or hours. In fact, "the dying" are spoken about as if they were a separate kind of person. The usual "non-dying" person seems to have an indistinct horizon, of no importance right now. Only when people have the label "dying" or "terminally ill" are they expected to do certain things — to say goodbye, make peace with God, take strong drugs for pain, or enroll in hospice. We use the label "dying" as if it were a distinctive characteristic, with no ambiguous cases. We talk as if being a "dying person" is as obvious and uncontroversial a fact as it is to be a man or a woman.

> *It is difficult*
> *to get the news from poems*
> *yet men die miserably every day*
> *for lack*
> *of what is found there.*
> *Hear me out*
> *for I too am concerned*
> *and every man*
> *who wants to die at peace in his bed*
> *besides.*
>
> WILLIAM CARLOS WILLIAMS
> *from "Asphodel, That Greeny Flower"*

This use of language is becoming increasingly misleading. Most of us will accumulate serious illnesses toward the end of life. One person might have a heart attack at age 60, then years of slowly progressive heart failure, eventually complicated by diabetes or hypertension, and finally a stroke and its complications, with death at age 80. Another might live with breast cancer for two decades, or be slowly disabled by Alzheimer's dementia. No longer is it clear who is "dying." Most of us will live with serious chronic disease, slowly worsening for years before eventually causing death. And the timing of death will often be quite unpredictable, even when the illness is far advanced.

Perhaps the classification as "dying" is really more like height than it is like gender. Some people are clearly "tall" or "short," but many are "in between." Likewise, some people are clearly "dying" or "fully healthy," but many are "in between." In fact, most of us will die without having a period when we could readily be recognized as "dying" or "terminally ill." The new reality is that most of us will die from complications of a serious chronic illness that we will "live with" for years. There will only occasionally be a transition from that "living with" to a time of "dying from."

Thus, this book aims to help those who face serious chronic illness that eventually will cause death. Getting to live for years with serious illness is a major triumph of modern medicine and social arrangements. Our society has largely managed to change what were once causes of rapid death into problems that one can live with for years. Consider how heart disease and cancer once killed quickly and now usually allow survival for years. However, we are not yet good at providing the right kinds of care or the most helpful conversation.

In writing this book, we have tried to give you enough straightforward information to help you to feel that you are familiar with the issues. We have focused on giving you the words and questions that will help you give voice to the issues that trouble you. Perhaps most important, we have tried to share the images of the human spirit that you will find helpful when dealing with serious illness and death. You will find poetry, stories, vignettes, and quotes that are favorites of the writers and their patients and families. We have combined a practical guide to the issues with words that speak to the spirit.

This book is a good start, or a good companion to other materials you may have used. But many will find that they want more. Our last chapter helps you to find additional resources to address a wide variety of needs.

Our first chapters give a general framework about how one might think about the last phase of life. Modern people often deal with life as if its end were sometime far in the hazy future, of no relevance to this day. And we often discard any idea that the time while seriously ill or dying might be especially valuable time. Our first few chapters here will illuminate a very different way of thinking about the end of life — that it is often a phase that lasts years, that the time of death is ordinarily quite unpredictable, and that this last phase of life offers unique opportunities for growth of the spirit, of the family, and of the community. It is not a time of life to be discarded as worthless!

Later chapters guide you through practical issues such as effective conversations with your doctor, making plans ahead, handling symptoms, stopping treatments, and dealing with the time just around death. You will find that most of the book is just as useful for people living with advanced stages of any one of a variety of illnesses. One chapter supplements this generally useful information by giving some specific information and advice about some common illnesses. We also discuss the issues around suicide, both because many patients think about suicide and because it is such a widely discussed topic in the news.

We have included two chapters on less common ways to die: the dying of children and dying suddenly. It is a mercy that these once usual ways to die now have become uncommon.

In general, we address this book to the person who is facing serious illness. So the word "you" refers to the person whom the doctor calls the "patient." We have found that family members and professional caregivers can easily make the translation to their situation. We expect that people may start reading this book for topics of special interest to them, and that they will skip around and skim. The headings, boxes, and quotes will help the reader find what is important at the time. In addition, there is a helpful index at the back.

> *Death is different from what*
>
> *anyone knows, and luckier.*
>
> WALT WHITMAN
> *from "Song of Myself"*

Living with serious illness

Trust yourself. You know more than you think you do.

BENJAMIN SPOCK
from Baby and Child Care

Over and over, as they realize that they are facing serious and incurable illness, patients and their families ask doctors and nurses: "What do I do now?" And they really mean that they do not see what comes next, or how a good person should act. Most Americans get a serious illness at a time when they have very little practical understanding of how to live with illness and very few images of how things could — or should — turn out. The first thing to remember is that you really *do* know more than you might think. You *can* trust yourself. Before in your life, you have made decisions, faced challenges, and found what is important to you. You will now, too. This book aims to help. It builds on a quiet conviction that people, even very sick or very burdened people, have remarkable spirits, inspiring creativity, the capacity to cope with illness and mortality, and the wonderfully human drive to find one's own life's meaning.

Living with a serious illness can open up an unexpected variety of new possibilities. You may feel freed to do those things you put off until *someday*, even though your activities are likely to be restricted by the unpredictability of good days and bad days. You may open yourself up to the love and care of those around you, even as you try not to overburden others with your needs. You may find deep meaning in the smallest of things, even if you question your faith in the greater powers of the universe. And you may glimpse, even face squarely, the certainty of earthly mortality, no matter your beliefs about what is to come. You will often confront the uncertainty of not knowing exactly when death will come.

Serious illness can be a time of growth, meaning, and healing. Many people find, often to their surprise, that the period of time when life may be short is a very precious time. When you are dying, you should do those things you have always wanted to do. Families and friends may want to hear your old stories one more time and to share with you their hopes and dreams and worries. They may look to you for blessings and advice. You and those you love will often look to a shared faith in God, nature, and each other to make some sense of life and death.

You may find the opportunity to heal relationships that were torn apart long ago. This time will not always be comfortable or rewarding. But coming to terms with the limits of life is a job that each thinking person has to undertake, and it can be so meaningful to you and to those around you.

You may not think that you have taken on a "search for meaning," but that is one thing that most people actually do when dying (though you may say it differently). For some, the search reassures them that they have lived life as well as they could. Others find new insights and make commitments to live the rest of life a little differently. Either way, your loved ones will remember your experience and use it to shape their own when their time comes. This book is full of people, stories, ideas, and advice to help you find more of this kind of meaningfulness in the final phase of your life.

Dying, though, can also be a time of frustration, fear, poor communication, and physical discomfort. This book offers stories and practical advice on getting through these problems, too. You will find help for managing pain and other symptoms, talking with your doctor, and wrestling with some of the difficult issues that may arise.

Death

I have seen come on
slowly as rust
sand

or suddenly as when
someone leaving
a room

finds the doorknob
come loose in his hand

JOHN STONE
from In All This Rain

THINGS TO DO WHEN TIME MAY BE SHORT

Very important

- *Spend time with people who are important to you.*
- *Create a legacy for those who care about you — letters, a tape recording, or a video can be a special gift for your children and grandchildren.*
- *Call or visit an old friend and tell your story to those who will live on.*
- *Accept some compliments and gratitude (don't make people wait until the funeral!).*
- *Forgive yourself, and seek to make things right within your own faith.*
- *Say "I love you," "I'm sorry," "forgive me," and "I forgive you."*
- *Right old wrongs.*
- *Take a "last trip" or two (and do it again if time allows).*
- *Make time for spiritual issues and struggles.*
- *Say goodbye (or "until we meet again").*
- *Eventually, be at peace with the end to come, and the uncertainty of when you will die.*

Important

- *Make plans so that care and treatment will be as close as possible to what you want (see Chapter 10).*
- *Specifically decide about resuscitation, hospitalization, and, if it might be important, artificial feeding (see Chapter 11).*
- *Choose someone to make decisions for you if you are too sick to make them for yourself.*
- *Write a will and help pass along obligations for your job and finances.*

DRAWN IN PART FROM THE WORK OF IRA BYOCK, M.D.

Am I "living with" or "dying of"?

If dying is to be meaningful, spiritual, or even just peaceful, it does seem that we should know when we are dying. But how will we know? In the movies, the last minutes are so obvious. Whether hero or villain, profound words and meaningful glances are offered before the eyes close and the last breath escapes from the lips. But if we wait for the obvious in real life, we are likely to miss the chance for any meaningful expressions. Most of us will die of chronic diseases such as heart disease, cancer, stroke, or dementia. Many will live with these diseases for years before dying of them. Often, your diseases and their related symptoms are treated with medicines and procedures and all the while you feel mostly well. So when do you stop seeing yourself as "living with" these diseases and start seeing yourself as "dying of" them?

Those things that people do while dying have a special meaning. Deathbed requests and confessions are particularly powerful. Getting one's affairs in order, taking one last trip, and saying goodbyes are especially poignant — and to be encouraged even if very difficult to do. Yet, if you don't know when you are "dying," you might miss the opportunity to do these things. And doing them before you are really "dying" often might seem out of place, premature, even irresponsible!

How we die — then and now

A hundred years ago, most adults died quickly from infections or accidents. While there was not a lot of time for goodbyes, there was little doubt when good-byes were appropriate. Now, death may not come quickly, but the time for good-byes can pass by without notice. Often, missing this opportunity doesn't arise from the lack of time, but from lack of certainty that the time has come.

You probably expect that you will either die suddenly (from a heart attack, for example), or be sicker and sicker before you die. With chronic diseases, however, you often experience episodes of being really sick; but, in between them, you get along rather well. During any of the really sick times, you could be sick enough to die. But, if you survive several of these episodes, then you hardly know when you are really going to die. Is dying going to be just the end of those really sick times? Will it be something altogether different? If you die during one of the otherwise "well" times, your loved ones may feel as if you died "suddenly," even though you had been "living with" your disease for a long time.

Think of people that you have known who were said to be "dying." Nearly everyone knows someone who has outlived the time a doctor said was left. And nearly everyone knows of someone who believed she had much more

"Am I dead yet?" he asked the nurse.

"No," she replied. He thought for a moment,

"How will I know?"

PATIENT WITH A SERIOUS ILLNESS

time left than she did. Just as we have no guarantee that we can sense when time is short, our doctors cannot be certain either. In fact, there is no medical definition of what "dying" or "terminal" is, or how soon before death someone should be considered "dying."

In one study of nearly 10,000 seriously ill patients in hospitals across the United States, nearly half of the patients died within six months of their enrollment in the study. But the best medical predictions by statistical methods and by the patients' doctors had trouble sorting out who was "dying." One week before death, the average patient still had a 40% chance of living six months. Even on the day before death, the average patient still had a 10% chance of living six months.

Many people have a tough time saying that someone is "dying" if he has a 10% chance of living. (It is so easy to ignore the 90% chance of "not living.") And 40% is not even close to being sure that someone will not recover. In general, we do not want to say that someone is "dying" until we are almost 100% certain of death within days or weeks. To do so sounds like giving up on someone we love. We might even feel guilty if we give up on them and they get better.

This leaves us in an awkward position. If we want the end of our lives to be a time of growth, meaning, or even merely comfort, how do we know when that time is? How can you "say goodbye" if you might be living longer? If you have been pursuing all kinds of treatments and technology that are uncomfortable, how do you know when to let go of these and make different plans for how to spend the end of your life? An old saying calls on us to "live every day as if it were your last." While this may sound rather grim, especially if you are seriously ill, there is some useful wisdom here. Even though you usually will not know exactly when you will die, you can try to be prepared. Planning is good, and practice may make it better. But the planning and practice have to be realistic about just how uncertain the timing of death is likely to be.

Practice, practice, practice

If you have episodes of being really quite sick, you and your loved ones might look on them as rehearsals. If you had died, what would have been left undone? What goodbyes would have not been said? What business would have been left unfinished? What goals would not have been met?

You do not have to begin every day anxiously wondering if it will be your last. But you can take advantage of these rehearsals to be sure that you have done what you most want to do in the time you have.

"I had my nails done — how do you like them?"

HOSPICE PATIENT
who died one hour later

Planning for uncertainty

If no one can know when you will die, that doesn't really get you "off the hook" in dealing with dying. It just makes the job a little complicated. What would you do if you knew that Uncle Sam was going to draft you with only a few days' warning, but you did not know when the notice would come? You would probably try to visit family and friends, wrap up business affairs, and write some long letters to leave for loved ones in case you were gone long or were killed. You might also find that you were especially sensitive to the joys of nature and family, and especially eager to heal old rifts and wrongs.

You can approach your uncertainty about dying in this way. No one can tell you whether this Thanksgiving is going to be your last one, but why not make it special anyway! Just because you might live another few years is no excuse not to tape record (or video record) some stories and advice for grandchildren or great-grandchildren. Everyone has some rift among family or friends. Just having a serious illness is enough reason to re-establish contact. You don't have to wait until later.

"Wait," you may say, "it will be embarrassing to do all this and then hang on! What if I find my brother and we hug and forgive one another, and then I am still here, weighing on him some years later? Or what if I tell my granddaughter that my mother's silver pin is hers when I die, but I don't die?"

Surely you will see that it is really fine to have re-connected as a family, and that the heirlooms can wait. The profound sense of impropriety that demands that you die "on a schedule" and do things in just the right order is really silly. Do things that are important just because you are a mortal who will die someday, and you know it. You probably cannot "put your affairs in order" and then live for a few years without some affairs becoming disorderly. Don't worry. It is a job that can be redone periodically.

When you have a serious illness, you may not be able to count on having a short time when you are "dying," when friends and family can gather and say farewells. You may have to take the opportunities that you create to do what is important, despite the uncertainty. It is, after all, better to have told people that you love them more than once than to have missed the opportunity while waiting for just the right moment.

WORDS TO TRY
FOR FAMILIES, TALKING WITH A SICK PERSON

When you think you want to say:	Try this instead:
Dad, you are going to be just fine.	*Dad, are there some things that worry you?*
Don't talk like that! You can beat this!	*It must be hard to come to terms with all this.*
I can't see how anyone can help.	*We will be there for you, always.*
I just can't talk about this.	*I am feeling a little overwhelmed right now. Can we take this up later tonight?*
What do the doctors know? You might live forever.	*Do you think the doctors are right? How does it seem to you?*
Please don't give up. I need you here.	*I need you here. I will miss you terribly. But we will get through somehow.*
There has to be something more to do.	*Let's be sure we get the best of medical treatments, but let's be together when we have done all we can.*
Don't be glum. You will get well.	*It must be hard. Can I just sit with you for a while?*

The power of words

The words we use to talk about death and dying make it very hard to talk about death and dying at all. If you try to plan for your death, you are urged not to "talk that way." If you are considering stopping certain treatments, you may be urged not to "give up" or "give in." If you are thinking about whether or not to have resuscitation attempted when your heart stops, you may be asked why you don't want "everything done." In our society, it is more common to hear that someone "is gone," "was lost," "did not make it," "passed away," or "expired" than that he or she "died."

From all of these phrases, it is obvious that death is to be avoided. Even talking about death may be discouraged, as if the words themselves might somehow steal life and bring death quicker. Words will not hurry death, but they can cast a different light on life.

If you are told not to "talk that way" when you are making plans or saying goodbyes, remember that you are making plans to ease your own worries. Your plans or actions help you to live well, not to die more quickly. If you decide not to use a particular treatment and others tell you not to "give up" or "give in," suggest that you are only giving up one course of action so that you can follow another one. And if someone asks if you want "everything done," remind them that you want "everything done" to treat pain, minimize suffering for you and your family, and enjoy life to its fullest. Certain high-tech interventions may not be worthwhile if they get in the way of a full life and a peaceful death.

> Late in her life, when we fell in love,
> I'd take her out from the nursing home
> for a chaser and two bourbons. She'd crack
> a joke sharp as a tin lid
> hot from the teeth of the can opener,
> and cackle her crack-corn laugh. Next to her
> wit, she prided herself on her hair,
> snowy and abundant. She would lift it up
> at the nape of the neck, there in the bar,
> and under the white, under the salt-and-
> pepper, she'd show me her true color,
> the color it was when she was a bride:
> like her sex in the smoky light she would show me
> the pure black.

SHARON OLDS
"Grandmother Love Poem"

Not particularly interested in dying . . .

People who are said to be dying often have a lot of living left to do. There is no requirement that someone with a serious illness spend all of his time thinking about how close he may be to death. While some observers may think that this behavior is some kind of "denial," it is actually healthy to continue to focus on living.

Feel free to refuse to dwell on the nearness of death. You do not have to talk about dying when you have better things to do. After all, most of us have many roles to fill, dying or not. As husbands and wives, parents and children, friends and colleagues, we work, play, love, and argue. Your interests and concerns do not suddenly disappear because you are ill. In fact, some issues may become much more important to get resolved while you still can. Often you will appreciate ordinary daily life and its stresses and troubles even more.

Patients with fatal illnesses may pursue medical treatments for a variety of conditions. These conditions may or may not be related to their fatal diseases. As one nurse noted, even hospice patients are not particularly interested in dying early from a treatable problem. Prolonging living can go hand-in-hand with accepting the inevitability of dying.

Decisions to make, decisions to wait

In the course of a serious illness, there may be lots of possible pathways. Treatment choices — tube feeding, cardiopulmonary resuscitation, diagnostic tests — are likely to be brought up for discussion and decisions. It is good to have a general idea as to how and when you might want them used (see Chapters 10 and 11). But almost none of the decisions that you might be called on to make have to be made immediately. Sometimes you need time, experience, and advice to

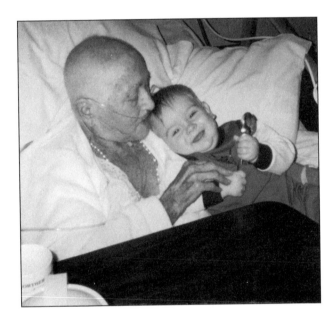

choose a plan. Sometimes the actual plan is less important than what you talk about and who you talk with when you discuss alternatives. And usually, the important decisions are not the ones that show up in legal forms.

Decisions to make include choosing who should speak for you if you are too sick to let the doctor know what you want for yourself. If there is a particular hospital you always want to go to, or a set of procedures you already know that you would never undergo, let everyone around know about it. But there is often no hurry to make a lot of other decisions. Issues need decisions only if and when certain situations arise, and often only then will you know all the details that could influence your choice.

No one "right way"

There is no one right way to live with or die of a serious illness. It may be more important that you are comfortable with your situation and your choices than that you have made perfect plans. Most of the really wonderful things that happen as time gets short could not have been planned. If you have a trustworthy nurse or doctor and some folks who will miss you, all the rest can be quite manageable.

Enduring and changing

"Everyday something else changes. It's like being on a roller coaster, sometimes riding high and then all of a sudden, plunging to the bottom. Knowing I'm going to die is not as terrifying as the getting there and wondering how it will happen."

NORMA
facing serious illness

It is little wonder that those who are dying, like Norma, dread the process of dying as much as death itself. At the same time, most people who are dying are struck by the wonder of life. "For everything there is a season, and a time for every matter under heaven: a time to be born, and a time to die" (Ecclesiastes 3:1-2). You may want to fight your illness, or deny it, or do both at different times. You may feel as though you should accept your illness without complaining and simply take whatever comes your way. Or you may be too confused, frightened, or sick to deal with anything for awhile. This chapter offers ideas on how to cope, and describes how other people came to terms with their illnesses and their fears.

From the time that you learn that you have an illness which is expected to take your life some day, the rhythm of your life changes. When you face a serious illness, you also face the challenges and worries that go along with it. You, and those who care for you, may wonder how you will cope with your life as it changes in so many ways.

Hold fast to time! Guard it, watch over it, every hour, every minute! Unregarded, it slips away, like a lizard, smooth, slippery, faithless. . . . Hold every moment sacred. Give each clarity and meaning, each the weight of your awareness, each its true and due fulfillment.

THOMAS MANN

from The Magic Mountain

One place to start — and, from there, to cope — is to look at your particular situation: What is the nature of the disease? How old are you, and what are your relationships with others? How have you dealt with illness in the past? What do you know of dying — have you cared for someone else who was sick, or lost someone you loved? Your experiences are likely to shape your experience at the end of life.

Knowing that your life is threatened raises lots of concerns and questions about the future. You are not alone in desperately wanting answers to these questions:

- How long do I have?
- How sick will I get?
- Will I be in pain?
- What will happen to my children, my spouse, my projects?
- How long can I keep on working?
- How will I pay for everything?
- Who will care for me?
- Can I stay in my own home?
- Will I be a burden?

You may feel very troubled, worried, and afraid. Worse, you may not know how to express your concerns, what to do, or what to say. The uncertainty and the distress can be just as troubling as other symptoms of your illness. In fact, your emotional state — the stress you are under — can profoundly affect how you feel physically.

Norma had lived with congestive heart failure for several years, and although she was weary of her illness, her primary concern was for her elderly husband, who suffered from advanced Parkinson's disease. "I worry about what will happen to him when I'm gone. The children are close by, but they have their own lives, so I have to hang on as long as possible."

Janie, a 28-year old, suffering from advanced breast cancer, worried constantly about her 6-year-old daughter. "This has all happened so fast and I don't think Lisa understands what's going on. She gets so upset when I can't do things with her. There doesn't seem to be anything that I can do."

A young corporate executive, Tom, struggled enormously with his declining physical ability, the result of an aggressive lung tumor. "I once managed hundreds of people and everything ran efficiently. I was never sick and now I need help with everything. This can't be happening to me."

Much of the suffering that comes with life-threatening illness arises from overwhelming feelings of loss on all levels of human experience. These feelings can be complicated by the ambivalence that so commonly directs the ebb and flow of emotions in the course of a long illness. Norma longs to be free of her restricted life but is afraid for her spouse. Janie admits that sometimes death seems preferable to the terrible pain she has at times and yet cannot bear to think of her child as motherless. Tom can't imagine a time of "not being." Your life may be a series of ups and downs. When you feel well, you may feel that a mistake has been made and that life will continue uninterrupted. Then, as if on cue, some change occurs, reminding you of your illness.

As dismal as your situation may seem at times, there is reason to be hopeful. Knowing that changes will occur and that anxiety and ambivalence will sometimes disrupt your life can also free you to make choices about how you will respond. You may not be able to change the outcome of your illness, but you can decide how you want to react to the emotional and spiritual pain, the anger, the frustration, the losses — the emotional roller-coaster ride you may sometimes experience.

RITUALS TO MARK TRANSITIONS

Ritual is one way cultures and individuals give meaning and continuity to their lives. You may want to use rituals to mark your changing body and life.

If you are religious, a prayer service can allow you to acknowledge the gift of your body, thank God for the use of it and symbolically surrender the part(s) no longer useful. This can be healing for the body, the mind, and the spirit. A member of the clergy or a chaplain can help you plan this service.

Another ritual involves making something that is uniquely yours, to leave for your children or their children. In a simple ritual, Janie gathered all the photos of herself and, together with her family, reminisced about old times. Afterwards, she placed the photos in a small box, requesting that they be put away and not shown again until after she had died.

You might go through photos and label them, especially if others will not readily recognize people from the past.

You might make gifts of items that have been special to you, or that are significant to members of your family.

All of these activities are helpful ways to change focus. Physical decline is often inevitable with terminal illness, so dealing with the changes is crucial. By trying to keep a positive view of yourself, you may be better able to endure the changes you experience.

Mourning your losses

The downward spiral of emotion and the roller-coaster feelings are the natural consequence of loss. Like most, you have undoubtedly experienced loss in the past. Perhaps you lost a pet as a child. You might remember the loss of a "first love," or friends left behind when your family moved away. You will often have lost important relationships through separation, divorce, and death. Now you are confronting the loss of your life as well as your dreams for the future.

Norma summed it up well. "Death is the least of my worries. I always knew it would happen someday. But it's watching part of me die each day that is so terrifying." Of course, she is referring to her succession of physical losses. Your losses may be different. You may not have the energy or spirit to function well as a parent, spouse, or friend. You may not have the strength to work or pursue activities you once enjoyed. You may often want to be alone. Medications may make you very tired. You may be alone because family and friends begin to distance themselves, in part as a way to cope with their own loss. It is then that you will realize that life is propelling you to the finish line over the roughest terrain you could ever have imagined. Can you recover from the changes and disappointments? It is possible to survive the "little deaths" if you are able to mourn your losses as they occur.

In spite of what our society suggests or well-intentioned friends offer, mourning is a normal, healthy response to loss. It helps us to survive all kinds of troubles, so that we can make the necessary adjustments to changes. It's generally easier to mourn for another and perhaps it feels a bit self-indulgent to mourn for yourself, but letting yourself do so can be healing for your body and your mind. What's especially important is that you find a way to mourn that makes sense to you and ultimately brings you some portion of comfort.

You may find that crying provides the best release, especially when sadness overwhelms you. Far from being a sign of weakness, crying is often an effective way to soften the emotional pain brought on by the changes in your life. Whether you are able to cry and how often depends on whether crying was acceptable when you were growing up; it will depend, too, on your particular temperament and the significance of the loss. The need to grieve for your losses in this way — or in whatever way you are comfortable with — will recur at different times in your illness. Norma, who referred to "little deaths" happening each day, said, "I find that every time my body lets me down or I see myself getting thinner, I become inconsolable. I wish that I could pull the covers over my head and disappear." Crying can be a good way to mourn the "little deaths." Other ways can be just as effective.

Gloria was in her late forties when she was diagnosed with breast cancer, a disease that had killed her mother when Gloria was 17. Now, her own children were in grade school, and she needed ways to reassure them about her health while preparing for just how sick treatment would make her.

Because chemotherapy would make her hair fall out, she had tried to prepare herself for that eventuality by cutting her luxurious, long black hair. One day, though, while talking to the children about what it would be like to see Mommy bald, she decided to let them cut her hair. She herself had always wondered how it would look cropped, or cut stylishly short.

Her daughter was given one side to trim as she pleased. Gloria's husband asked to do the other. In the end, her hair was a little ragged and uneven, not quite professional or stylish — but lovingly styled and, for a while, beautiful to Gloria and her family. The love, and the story, are what matter, and what will be remembered.

Seeing yourself more clearly

Seeing yourself and what is important to you more clearly will mean:

- Being honest with yourself
- Knowing your limitations, but living fully
- Being open to the lessons and gifts life continues to offer, despite the difficulties of being ill

Making adjustments in your life will require that you be honest about what you are feeling and experiencing, in both good times and bad. You don't have to hide or be embarrassed by tears, anger, and frustration. A touch of humor may help you cope. Janie would post a sign on the front door, either "Mom's Having a Good Day," or "Mom's Having a Bad Day," depending on her mood. She said, "I guess folks ought to know what to expect when they come to see me. This gives them an out if they're not up to the challenge." Your own challenge is also to be honest with yourself and to live within your limitations, but to live fully within them.

In addition to determination and honesty, be open to what life has to offer now. Tom said, "You know, I never stop being afraid of dying. But I'm more afraid of not living. I've got just so much time, so I have to make the best of it." He started painting again, a hobby he had long ago put aside. It served as a powerful antidote for the depression that haunted him.

No longer able to participate in her regular activities, Janie learned to knit and taught her daughter some simple stitches. Eventually, their "knitting time" became their special time together. Learning new skills or finding renewed pleasure in interests long forgotten can be a wonderful affirmation of your spirit. Tom and Janie would quickly say that it wasn't easy to find their way through the "shadow of the valley of death." They discovered that they had to turn to others who gently helped them see a different direction, nurturing the determination that lay quietly within, waiting to be summoned.

Coping with changes in appearance

Changes in appearance can be devastating because they are so undeniable. Surgical procedures can disrupt your self-image, and weight loss or gain can be difficult to disguise. The effects of medications and treatment can also take a toll on your appearance. Your skin, for example, might become much more pale than usual, or have a yellowish cast to it. The hair loss associated with chemotherapy can be especially disturbing.

These physical changes sometimes have a profound effect on how you feel about yourself. Our culture places so much value on "looking your best!" When your health care providers and everyone else around you focus on your body, assessing the effects of illness and treatment, it's not surprising that you may also be preoccupied with your body. Befriend the new face that you see in the mirror. A necessary first step will be to let go of your "old self," or at least of your image of that self.

"Look Good, Feel Better" is a special program designed especially to help you adapt to your appearance and is available in many communities. Hospitals or other sponsors bring in professional beauticians, cosmetologists, and stylists to advise people on how to wear make-up, turbans, and wigs, not only to minimize changes, but to look truly good.

Many people lessen the effect of physical change by changing their wardrobe. If you have lost a great deal of weight, your old clothes may be uncomfortably baggy. If your skin is fragile, certain fabrics may irritate it. Soft cottons, velour, and chenille may feel better than wool and nylon. Clothing can disguise many changes, and makeup and wigs work wonders. Janie had a number of brightly colored loose-fitting robes that she wore frequently because, she said, the colors lifted her spirits and hid what she described as her "bony body."

"It's so strange, when we become aware that we're talking about a very short period of time together, how the extraordinary becomes ordinary and vice versa. A good meal or a long walk has never meant so much before."

ALAN MARKS
facing death within a few weeks

Taking care of yourself

When you try to live your life fully, making the most of each day, you will need to focus some attention on taking care of yourself. It may seem as though the effort isn't worth it, that you're "too sick" or there "isn't enough time." Not true, but how you care for yourself will depend on how your illness affects you and what makes you feel your best.

Your ability to take care of yourself — your appetite, energy level, and fatigue — can be affected by troubling physical symptoms, so getting good and reliable help from your doctor is crucial. You will need to be honest about how you feel and persist in your requests for whatever medication or therapy will be helpful in alleviating these symptoms. In the majority of situations, adequate relief from troublesome physical symptoms is possible.

Even though you may slip into despair from time to time, enjoy what you can and maintain your connections with family, friends, and colleagues for as long as possible. Above all, don't give up hope — not the "wishful thinking" variety, but the kind that looks forward to security, comfort, and meaningful time for you and those you care about.

Pick up the pieces of your life and make something good out of them.

SELF-CARE: THE
BASICS

Just like any other time in your life, try to:

- ◆ *Eat as well as you can*
- ◆ *Exercise, within the limits of your disease*
- ◆ *Get adequate rest*
- ◆ *Enjoy the time you have*

SELF-CARE: PART TWO

- **Ask for help when you need it.** *Getting assistance in tough times can reduce your experiences of frustration. Tom fought the idea of getting help with his personal care until he realized that trying to do what needed to be done for himself left him with little energy for anything else.*

- **Identify sources of strength that you can summon during moments of despair, when the world looks bleak.** *For some, strength is in religious faith; for others, in nature.*

- **Find ways to feel useful and focus on interesting or pleasant activities.** *Distraction is a wonderful way to reduce stress. Music can be comforting, as can a warm bath or shower.*

- **Reduce your isolation by finding a support group.** *Living with a terminal illness can be an isolating experience. Within a support group, you might discover friendship, as well as a sensitivity and understanding that is hard to find among people who haven't shared your frustrations, fears, and losses. Support groups allow you to share your thoughts and fears, providing a chance to hear how others find strength and learn new ways of dealing with the changes in their lives. Others, no doubt, will learn from you. Even if you have never been a "group person," joining such a gathering is worth considering.*

Turn to a family member, a trusted friend, or a member of the clergy for support and guidance. Find a support group or trained counselor who can help you explore your options. If you prefer books and libraries, there are some excellent resources that can further guide you (see Chapter 17). The goal is to find a way for you to *live* with — or despite — your illness and dying. Finding your way will help you live on your terms.

If you are in a support group, listen to what others say about what is helpful to them. If you are still able to be physically active, continue to exercise. This can be especially helpful if exercise has been a tension reliever in the past. If solitude has brought you peace of mind, spend some time alone. Meditation, listening to relaxation tapes, and guided imagery can be useful, but their effectiveness may depend on whether you are already familiar with such exercises. If you have the time and inclination, ask your doctor to recommend a relaxation class in your community; often, hospitals offer them as a community outreach program. Or your faith community might have programs on how to meditate or pray.

Setting realistic goals

It's important to be clear about what you will be able to achieve. Many a noble venture was sabotaged by overly ambitious goals. Sometimes you try far too much, perhaps due to denial, but more often you just don't consider all that is necessary to achieve your goal. You may find it most helpful to set daily goals. Aim for something each day — something modest that has a good chance for success, like doing a little exercise, performing specific tasks, or making phone calls. Accomplishing goals will do wonders for your self-esteem and can serve as a way to find meaning for yourself.

It's horrible to watch my body slowly wilt away to nothing. But it's also wonderful because of all the time I get to say good-bye.

MORRIE SCHWARTZ
from Tuesdays with Morrie by Mitch Albom

You may wish to set a much more complex goal, but you will need to be realistic about how you are going to accomplish your objective. Janie decided that she wanted to have a surprise 60th birthday party for her mother. Once she realized that the planning would be an enormous task, well beyond her capability, she engaged others (at the suggestion of members of her support group) and the party was a success.

One man decided he wanted to complete his woodworking projects, which had always given him satisfaction. He no longer had the energy to do everything alone, so his wife was able to follow his directions and help complete the projects.

If you are setting long- or short-term goals, flexibility is a valuable ally. It helps if you expect the unexpected. Plans will have to be altered when your energy level is not up to the task or your illness causes an unexpected problem. You may need to shift gears. The disappointment of letting go of your original plan will be somewhat easier to deal with if you can appreciate the pleasure you had in planning something and imagining it done. Just realize that it was good to have made the plans and imagined the outcomes, but then let it go and make new plans within the new possibilities.

About relationships

By nature, we are social beings and define ourselves by our relationships: parent, child, spouse, sibling, friend, and so forth. These relationships remain crucial when you are ill. But your illness can improve them or shatter them. How these relationships emerge from this experience will depend on how healthy they were to begin with and how open all those involved are willing to be. Maintaining connections to those you care about is conducive to a feeling of well-being. The practical support that others are willing to give you, along with their love and concern, can be an important source of strength and comfort.

Judy was 45 when her kidney cancer returned. In the course of chemotherapy, she attended a family picnic — and laughed heartily when all of the men removed their baseball caps to show off their newly shaved heads, a sign, they said, of their solidarity with her, and their enduring love.

You will probably discover that many people will feel uncomfortable because of their own fears of dying and awkwardness around the subject of illness. They may distance themselves. If you can be open and share your feelings, including your frustrations and your fears, you may give them a way to deal with their own apprehension. Be prepared, though; some people may never want to deal with your illness and your only options will be to adapt or to let them go. Over time, you will know those with whom you can be most comfortable, and you can focus your energy on sustaining those relationships for as long as possible. You can avoid offending those in the distance by offering information or sentiments by note, by phone, or through a mutual friend.

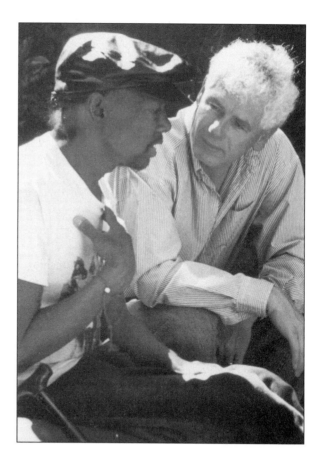

If conflict has strained an important relationship, it is worth the effort to try to mend the differences. If you feel inept at attempting this on your own, or your illness has depleted necessary physical and mental resources, seek the help of your clergy or another professional. There are counselors trained to facilitate discussions around resolving conflict, but anyone with interpersonal and communication skills can probably be of help. Working toward mending rifts among family or friends can be an important gift to those you love, as long as you recognize as well that some relationships are beyond repair.

Norma was able to benefit from just such an intervention. She had long thought her children were indifferent to her and became resentful of their behavior. A social worker from the hospice gathered the family members together. During that time, they realized that most of what divided them was not so terribly important and often was based on misunderstandings. This left the family much closer and more supportive than they ever could have been if things were never said and sentiments were never explored. Although your life is ending, those left behind will have memories to sustain — or overwhelm — them. Those memories can often be freed of bitterness.

Life is changing, but . . .

Consider how you can best meet the challenges that await you. Be compassionate toward yourself. Allow yourself to find a measure of joy in your life, despite the sadness you are sure to feel. Extending the same respect, concern, and affection to yourself that you would offer someone else will help you live fully while dying.

It's terrible to die if you're angry with someone, or if you have a misunderstanding. The person left alive feels guilty, and it's hard for them to grieve for the dead person. Grief is necessary. You have to be able to mourn.

REBECCA BROWN
from The Gifts of the Body

Chapter 3

Finding meaning

You need to know me and my spirit — that I seek meaning in suffering . . .
somedays I am able to make meaning of suffering.

STEVEN A. SCHMIDT
from When You Come Into My Room

We each get our "brief time on stage," and then we are gone. Some-times everything can seem so pointless. Why bother to live? Nothing is so deeply human as the search for meaning.

Most of us seek life's meaning beyond the boundaries of our physical life. Many discover that finding meaning that transcends physical limits becomes important to them as they try to live fully despite serious illness. Such search-ing takes many forms. Some pursue meaning through their religious faith, some in family and friends, others in good works or the goodness of humanity, and others in nature. However you find meaning, your search for it is ordinarily one of the most important projects for the end of life.

When you have an illness that will eventually cause your death, a door closes on what had seemed a future of endless possibilities. Everything may seem beyond your reach to you. Things once taken for granted are now uncertain, and new and unfamiliar issues arise. While others go about their activities and the business of the world continues, the road you travel may suddenly seem unfamiliar, its signposts poorly marked. At this crossroads, you are likely to question issues you once felt were settled.

"My dad always worried, as he got older, that he had no money to leave his children — and in the end he didn't. We always told him that it didn't matter . . . while my father suffered much illness in the last few years of his life, he died secure in the respect and love of his children."

GARA LaMARCHE

Religion and relationships

One Catholic monk has said that all religion is about the same thing: death, and trying to make sense of it. Indeed, the connection between spirituality and end-of-life may seem obvious to people who have strong roots in organized religion. Religion gives believers a pathway with clear road signs and expected activities. If you have faith, you may take comfort in the milestones that mark the way, no matter how troubling the journey.

If you have been actively addressing spiritual issues throughout life, with or without formal religion, life's last journey may feel like the natural conclusion to a lifelong journey, not requiring particular attention.

But most of us are caught up in the challenges of daily life, and arrive near the end of our life's journey with more questions unanswered than we would like. It is helpful to see the spiritual journey at the end of life — despite its challenges and troubles — as an opportunity to learn and grow.

Serious illness often requires an important redefinition of self, because it lets us get beyond the usual "currency" of being worthy, whether that's making money or being a good citizen. Serious illness, like other significant life challenges, forces us to rethink what it is that really matters. Often, we discover that what matters most are relationships with others, with ourselves, and with the world that surrounds us.

Spirituality goes beyond readily defined social roles and relationships and focuses on one's relationships with an interior world — the soul — and with a limitless, external world. Those infinite worlds, both within and around us, and our relationship to each shape our spiritual world. These are the relationships that may concern you as you approach death and question God or the universe: Why me? Why now? Why this? The way you come to answer those questions, or understand what is happening to you, also shapes your spiritual life.

How do you handle the urgent need to find meaning for yourself in what is soon to be a completed life? First, it helps to see this search for meaning as an important "task" for the end of life. In a sense, this is the valuable opportunity that dying with some forewarning offers: you have the chance to seek and find your own meaning. The fact that most people find this search to be terribly important and rewarding means that it is worth resisting the temptation to spend all your energy on medical treatment or on relatively unimportant tasks. It is as important to seek space and time for spiritual concerns as it is to seek the right treatment or therapy.

Second, it helps to seek spiritual companions. Perhaps you can talk to your spouse, or someone else who is close to you. He or she may be on a spiritual journey, too, and sharing thoughts can help you both along the way. Often, it helps to seek out others who have more experience — including religious advisors, older persons, or groups of people who have taken on these issues together. Perhaps you will find it especially meaningful to share your journey with someone much younger who is not yet driven by a search for meaning but senses its importance. You may find this list of "Four Rs for the Spirit" helpful in your search for meaning.

FOUR Rs FOR THE SPIRIT

- ◆ REMEMBERING. *Take time to reflect on your life and its events. What were your accomplishments? What must be left undone? Who influenced you, for better or worse, and whose lives did you influence? Who did you love? Who do you love? What do those relationships mean to you now?*

- ◆ REASSESSING. *Take time to see your life as a whole. You may ask what your life really added up to, or who you really were. You might share your thoughts with those who know and love you. Even if you accomplished much in the worldly sense, you may feel you really came up short on doing well with your life. And if life was really tough, you may feel unfairly denied your chances. This is the time to be honest and thoughtful. You are likely to find that you did pretty well, on the whole, and you will probably find ways to forgive yourself and others. Surprisingly, you will even find ways to see and complete important tasks — instructing a grandchild, affirming the goodness of someone who really needs your support, arranging your finances to protect your spouse, or creating something, whether it's needlepoint, woodworking, or fine art.*

- ◆ RECONCILING. *Try to be at peace with yourself. You may need to reconcile yourself to not having done the things you always wanted to do. You may need to forgive yourself for your shortcomings or transgressions, or forgive those who hurt or disappointed you. You may need to ask others to forgive you. Reconciliation with your imperfections — and those of others — can help you find peace.*

- ◆ REUNITING. *Try to be at peace with those you love. Most of us have had various relationships disrupted over our lifetime, from death, anger, relocation, and the many forces that push people apart. As serious illness threatens, it is important to come together with family and friends, when you can, and to have the chance to say farewells. Don't wait too long to try to see that long-estranged sister or son, or even to sit awhile with a friend from long ago.*

Meaning and loss

You are likely to experience many emotions as you recollect aspects of your life, think about accomplishments or disappointments, contemplate what lies ahead, and consider how illness affects who you are. Among the most powerful of these feelings are grief and anger. People with life-threatening illness have to confront their illness, their approaching death, and all of the loss they must face. Grief is a normal, human reaction to devastating news. Grief will take its time with you — and you must take time with your grief. Some days, it may feel like a tidal wave of emotion, threatening to overwhelm you and knock you off your feet; on other days, you may feel gently rocked on a calm sea.

You are likely sometimes to feel very angry at the universe, at God or fate, at your own body or its illness, and at your family and others whom you love. For people who have been taught to worship and revere God, or trust in His will, feelings of anger can be very upsetting. However, as Rabbi Earl Grollman has described it, "Don't worry. God can take it." Feeling angry is also a normal, human reaction to a life-threatening illness. You may feel that your spirit is subsumed by anger — like grief, this anger can stay with you for a while, but watch for the ways to let it go.

At those times when anger is not the dominant emotion in your spiritual landscape, you can stop to consider spiritual questions. Your whole life is, of course, a spiritual journey, and it is as important to seek space and time for spiritual

> *Is it so strange that we want*
> *to meet again for the last time,*
> *to look at each other, to listen to*
> *each other's voices, ever*
> *so gently to touch hands?*
>
> JAMES LAUGHLIN
> *from "The Least You Could Do"*

When my mother died, I inherited her needlepoint tapestries. When I was a little boy, I used to sit at her feet as she worked on them. Have you ever seen needlepoint from underneath? All I could see was chaos, strands of threads all over, with no seeming purpose. As I grew, I was able to see her work from above. I came to appreciate the patterns, and the need for dark threads as well as bright and gaily colored ones. Life is like that. From our human perspective, we cannot see the whole picture. But we should not despair or feel that there is no purpose. There is meaning and purpose, even for the dark threads, but we cannot see that right away.

RABBI KENNETH L. COHEN

concerns as it is to seek the right treatment or therapy. Spirituality is an integral part of our lives, and you and your family can insist that caregivers and health care providers respect your spiritual needs, that they give you time to pray, meditate, reflect, and worship.

SHAPING MEANING: A FEW IDEAS

There are many ways to find and give meaning to your experience. These are offered as examples of things others have done to heal and grow.

MEDITATING: Meditation is a way to center yourself and your thoughts, to quiet your mind and connect with the Infinite. Tapes can help you learn to meditate; you might also ask the hospice or hospital chaplain or a social worker to help you find ways to meditate.

GATHERING: Gathering with people you love and who are important to you can be enriching to you and to them. One man, told he had but four weeks to live, organized a party and invited his many friends to come. Family and friends made tributes and shared memories and stories. Such gatherings can be surprisingly happy and can give you a chance to say goodbye to people you have enjoyed and loved.

CREATING: Making a tape of stories or memories, sharing your experience with family members and friends, is a wonderful gift to you and your family. By making a tape, a special photo album, or a scrapbook for those you will leave behind, you can help create memories of times you shared. Some people, especially parents, write letters to the children who will survive them.

GIVING: Some cultures and traditions emphasize gift-giving. Native Americans, for instance, give valuable keepsakes to signify the end of life. This ritual allows the giver to show appreciation for the relationship shared.

LEAVING A LEGACY: You can give more than your material treasures to those you love through an "ethical will." Leave a letter or tape recording sharing your values, hopes, insights, beliefs, and wisdom. Even just tell your story. Your bequest becomes both a cherished memento and a way to continue your good ways.

Chaplains and others who can help

If you are in a hospital or hospice program, a chaplain can offer support, prayer, and spiritual guidance. Hospital chaplains are people ordained or consecrated for religious ministry and who have a special commitment to work with people who are seriously ill. They come from various religious backgrounds, but provide care regardless of religious affiliation. They can join you, your family, and your friends for prayer or worship services, or for other rites and rituals that honor your faith. If you would like assistance from a religious leader of your own tradition, a hospital or hospice chaplain will work to make that possible. You also may want to invite health care professionals to join you in prayer or ritual; often, they are willing and even happy to do so.

He did not say: You will not be troubled, you will not be belabored, you will not be afflicted; but he said: You will not be overcome.

MOTHER JULIAN OF NORWICH

Many, but not all, hospitals have chaplains whose job it is to counsel and support the very sick and their families. Some people feel reluctant to talk to chaplains for fear that the chaplain will preach at them or attempt to convert them. This situation should not occur. Hospital chaplains participate in rigorous clinical pastoral education (CPE) programs, and their desire will be to help you and

---

QUESTIONS TO ASK OF HOSPITALS AND HOSPICES

- *Do you offer chaplaincy for spiritual issues?*
- *If you do, how are chaplains affiliated with you? Are they full-time staff, contractual employees, or local clergy?*
- *Have the chaplains participated in clinical pastoral education? Has their experience been introductory or has it included clinical residency?*
- *How does the chaplain approach care for people from religious traditions other than his or her own?*
- *If I have fears, doubts of faith, and other concerns, is the chaplain able to help me talk about them?*
- *Where does my past religious advisor fit in?*

to offer you comfort and care that is centered in what you believe and value — not to persuade you toward any particular religious faith. Because chaplains have been trained to listen to your concerns, you may find that they are easy to talk to, and that you can lean on them to help work out problems or issues that trouble you.

Most hospital chaplains participate in clinical pastoral education programs approved by either the Association for Clinical Pastoral Education or the National Association of Catholic Chaplains. The time commitment for this process varies but includes at least 400 hours of study, service, and reflection for an introductory program. People who become hospital chaplains generally spend one or two years in a residency program devoting their full time to preparation for the chaplain's role. The Association of Professional Chaplains (and other national and denominational groups), a respected national professional association, provides a process for board certification of chaplains. Board-certified chaplains must complete at least one year of training and also pass a rigorous peer review process.

As is true in so many professions, credentials are no guarantee of quality. However, people can ask questions of chaplains, such as the level of formal training they have received and the focus on interfaith care.

A religious leader in your own faith is obviously someone you might turn to for help. Your own community's ministry may have recommendations on how to seek spiritual support and care for end-of-life issues.

When you leave the hospital, you may want continued professional support and guidance. Pastoral counselors are well-suited to help. Pastoral counselors are individuals who have training in theology or ministry, and who have formal training in counseling and psychology. They can help you and your family work through spiritual concerns, fears, and problems, and can counsel those who may be depressed, overwhelmed, and under a great deal of stress. They can help you put issues in perspective. If you are uncomfortable discussing your spirituality with your family, pastoral counselors offer the security and privacy you may need. If you want to bring up spiritual concerns, but don't know how, pastoral counselors can help with this, too. Most pastoral counselors accept payments according to a sliding fee scale, so the cost should not be a barrier for you.

The nearer she came to death, the more, by some perversity of nature, did she enjoy living.

ELLEN GLASGOW
from Barren Ground

Your worship or faith community (meaning your church, synagogue, temple, or other site) may have prayer support groups and lay ministers. One widespread lay group is called the Stephen Ministry. People from your church or congregation may visit you at home or in the hospital, pray and offer sacraments, and provide practical support, such as respite care for your family or grocery shopping. Some communities have prayer support groups that meet to pray together, but that also pray on your behalf. People who participate in these groups find them supportive and comforting. In fact, such groups can even be found on the Internet. And emerging research shows that people who are active in their church, have a relationship with God or some spiritual being, and pray seem to cope with illness and dying more easily than those who have not yet focused on their spirituality.

You may also find support and comfort through practices such as yoga, relaxation therapy, meditation, healing rituals from other cultures, writing and journal exercises, or spirituality courses offered by local colleges and adult education programs. Ritual and tradition give form and focus to faith and strength, and support to many people and families. You may find that praying alone or with your family or other caregivers (even if this is not something you have ordinarily done) is comforting. When you are gone, shared prayers and rituals will offer a way for people to reconnect with you and the love you shared. In fact, you might think of creating some more family rituals while you are very sick. How do you say goodnight, how do you say goodbye on a daily basis? Sometimes it makes time

RELIGIOUS RITUALS: A SAMPLER

PRAYER: *Most denominations include prayer. Prayer can be formal, recited or read by an individual such as a member of the clergy or congregation, or informal, created spontaneously to give thanks or praise or for specific needs. For some people, meditation and silence are forms of prayer.*

CONFESSION: *Many religions, including Christianity, Judaism, and Islam, have a form of confession. Christians, including Catholics, usually make private confessions to a clergy member, while Jews and Muslims may confess sins to family or in ritual prayers. All who confess do so with the expectation of forgiveness.*

COMMUNION: *Christians often partake of bread and wine as a ritual remembrance of Jesus' death and resurrection. The Eucharist, as it is often called, is meant to nourish one's soul. Communion is usually given by a clergy member or lay minister.*

ANOINTING: *Priests and ministers in many faiths bless the sick by anointing them with sacred oils, often touching them on the forehead, hands, or diseased part of the body. Once called "the last rites," Roman Catholics now receive "the sacrament of the sick," in which communion, confession, and anointing occur. This sacrament, which is considered to be a healing one for the soul, can be received several times during an illness.*

RELIGIOUS ARTICLES AND ICONS. *For many people, items such as statues, rosaries, medallions, prayer beads, and prayer wheels offer a comforting connection to their beliefs.*

seem much more meaningful and orderly if there is some little prayer or another action that marks important times each day. The story below describes how one woman, in learning to pray with her dying grandmother, supported her grandmother and learned to cope with her own loss.

When I was a preschooler and afraid of the dark, my grandmother — whose house my family lived in — would leave an M&M trail through the house from my bed to hers. I would set forth through the dark house to the night light of her room. Once I'd eaten one M&M, I could find the courage to search for all of them. My presence in her room always woke her. She would say, "Hello, doll. Dark getting to you?" Then she'd turn back the blankets to make room for me.

It was many years before I believed, as my grandmother often said, that there was nothing in the dark that did not exist in the light. Thirty years later, when a doctor told my grandmother she had widespread kidney cancer, we found ourselves in a different dark.

My mind played with the terrible anticipation of her absence, the way your tongue cannot avoid exploring the pain of a fever sore.

I wanted to become some sort of light for Grandmom, to blaze a trail from the dark room of her illness, fear, and pain to the light of my love and the love of our family. But as the days wore on and cancer took her life piecemeal, I clung to what little we could still share. I held her hand and stroked her head. In those last weeks, I sang for her: hymns, spirituals, Irish drinking songs, sea chanteys, "Amazing Grace," and "Lord of the Dance." When I tired of singing, I read aloud: trashy novels, magazine articles, newspaper stories, reports I was writing. The content was meaningless, but my voice calmed her.

During the last two weeks of her life, she taught me to pray the rosary, a ritual I had somehow missed, despite years of Sunday school and church. To her, the rosary was a daily obligation. To me, it was an odd and time-consuming task from an archaic world. She could no longer recite the entire litany aloud and could not keep count of the prayers she had said. She wanted someone to pray it for her. I volunteered.

The rosary connected her to her faith and to the past, her parents, her brothers and sisters. Praying with her as she lay dying became a way to connect and comfort us. I had to concentrate to say each of the prayers on each of the beads, moving them through my grandmother's sore fingers. I could think of nothing else. When we began to pray, it was usually in the midst of her pain and my fear. But by the time we had come full circle, she would be asleep and peaceful, and I would have forgotten, for a while at least, how awful things were.

On the last day of my grandmother's life, she lay in pain in a hospital bed. I could not see the world without her in it, yet I could not bear the world that kept her now. I wanted to say something to release her, and so began to whisper names. I named my sisters and brother, my cousins, my grandmother's siblings; I named streets we had lived on, countries where she had traveled. I whispered and prayed that her tight grip on this life could be loosened by memories of how much she had loved this life, and how well she was loved.

She began to grow calmer later that evening. A priest suggested we play a tape of Gregorian chants for her, and the music stilled her. I went home. My mother and sister were just falling to sleep in her room when she stirred for a moment, sighed, and was gone.

As I drove back to the hospital that night, my loss was as overwhelming as the darkness had been 30 years earlier, on my M&M trail to safety. I made that late-night drive to the hospital because I so desperately needed to see my grandmother at peace; it was her turn, again, to guide me through the night, to teach me to walk without fear into the hard moments of this life. I held her rosary beads in my hand and let them rattle against the steering wheel.

When we walk to the edge of all the light we have and take a step into the darkness of the unknown, we must believe one of two things will happen — there will be something solid for us to stand upon, or we will be taught to fly.

ANONYMOUS

Helping family make decisions and give care

"[This story] is worth telling because it reminds us that successful dying, like successful child-rearing, depends on family."

ROBERT J. SAMUELSON

The person dying is never the only person who is affected by illness and death — family and dear friends are, too. Often, entire communities mourn a death. Many will feel your losses and their own. They will have to make decisions and support one another. And they will have to make practical arrangements to help you. It would help if everyone recognized that families and close friends are really "going through it" with a seriously ill or dying loved one. In Chapter 16, you will find thoughts and insights on grieving. Here you will find some stories and advice about family togetherness and caregiving.

Families deciding together

Serious illness can suddenly make families come together more closely than they may have been for years. Adult brothers and sisters may have to understand what is happening to their parents and to make decisions. In some situations, it is clear who will decide and how. In others, there are too many options, too much friction, and too little practice in making decisions together (and the patient and the family suffer for it). Think about how your family operates. Could you make a decision about a business matter without one of you being in charge? Are you still arguing about what to have for lunch when it's time for supper? Do you tolerate one another's shortcomings and habits or annoy one another endlessly?

"Even the kids say they wouldn't have missed being there, caring for Pops, for the world."

DAUGHTER OF A CANCER PATIENT

How your family and closest friends will unite is something that they and you can plan. Perhaps it will be best for you to make many decisions in advance, or to name one person who has final authority. Perhaps it will be fine to let things go, trusting them to work out. However, it is almost always best to check out ideas with each other first. Let your family learn what it is to pull together on some early issues that really don't matter too much. Rather than letting the first family decision be something really shattering, like selling a family home or stopping a ventilator, start by figuring out how to make decisions on which doctor to stay with, or whether to take a trip.

Reflect a bit on how the family is working and how it will do without you. Encourage family to think about who will fill some of your roles. If you are the one who always remembers birthdays or hosts the celebrations, encourage others to start doing these things. Offer advice, or share your address book or calendar. If they say that this is uncomfortable while you are still alive, be glad to keep the role while you can but be gently forceful about passing it along, too. Remember, these are the same children who were so eager to learn to drive, get a place of their own, or stop calling if they were going to be late. They *can* take on some of your responsibilities now when you are ready for them to.

Sometimes families really are too distant — emotionally or geographically — to work together. Then, the best you can hope for is some comradeship and contact. And, of course, some people have no family or friends at all and rely on volunteers and health care providers.

At times, families get into fierce disagreements over the treatment of a seriously ill family member. All too often, it is a caregiving family member pitted against a distant family member who may feel guilty for not "being there." If there has been a history of feeling left out, arguing, or providing an unfair share of caregiving, there can be deep resentment, too.

Often, family members need some perspective. Starting a conversation with a prayer, if that is in your tradition, may set the right tone of humility, service, and working together for something important. Turning to a professional for help is also worthwhile. A chaplain, social worker, nurse, or doctor may be able to listen and advise. It is not as important to be "right" as much as it is to be dedicated, helpful, and forgiving.

Family caregiving

Watch for serious, long-term illness on television, in the newspapers, in the movies — it is almost never there. One would think that America is made up of vigorous young people who never grow old and never get sick. Very few people realize that almost all of us will have a substantial period of our adult lives in which we are responsible for the care of an older relative who cannot live independently any more. At any one time, one in four American households is providing unpaid care to an older relative for a substantial period of time. The family that does not have this experience is rare.

TENSIONS FOR FAMILIES

You will often find your family torn by emotions. People deal with tension in all sorts of ways, but it often helps just to be able to name the problem. Note that the best "place" to be is not usually at one end or the other, but somewhere in between.

Hope ←→ Despair

Denial ←→ Acceptance

Meaninglessness ←→ Meaningfulness

Independence ←→ Accepting dependency

Family burden ←→ Opportunity to serve

Ambiguity ←→ Certainty of outcome

Making plans ←→ Experiencing emotions

Holding on ←→ Letting go

Speaking openly ←→ Not talking

Family as it was ←→ Family as it is becoming

Caring for children is expected and fairly predictable in onset and in completion. However, the need to care for a sick elderly relative often happens unexpectedly and is certainly an unpredictable way of life. Caring for one another, though, is probably the defining trait of families. How families provide this care challenges creativity, commitment, and virtue. In some families, taking care of one's relatives is absolutely expected, and people can take on extraordinary burdens to honor that expectation. Other families, however, find it to be sufficient just to keep in touch with one another and to oversee paid caregivers.

Eight of every ten family caregivers are women and most will be caregivers for more than ten years. No matter what social class or status a woman has in the workplace, it is she who will most often be expected (in her own eyes as well as by others) to take physical care of family members who are sick or dependent. Sadly, having lots of daughters and daughters-in-law still gives one the best chance

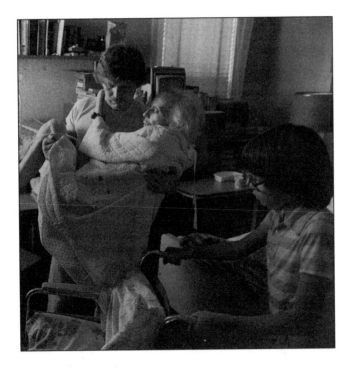

to stay in a family home when one is dying. In the past, having sons (unless married) did not help you much. This may be changing, though, as men get more skills in homemaking and live longer, and as they find themselves in situations where they are the best persons to provide the care.

Caregiving often starts rather abruptly — after a stroke or a fall, for example. After an initial period of adjustment, which often comes with no instructions or help, caregiving settles into a rhythm of coping with the day-to-day. It can become easier to get breaks and support in this stable phase, but only if the caregiver is encouraged to do so. Caregiving for someone who is seriously ill often ends with death, though it might also change if the dying person is admitted to a nursing home, hospital, or inpatient hospice. While the caregiver may feel relief when this work is done, it is another major life transition which is often quite uncomfortable and disorienting.

Caregiving for a dependent adult is often most difficult for the person needing the care. If the person is mentally sharp, he or she is often quite offended by dependency and troubled to impose a burden on younger relatives or a spouse. Needing help with private matters like using the toilet and dressing can feel terribly humiliating. If the person is not mentally sharp, he or she may be upset by needing help, but may be unable even to understand why there is no choice.

Caregivers have problems of their own. They can wear themselves out, cut themselves off from most of the world, and sidetrack their own career prospects. They can lose their job, their health insurance, and their economic security. So, why do they do it? Because it is such an essential part of what it is to be a caring person — to take care of those who are part of your family or those you love.

One after the other they came bounding up the steps to lean and kiss her. I saw her hand, the half-clenched one, fold over each bent back in turn, pressing, and it struck me in a way it had never struck me before (why not? why ever not?) how touching and attractive the gestures of human affection are.

WALLACE STEGNER
from Crossing to Safety

REST AND RENEWAL FOR CAREGIVERS

- *Hire a sitter or an aide for occasional events or on a regular basis.*
- *Arrange for other family members to provide care.*
- *Use a nursing home or assisted living facility for planned vacations of a week or more.*
- *Use a day hospital or adult day care.*
- *Get a family member to take on some responsibility regularly — paying bills, taking your loved one for a daily walk, giving a bath and shampoo.*
- *Change your expectations for yourself — let the housework go more than you like, for example.*
- *Meditate or pray.*
- *For some people, nursing homes or assisted living facilities are the best option.*

If the person facing dying is likely to have only a few months, and the caregiver has a large employer (or an understanding one), caregivers can often arrange to have their job back when they return. However, if the caregiver had a job with a small employer, or needs to take a longer and more uncertain time off, it can be very hard to be sure of having a job to come back to. Likewise, the caregiver may have health problems and have problems getting insurance if she leaves her job. The federal Family and Medical Leave Act may ensure that a caregiver has some unpaid leave to care for a sick family member — be sure to ask. Often, other workers are willing to pool some extra leave, or an employer will make some accommodation if you ask.

Since most caregivers have had little experience with friends or family who have provided similar care, many feel they need "a road map," some sense of what it is to do this job well. This guidance is made even more difficult by the fact that many of these caregivers also must keep working in conventional employment. Juggling multiple obligations becomes the routine for most.

How can a caregiver know if things are out of control?

Having some perspective is one of the hardest things for caregivers to do. Caregiving is often stressful, yet people do it and do well. On the other hand, some caregivers really do stay in situations where they cannot possibly give good care, where the needs are overwhelming. When the caregiver notes that the patient is suffering from some inattention, such as skin problems or overmedication, the caregiver should be concerned. Other trouble signs include when the caregiver becomes more and more exhausted, depressed, angry, and unable to sleep or eat well. Another important sign is when the caregiver feels that there is no other person to call on for help. The terrible isolation that many caregivers feel is both a

HELP FOR THE CAREGIVERS

- *Ask the doctors and nurses: What will the patient need? Who can help? How does one become a good caregiver?*

- *Consult a social worker or case manager, especially to understand Medicare and Medicaid rules and what facilities and services might be available.*

- *Use a support group. Even if a caregiver is a little uncertain about meeting with others, try it a few times. Most people find it enormously helpful to hear how others have met challenges and to share stories with others who have really "been there."*

- *Get information from the relevant national organizations. All kinds of good information is posted on the Internet, and a librarian can help you get it if you don't have access. Some groups also have toll-free phone numbers. See Chapter 17.*

- *Contact a local hospital or hospice to locate support groups and special services that they might have for people who face similar challenges.*

- *Do some research — in the library, on the Internet, in getting second opinions. Try to become something of an expert on the particular illnesses affecting your family.*

- *Call on family and friends — don't do it all alone.*

ADAPTED FROM ROSALYNN CARTER WITH SUSAN K. GOLANT, *HELPING YOURSELF HELP OTHERS.*

symptom of an overwhelmed caregiver and a sign of a community that does not know how to care for one another.

What to do when the caregiver is overwhelmed

Few caregivers maintain their connections with the rest of the community. Often, just re-establishing some relationships helps. If the caregiver was active in a church or social organization or has a fairly stable neighborhood, these friends will often be eager to help if someone just gives them permission and encouragement. Isolation can really sap caregivers' self-esteem and their ability to reach out for help. If at all possible, join some sort of support group and get together with people who are "in the same boat." Even if you have to hire a sitter for a few hours or bargain with a neighbor for help, try hard to get a break and get out in the world.

How do you find support groups?

Ask around. Try your doctor, nurse, and social worker. Try hospitals and nursing homes in the area. Call national organizations to ask how to contact a local chapter. Check with your local Area Office on Aging, which may have a list of a variety of help that is available to the elderly; those services are often available to younger persons also. Call your church or other religious institution. Call other religious institutions that are geographically close even if they are not associated with your religious tradition. A support group at any church or synagogue is usually quite welcoming to persons of all faiths. Then, try it out a few times. If you don't find it supportive, move along and try something else. Some people are finding a great deal of support by joining in chat rooms or listservs on the Internet. If you do this, be careful — it is hard to know whether the information being given is honest or accurate.

Is there anything good about caregiving?

Yes. Many family caregivers say it is the toughest job they ever had, and the most rewarding. Dedicating yourself to an elderly relative or spouse certainly affirms your virtue and good character. Caregiving often helps reorient a house-

hold around matters of enduring value, such as faith, prayer, and love, rather than the material issues that often dominate home life. Once the dependent person dies, persons who have been caregivers generally are more confident that they have "done well." They have "been there" and know what the person went through, and that they, the caregivers, were loyal and trustworthy and kind.

Family caregiving usually saves the family money, too. Round-the-clock service by a combination of a nurse and an aide would cost upwards of $50,000 per year.

Getting the help you need

And that's just the point: we will have another month like this — and then how many more? . . . How many hundreds, how many thousands this month; how many "next months" will there be? How much of that is our "co-pay?" I know I'm not supposed to be thinking about money in a crisis like this, but where will we get the money?

ROBERT STINSON
from The Long Dying of Baby Andrew

Most people want to be well-informed about things that are important in their lives, but it is very difficult to know everything you need to know about the kinds of health care you might need. Coping with a serious illness, our own or a loved one's, causes a lot of anxiety and confusion. This can be made worse by our health care system — which is really not a system, but a mix of disconnected, and sometimes dysfunctional, groups, plans, services, and professionals. If what you need is a little help for a short amount of time, you might find that no program or service is available. At another time, when you need extensive care for a long time, that's not available either! Sometimes it seems that the array of services and qualifications were designed to frustrate.

It is important that you have the proper tools to obtain the best and most appropriate care. Although many people are attempting to change the system to make it more usable, there are things that you can do now to ensure that the system works better for you.

How to find help and advice

Ask lots of questions — of everyone! The art of getting the information you need is to ask questions of different people who have a variety of expertise and experience. Talk to doctors, nurses, social workers, friends, neighbors, priests, 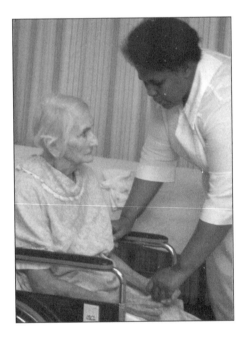 pastors, and rabbis. Call your local churches, hospitals, hospices, and civic or volunteer service organizations. Call your city, county, or state government officials. Talk to people who have gone through similar experiences. Join a support group, perhaps one that is organized around your situation. Tell them your story. Ask your questions, but also be willing to listen to thoughts, ideas, and suggestions that may not have occurred to you.

Call your local Office on Aging

Area Offices on Aging provide information and referral and match you up with services such as meals at senior centers, meals-on-wheels, transportation, financial help, telephone reassurance, grocery shopping assistance, income tax assistance, or any other special need you might have. You may also qualify for financial assistance through this office. If you do not know how to contact your local Office on Aging, call the national toll-free hotline at 1-800-677-1116. Often, the Office on Aging can send you a list of local services, their missions, and their phone numbers.

Getting the help of a case manager

The Office on Aging or various individual professionals or companies may be able to provide you with a case or care manager. You may want to consult a care manager early on to make plans and coordinate care. This person is usually a nurse or social worker who helps to coordinate the care in your home. For example, if your family members live far away, you may choose to hire a case manager to help hire persons to provide care in your home. The case manager will visit your home and find out what your specific needs are. A case manager, for instance, could hire one aide to help with laundry and cooking and another aide to help you with personal care, including bathing, dressing, and eating. She could assess whether you might need special equipment in your home such as a shower chair or a raised toilet seat.

"Without outside help, our attempt at caring for our parents would have been misguided and poor but wrapped in the best of intentions."

A FAMILY MEMBER

A good care manager will also help you adjust to having a paid household worker. Many people find having a household employee to be anxiety-provoking and need someone experienced to talk it over with. The cost of a case manager varies depending on your income. You may need to consult a care manager only once or twice, and some good advice at the beginning may well save anxiety and money in the long run.

When your family needs a break

Your local Office on Aging (see Chapter 17) can tell you where to look in your area for respite care. Respite care is temporary care provided by someone else so that the everyday caregiver can do other things such as shop, go to church, run errands, or just have a much-needed break.

Getting your wishes followed at home

Most doctors, nurses, and others in the medical world are focused on curing disease, or at least trying to stop it in its tracks. While cure is a worthy goal in many cases, the high-tech treatments that are commonly used may not be what you want at this stage in your life. There are some things that you can do to be sure that your caregivers follow your directions (see also Chapter 10).

- Whenever possible, decide in advance what circumstances warrant a call to "911" and when that should *not* be done.
- Talk with your doctor about what kinds of symptoms or sudden changes you might expect with your illness.
- Get the medications you might need for a sudden problem in advance, and keep them in a place that's easy to find.

- Have important phone numbers by the telephone with instructions about who to call and when.
- Keep a list of your medications (name, dose, how to take, and timing), illnesses, and symptoms.

When you have help in your home

If family or friends are distant or not available to help, you may find that you rely on paid caregivers, such as home health aides or chore aides, to help around your house or apartment. You may find that their schedules vary and that you cannot count on seeing the same person every day or even every week. You need to think through what it is that really matters to you in their work and their relationship with you and be prepared to choose agencies or personnel on that basis. You can't spend your energies on frustrations with hired workers!

Sometimes, a hired home caregiver comes to be your close friend, but often they will never know you well enough to understand what you hope for in life and in dying. It often is prudent to place a simple set of instructions near all phones and review them with all caregivers. Here are two contrasting examples:

> INSTRUCTIONS ABOUT JANE SMITH
> DO NOT CALL 911!
> If I die, I do not wish to be resuscitated (see my bracelet).
> Call John Smith at 555-1212.
> Call my physician at 555-1010.
> The funeral home number is 555-1111.

OR

> INSTRUCTIONS ABOUT MARY DOE
> I am not expecting to die.
> If I collapse, call 911.
> Call my physician at 555-0101.
> Call my friend Jane Smith at 555-2121.
> They will know what to do.

Whether your caregiver is paid or is a friend or family member, there is information that he or she will need to know. Once again, ask nurses and support group members who have cared for others what will make it easier to give good care. Also, call the National Caregiving Foundation for information, support, and a caregiver's Support Kit (1-800-930-1357).

What to do when things don't go well

When things seem out of control, try to find a sympathetic person who knows the care system well and who can help you see new perspectives and creative solutions. If you feel that you or someone you love is being treated poorly, you will probably have to find the energy and thoughtfulness to complain effectively. Hospitals and health care providers are not unfeeling or malicious — although you may sometimes think they are. It may help you to recognize that problems are often the result of systems and procedures designed to cure disease, or at the very least, prolong life. If you can imagine yourself in the doctor or nurse's place, you might be better able to state your concerns constructively, without creating tension and hard feelings.

When you complain, try not to just "take it out" on whoever is closest. Probably the person who has to be persuaded that something is wrong is not nearby. Find out who supervises the care you find troubling. Then set a time to talk with that person. Write down the key facts to remind you of the things that will make the person see just how important the problem is.

A guide to settings and services

Hospitals

What is a hospital? This question might appear to be an elementary one. However, at the rate that our health care system changes, it is worthwhile to know just what kind of care hospitals provide and how to find out if that care can meet your needs. The traditional hospital is a health care institution that has an organized staff, inpatient care, and nursing services. Generally, hospitals are designed to provide aggressive and curative care. Because we are most familiar with hospitals, they might be the first place that we would turn to in an emergency. But a hospital might not be the appropriate place for everyone. While the hospital usually provides good emergency and

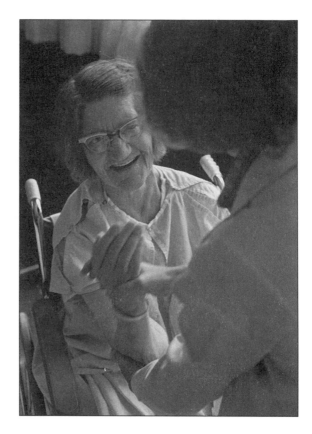

rescue care and life-prolonging treatments, hospitals may not be the best place to get good symptom relief and care planning. As with any important decision, the first thing is to think about what kind of care you would like and discuss your choice with your family.

Your doctor might be the most appropriate person for you to talk with to find out if the hospital is the place that fits your needs. Most often, doctors are trained to cure illness within a care system that generally pays well for brilliant performances in something like surgery, but does not pay well for hearing aids or medications. The ways that doctors and hospitals are paid for the services that they provide create gaps when you need care over an extended period or at the end of life. If the questions you have are medical, like those about medication for pain, calling your doctor is the best option. If the questions are about how to pay for services or plan for care, asking advice from a nurse or social worker from the hospital may be the better choice.

> *. . . we need to find hope in other ways, more realistic ways, than in the pursuit of elusive and danger-filled cures. . . . Hope should be redefined. Some of my sickest patients have taught me of the varieties of hope that can come when death is certain.*
>
> SHERWIN B. NULAND
> *from* How We Die: Reflections on Life's Final Chapter

Intensive Care

Critical care units for heart disease, surgery, brain injuries, or just overwhelming illness are very special settings. Most patients are so sick that they require all manner of tubes and treatments. It can be quite intimidating. Try to find a few identifiable people — your nurse, for example — and have one of them tell you how the system works. You will usually find that it makes sense, once you have a "translator."

Hospice

Unlike a hospital, which is an actual building where care is provided, "hospice" is more of a concept or a description of a type of care. Some communities do have hospices that care for patients in a designated facility, but the majority of hospice care is provided to patients and families in their own homes, whether that is a private residence or nursing home. Hospice care emphasizes physical comfort, pain relief, and symptom management, and addresses the patient's spiritual, psychological, social, and financial needs. Bereavement care for the family is also an integral part of hospice care.

At the current time, most patients suffering from chronic conditions cannot use hospice services. Under current restrictions, a patient must be expected to have less than six months to live before most insurance, including Medicare, will cover these services. Hospice provides many benefits for patients. People who might want hospice service and who believe they qualify should not assume that a doctor will automatically refer them to hospice at the right time. It is often up to patients and families to ask questions and take an active role in defining what kind of care fits them best.

Beneficiaries can find out about the specifics of the Medicare hospice benefit program by calling the Medicare hotline at 1-800-638-6833.

Long-term care

Long-term care describes a type of care, rather than an actual place. Long-term care is the range of health, personal care, social, and housing services provided to people who are unable to care for themselves independently as a result of chronic illness or mental or physical disability. Not all individuals will require the highly skilled, intensive care that some nursing homes provide. Many can remain fairly independent and may only need assistance with a few activities of daily living. These activities could include a range of things such as help to bathe, help getting in and out of bed, or other daily functions such as grocery shopping, housekeeping, and balancing a checkbook. Some may prefer to remain in their home and receive services there. With the advances made in technology, this is becoming more available, even to individuals who may require intravenous or nutritional therapies. Your care manager or local Offices on Aging can help answer any other questions that you might have about the different kinds of facilities and services in your area.

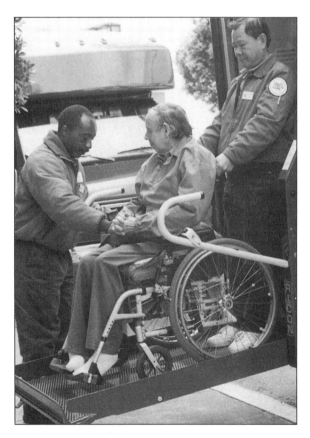

Long-term care services can be as basic as assistance for daily living activities, or as complex as skilled therapeutic care for the treatment and management of chronic conditions. Like hospice services, long-term care can be provided in a variety of settings, such as nursing homes, assisted living facilities, or a patient's own home. Finding the services that fit your needs can be difficult. Information will be your best tool. Start with asking your doctor. Although many doctors don't really have much experience working with nursing homes and home care, they at least know the organization's reputation. Doctors can also help work out a description of what services you probably need now and in the near future.

Home health services

Home health care can help for a short time during recovery from an illness or a procedure, or it can be a long-term arrangement that provides an alternative to institutional care. These services aim at allowing individuals to remain at home and be independent. Advances in technology have also directly affected the growth

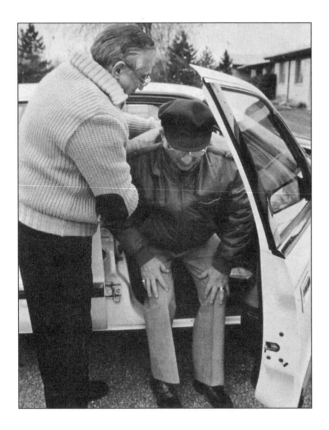

in home health care services. Many types of organizations and agencies provide home care services to clients and their families. Some are more regulated than others. Some may or may not be Medicare-certified.

Home health agencies provide skilled home care services through physicians, nurses, therapists, social workers, and homemakers that they recruit and supervise. In order to be covered by insurance, however, a physician must prescribe that the services be delivered. Don't hesitate to ask your physician or social worker if she thinks that this kind of service would benefit you and your family.

Medicare will cover some home health services. To qualify, the person must be confined to the home and require part-time intermittent nursing care and physical or speech therapy. Some services are not Medicare-certified. The clients receiving these services will generally pay out of their own pockets.

Home care aide agencies provide more informal assistance such as meal preparation, bathing, dressing, and housekeeping. Some states require that they meet minimum standards established by the state. These agencies recruit, train, and supervise their personnel. These services enable people to remain at home and be relatively independent.

Adult day services

Adult day care programs combine personal services and light medical and nursing care in a "center" that is used daily or a few days each week. Such centers are typically open long hours during the day so that family members can work and raise children. Adult day care centers can provide important support to family caregivers and enrichment to patients.

There are two types of adult day services. One is more informal with no legal requirements, required activities for the clients, or staff qualifications. Medicaid and other insurance do not cover these "social day care centers," therefore, most clients are funded through private payments.

"Medical adult day care," in contrast, is regulated, licensed, and often paid for by Medicaid. The center can be freestanding or affiliated with a nursing home or a hospital. Participants are similar to those usually found in a nursing home. This service allows people with mild to moderate dementia, chronic physical problems, or other conditions requiring daytime care to live at home because the daily burden of care is reduced for their caregivers. Licensure is mandated, along with requirements for certain services including transportation to and from the facility, medical monitoring, group activities, and medication administration.

Providers sometimes specialize in specific conditions. For example, there are day programs for people with AIDS or multiple sclerosis. Others are operating like outpatient sub-acute care centers, offering services such as occupational therapy, intravenous therapy, speech therapy, and wound care. Clients may need these services for just a month or two, and day care can be a good alternative to the more expensive and restrictive care one could receive in a nursing home.

Sub-acute care

Sub-acute care is a relatively new and rapidly growing medical care service in America. It focuses upon care right after a serious illness in a hospital, when you still need antibiotics or physical therapy while recovering. Nursing facilities are dedicating entire wings, even entire facilities, to provide high-tech, hospital-like medical care to seriously ill patients of all ages. Generally, the individual's condition is such that the care does not depend heavily on high-technology monitoring or complex diagnostic procedures.

Sub-acute care facilities are sometimes reimbursed by Medicare or other insurance, but the situation is changing and complicated and you would do well to make arrangements and decisions ahead of time. Sub-acute facilities are usually licensed as nursing homes, not hospitals.

Assisted living

Based on a Scandinavian and Dutch model for senior living, assisted living first emerged in America during the mid-1980s. Assisted living combines housing, personal services, and light medical or nursing care in an environment that promotes maximum individual independence, privacy, and choice. Clients can receive help with personal activities, including eating, dressing, and bathing, as well as meal preparation, laundry, housekeeping, recreation, and transportation. While assisted living customers may be too frail to live alone, they are too healthy to need most of the nursing services provided in a nursing facility. Assisted living residences typically do not provide 24-hour skilled nursing care, but can help with daily tasks including the supervision of medication by a qualified staff person. The "typical" assisted living customer is an 86-year-old woman who is mobile, but needs assistance with some personal activities. Whether proprietary or non-profit, assisted living residences serve mostly a private-pay clientele.

Today, there are between 40,000 and 65,000 residences, housing up to one million people. Customers stay in assisted living residences an average of 34 months.

As needs change, elderly people leave assisted living residences, mostly because they need more intensive care.

How do I pay for these services?

Confused? You are not alone. Knowing and understanding how each kind of these services are paid for is not simple. Here is a brief guide of what is covered by traditional Medicare and Medicaid. As always, these services and how they are paid for vary depending on where you live and on recent changes in coverage. Ask your doctor, nurse, social worker, or case manager to guide you.

Service	Medicare	Medicaid	Private
Hospital care	usually	secondary	often part of bill
Emergency ambulance	usually	secondary	not usually much
Sub-acute care	often covers most	part	part
Nursing home	very little	commonly yes	common
Medications	usually no	commonly yes	commonly yes
Home health nurses	usually	usually	often part
Home health aides	usually not	commonly yes	commonly yes

Chapter 6

Talking with your doctor

"When the doctor asks, 'How are you?' and you say, 'Fine,' the doctor thinks he has gathered clinical facts, while you think you have been polite."

MOTHER OF A CHILD WITH CANCER

It isn't easy to talk about disease and dying. And talking specifically about your own dying is both harder and more important to do. Sometimes talking about it is hard because you don't know the words to use. That isn't your failure — our society doesn't have the words and shared stories that would make it natural to talk of death and dying. Sometimes it is hard to talk about your own dying because you are afraid to learn what might happen next. You might fear that if you talk about something bad, you will cause it to happen. Even if you know this "magical thinking" is illogical, it can still keep you from talking and asking important questions.

When you put something into words, sometimes it is more "real" than if you don't mention it. Often, however, the future becomes less threatening when you name and describe it. Until then, your thoughts and feelings are often too vague to confront and manage.

And, of course, you might be afraid of what kind of response you will get when you speak of dying, pain, and fear of what is likely to happen to you. Although doctors are supposed to take care of sick and dying patients, you might be afraid your doctor will think you are "giving up" and give up on you, too.

Was it your very predicament that made me sure I could trust you, if I were dying, to say so, not insult me with soothing fictions?

W. H. AUDEN
from "The Art of Healing"

It is not "giving up" or being overly anxious to ask questions. "What is likely to happen to me?" "What treatment options are available, and what are they likely to do for me?" "What do I do if my pain gets worse?" "What will happen to me as I die?" You can talk with your doctor and get information that will help you live more comfortably day-to-day. You can also improve the care you get by talking to your doctor about the issues that affect you.

There is no "right" way to talk with your doctor — there are only ways that work for you. And they don't always work perfectly either. When the lines of communication get crossed, despite your best efforts, it's okay to try something different. You can also shrug and say "oh, well" and see if the next conversation is better, especially if you and your doctor have usually had a good rapport. However, there are things that you should know and do to increase the likelihood that your conversations will be successful.

Know what you should expect from your doctor

When you are living with a serious illness, your relationship with your doctor becomes especially important. You should feel secure in that relationship, and you should know what you can expect. If you have many doctors, then you should identify one as your *primary doctor*. This is the doctor you call for emergencies, medication changes, new or changing symptoms, and even to clarify what other doctors may have told you. This doctor may be any of the doctors that you have. If you expect one of your specialists to fill this role, you should explicitly ask the doctor if he will do so. Many specialists expect to limit themselves to advising patients, family practitioners, general practitioners, and internists. Other specialists, however, are prepared to be the primary doctor who will see you through the frequent changes, complications, and treatments of a chronic, severe disease. Sometimes a nurse, nurse practitioner, or physician assistant will be your "primary doctor." Throughout this book — and throughout health care — these professionals function very much like doctors and we'll use the term "doctor" for all.

Often expectations are personal. Only you can decide if a doctor has a sufficiently pleasing personality, comforting bedside manner, and respect for you and your time to establish or continue your relationship. In fact, writing down what characteristics are important to you can help you choose a doctor (see p. 60). But other expectations are universal; your doctor should be competent, dependable, and have a professional demeanor. Your doctor should also have reliable coverage "after hours."

Competence can be judged in several ways. You can ask if the doctor is "board-certified" in his specialty or look for him in medical specialty directories found in many public libraries. Doctors who are "board-certified" have had additional training and passed an examination in their fields of medicine. You can ask how much experience your doctor has in caring for patients who lived and died with your disease. And you can ask how those deaths went. In addition, you should consider your previous experiences with the doctor, as well as opinions of friends or other doctors who referred you to him.

Dependability includes many different things. Your phone calls should be returned in a timely fashion by someone who can reasonably be expected to answer your questions. Dependability also means that getting information about

CHOOSING A DOCTOR

If you are looking for a new doctor, decide what qualities are important to you. Ask family members, friends, and other health care professionals for the names of doctors they recommend. Then find out the answers to some important questions.

- *Is the doctor accepting new patients?*
- *Is the doctor in a group practice?*
- *What days and times does the doctor see patients?*
- *How far in advance do I have to make appointments?*
- *How fast can I be seen if something happens that scares me? Who will likely see me then?*
- *Can the office do simple urine and blood tests?*
- *Who takes care of patients after hours or when my doctor is away?*
- *Is the office located close enough to be a comfortable trip?*
- *Which hospital does the doctor admit patients to?*
- *Does the doctor see patients at home? in nursing homes? in hospice?*
- *Does the doctor accept my insurance or health plan?*

Call the office of each doctor you are considering, tell them that you are looking for a new doctor, and ask the questions you choose. Also, ask if the doctor has introductory visits available for people who want to meet before deciding on a doctor. If so, ask what you should bring with you to such a meeting and what the fee will be.

When you visit a doctor's office for the first time, don't wait until you meet the doctor to begin forming your impressions. Take note of how attentive the office staff is to patients, how long you and other patients wait, how long the phone rings before it is answered, how organized everyone seems to be, and how easy it appears to be to arrange payment and follow-up appointments. Also, pay attention to see if other patients' personal information is handled quietly or is discussed loudly enough for everyone to know why they called. A beautiful waiting room is nice, but it can't substitute for polite, professional care from the staff.

ADAPTED FROM *TALKING WITH YOUR DOCTOR: A GUIDE FOR OLDER PEOPLE* BY THE NATIONAL INSTITUTE ON AGING.

yourself and your situation should be easy. Test results should be relayed to you promptly and in a professional manner. That may mean a phone call or mailed note, but not an eternal wait. Ask your doctor how you can expect to get this kind of information and how long it usually takes for different tests to be completed. If you are told, "We only call you if the results are abnormal," then you may be in for days of uncertainty that fades but doesn't completely disappear. If the "no news is good news" approach does not satisfy you, ask how arrangements can be made to notify you when results become available. Or, ask when you should call for the results, or give them a self-addressed envelope to provide a reminder.

Your doctor should be professional in all aspects of your relationship. That doesn't preclude a genuine friendship. It does mean that your medical information and personal concerns are kept confidential by the doctor and staff. It means that your care is not shaped by the doctor's self-interest. Your doctor should be able to handle emergencies at any hour and should be comfortable working in various settings: hospital, nursing home, home, and emergency room.

Your doctor should also accommodate reasonable requests to stay in touch with your family. For example, a particular family member could be called before the patient leaves, after any examination.

Getting the most out of each visit with your doctor

You can prepare for your visit in a way that helps you get the information you need — and manage the information you get.

PREPARE A LIST OF QUESTIONS AND CONCERNS THAT YOU WANT TO DISCUSS. This should include any new or changed symptoms that you have experienced since your last visit. It should also include any major changes or stresses in your life, such as changes in your living arrangements, difficulties getting your medicines, or the death of a loved one. Number the items on the list so you know which are the most important to talk about.

CONSIDER BRINGING A FAMILY MEMBER OR FRIEND TO HELP YOU. You may need only moral support or company in the waiting room, but having help is good. You may forget to ask something important (especially if you didn't put it on your list!) You may wait longer than usual and feel too tired to drive yourself home. And, if you get test results or treatment recommendations, it is helpful to have someone there to help you remember many of the details of what was said.

BRING ALL OF YOUR MEDICINES OR A LIST OF ALL OF YOUR MEDICINES. Although you may think your doctor knows everything you are taking, sometimes things get left out of the chart. This happens often when a patient is being seen by more than one doctor, and information about test results or new medications hasn't gotten from one doctor to the other yet. Bring any vitamins, nutritional supplements, or herbal medicines you are taking, too. While these usually do not require a prescription, they can still interact with other medicines you may be taking.

SET YOUR PRIORITIES FOR THE DOCTOR'S TIME. At the beginning of the visit ask, "How much time do you have for me today?" Then, address the issues on your list, beginning with the most important one. If you are not going to cover everything on the list in the time available ask, "How can I get 30 minutes (or whatever you need) to talk about the concerns I have that we don't have time for today?" This lets the doctor know that you have more concerns and that you are aware of the time constraints he may be facing.

BE HONEST. Telling the doctor what you think she wants to hear will not help her to help you. It is natural to want to seem to be improving, sometimes for your own well-being and other times to feel like a "good" patient. But this will only result in less than the best therapy for you.

ALSO, BE HONEST ABOUT YOUR PRIORITIES. It is often easier for doctors and patients to talk about medicines and treatments than it is to talk about what is really happening in the course of an eventually fatal illness. Do not be afraid to say, "We have talked a lot about the side effects and the schedule for the next round of chemotherapy. I really want to hear from you what it means that there is almost no change in the tumor."

ASK QUESTIONS. If you have questions about anything your doctor says, ask! Ask what unfamiliar words mean, why you need a certain test, or what to expect from a new medicine. Ask what new treatments and medicines are supposed to do to help you and how likely it is they will do what they are supposed to do. Ask whether the therapy being recommended is supposed to treat symptoms or prolong life. Ask what side effects you might experience. Ask what is likely to happen to you if you do not try the therapy. And do not hesitate to ask about the cost if that is of concern to you.

TAKE NOTES. Be sure to bring pencil or pen and paper to record the doctor's answers to your questions. You can assign this task to whomever comes with you if note-taking is hard for you or if you want to concentrate on talking to the doctor.

REPEAT WHAT THE DOCTOR TELLS YOU — IN YOUR OWN WORDS. Nothing tells you or your doctor what you think he said better than to say it back in

DRESS FOR SUCCESS

Although you may be a patient, you can preserve your identity, dignity, and control in your interactions with doctors and other medical personnel. Most of us would refuse to undress to talk to a complete stranger. Yet many people will mutely follow directions and put on a skimpy gown to talk to a doctor. This not only strips away your sense of identity, it distracts you from discussing important matters because you are threatened by the possibility of inopportune exposure!

- *If you are making a routine visit to a doctor you have seen regularly, you may feel perfectly comfortable in putting on a gown and waiting to be examined. But keep your clothes on to maintain some dignity and control during your first visit with a doctor or during a visit when you want to discuss something particularly important.*

- *If you are told to "put this gown on and the doctor will be in soon," say: "I prefer to talk to the doctor before being examined."*

- *If you are pressed to change clothes, say directly: "I'll change after I talk to the doctor." If you do not want to argue with someone who is probably following office procedure, then just don't change clothes!*

- *If the doctor or staff asks why you are still dressed, repeat, "I prefer to talk with the doctor before being examined."*

- *When you do undress, leave on your watch or jewelry. This provides a statement of your personal style. And such items rarely interfere with an exam.*

your own words. "If I understood what you just said, then I should increase my pain medicine to 120 milligrams every 12 hours and call back day after tomorrow if that doesn't help." This allows you to uncover and correct any misunderstandings.

MAKE CONTINGENCY PLANS. Doctors can't predict every symptom or complication that you might experience, but they should be able to tell you the major ones. And the ones you already have may change over time. Ask the doctor what to expect and what to do if you have a problem. Do you take more medicine? Do you call the office? What if it is 3 AM? Asking these questions and planning in advance can save you frantic trips to the emergency room when you have a problem.

Talking with your doctor — special situations

One of these approaches may fit you to a tee all the time. Some might fit at different times. Or maybe you have your own method of talking to your doctor, asking questions, or investigating new ideas. The most important thing is that you feel that your explorations and control are supported as you stay as involved as you want in choosing treatment or care options.

"THE SOCIAL PLEASANTRY"

Doctor: *How are you doing?*

Patient: *Pretty good, thanks.*

Doctor: *Good, good. We'll see what the tests today show.* (Leaves)

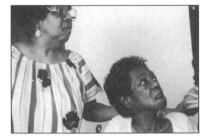

Have you had this conversation with your doctor? Was the doctor insensitive to your need to talk or ask questions? Did you feel you were not assertive enough in demanding some of the doctor's time? Did you think you were exchanging a social pleasantry while the doctor thought he was gathering clinical information? Or was nothing wrong with this exchange? Maybe all of the above, depending on your circumstances at the time.

If you needed to talk to your doctor about something important to you, then you probably felt slighted, hurt, even angry at the doctor's lack of concern for your needs. He should have known better. You were sick and obviously needed his attention. Of course you weren't "pretty good." That was a polite response, a prelude to real conversation. On the other hand, you might have blamed yourself for not speaking up and demanding that the doctor stay and listen to you or, at least, schedule a definite time to come back and talk with you. Both of these reactions are natural, but neither help you get what you really want — more time and consideration for something causing you distress.

If that was the case, there are several ways to avoid both the feeling that your doctor is insensitive or that you are suddenly incapable of speaking up for yourself.

Doctor: *How are you doing?*

Patient: *Not so good today. The nausea's worse, although my breathing is a bit better.*

First, consider that what sounds like a variation on "hello" may be a real question and answer it accordingly. It may feel awkward or impolite, but it will get your point across.

Doctor: *How are you doing?*

Patient: *I'm glad to see you. I have some questions about my breathing getting more difficult. Won't you have a seat?*

Second, offer an answer that suggests there is more to come. In a hospital or home setting, you can even combine this with a little old-fashioned hospitality that will encourage the doctor to hear you out.

Doctor: *How are you doing?*

Patient: *Pretty good, but I really want to talk about what I should expect if my cancer keeps spreading. How much time do you have for me today?*

Finally, ask a question to gauge whether your expectations of a lengthy conversation are realistic. This is very important to do if you have scheduled a "routine" or "follow-up" appointment, but you want to discuss a new problem or an especially troubling issue.

Even if the doctor doesn't have time to sit for a long conversation, you have put him on notice that you expect to talk further. If he offers to return to your hospital room later, ask: **"When should I expect you back?"** If you are at his office, and you have the time and energy, you can offer to wait. If that is not a good option, ask: **"What should I say to let the nurse or receptionist know that I need more time with you next visit?"**

But maybe you see nothing wrong with the question, answer, or doctor's response. You might have been in the hospital or office specifically for tests, and the greeting was meant to be social. You might have been feeling "pretty good" with no pressing needs to discuss. Or maybe you choose to discuss your medical problems with your doctor, but your feelings, fears, or other concerns with someone else. As long as your questions are being answered by someone knowledgeable about your condition and your plan of care — and your needs are being met — that is okay.

"I READ SOMEWHERE . . ."

Doctor: *Do you have any questions?*

Patient: *Doc, I know you said nothing will cure this disease, but last week I read in a magazine about something new . . .*

Some people like to be very involved in researching their illnesses, diagnostic tests, and treatment options. This may mean asking other people how they've fared with the same disease or doing research on the Internet or in a medical library. Your involvement may vary depending on how well you feel and how far along you may be in the course of your disease. The reception you get from your doctor may also vary.

She might listen intently, offer to take the information, and research it further. She might listen briefly, then tell you why such an idea is experimental, unsupported by the evidence, or just fanciful. Or she might cut you off, telling you that such articles are nonsense and she would have told you if there was something else to try. You are the only one who can decide which of these responses is acceptable to you on any given day.

If you are bothered that your doctor is not taking your concerns or ideas seriously (and you do not want to change doctors), you have several choices. You can try the "direct approach." **"I want to know more about this treatment that I was reading about."** But be careful of the "most direct approach": "I'm the one who's sick, and I want you to listen to this!" While it gets your point across, it is more likely to encourage your doctor to hide from you than to consider the alternative you are trying to discuss.

You might try the "curiosity approach." "I was just wondering about this treatment that I recently read about...." It is still an honest question. If this feels like a weak approach to you, you might be concerned that your doctor will not take your question seriously. If you feel that you or your question is dismissed, you can have an insistent follow-up ready.

SET THE STAGE FOR A SUCCESSFUL CONVERSATION

Although you probably can't rearrange medical office space (or even many hospital rooms), you can control some of your surroundings to maintain a feeling of being a partner in the medical process and not a wayward student being sent to the principal's office.

- *When you are ushered into an examination room, sit in a chair, not on the exam table.*
- *If you are asked to sit on the exam table for a blood pressure reading or other measurements, move to a chair when the measurements are finished.*
- *If you have a choice, choose the chair that is closest to the doctor's chair.*
- *If you are too weak to sit in a chair, have the head of the examination table raised to a sitting or half-sitting position.*
- *In a hospital room, if you are in bed, offer your doctor a chair. "Do have a seat here, doctor." The one nearest the head of the bed will allow the easiest conversation between you and your doctor. You can also offer a spot on the foot of the bed if that is comfortable for you to do.*
- *If you are sitting in your hospital room, offer the chair nearest to you.*
- *If your encounter is in the hall, say, "Let's go back to my room," then walk in that direction. This not only encourages privacy, but allows you to choose the most comfortable place to sit and feel in control.*
- *Extend your hand when the doctor walks into the examination room to begin the visit on a more equal level. This can even be done if you are lying flat on your back in a hospital bed.*

Doctor: *That's nonsense. I'll tell you about anything that will help you.*

Patient: *Well, I'd still appreciate hearing what you know about it.*

Being insistent is not being rude. It does not make you a "bad patient." Some doctors do become abrupt when questioned about new treatments. They may feel that their knowledge or judgment is being questioned. On the other hand, they may be worried that you are denying your illness by grasping at "treatments" that will not help you (and may harm you in some way).

Still, you should be comfortable asking your questions, even if you do not like the answers. If your doctor is unacceptably exasperated or brusque when you ask questions, you can be direct without being apologetic. "I hope it doesn't bother you to talk about other treatments, even if you don't think they will help. After all, it is important to me to feel that I've made the best choices I could." If you find your doctor to be frankly hostile, it may be time to save your energy and consider changing doctors.

"TELL ME WHAT TO DO!"

Doctor: *Have you thought about the different treatments that we talked about?*

Patient: *Yes, but I don't know what to do.*

Doctor: *Well, do you have more questions?*

Patient: *No, I just want to do what you think is best.*

Even if you are very assertive about knowing all there is to know about your illness and making your own decisions, there may be a time when you just don't know what to do. You might want someone else to make the decision. It may be a relief to have someone just tell you what you should do. And that's okay.

Having a serious illness, especially one that you are likely to die of, is overwhelming in at least two ways. First, the very thought of dying is overwhelming. Second, there are a multitude of decisions that must be made throughout the course of the illness. These can tax the healthiest of people, not to mention those feeling ill from side effects of medication, lack of sleep, or just being sick and tired.

Some people are very comfortable having others make decisions for them, or at least weighing others' opinions before making their own decisions. If that's you, then the best thing you can do

is identify family members, doctors, and other people whose opinions you trust.

Other people fear that if they reach the point where they are asking other people to make decisions for them, they are "giving up" either control or the will to live. Neither of those is a bad thing if it is what you need to do. In fact, it can be a relief. But if the need to let someone else take control, even for a while, distresses you, it may help to tell yourself a few important things.

Remember that you've made a lot of decisions up to this point. Choosing to let one pass is really a choice, not a loss of your ability, adulthood, or right to make future decisions. If you are truly unhappy with the decision, it is likely to be flexible; few decisions are one-chance-only opportunities. If you are relying on a family member or friend to make a decision for you, then you probably picked that person (and this decision for him to make) because you are comfortable with his judgment. If you are asking your doctor to decide for you, then you are relying on someone whose expertise you have sought because you believe her judgment and knowledge of you and your illness to be sound.

"I DON'T WANT TO KNOW"

Patient: *If it's bad news, I don't want to hear it. I especially don't want to know if my heart was worse on that last test. Tell my daughter, not me.*

Doctor: *Okay. I'm giving you this medicine to treat your pain. Take two pills three times every day, and come back in two weeks.*

The "don't ask–don't tell" policy is not much in vogue these days because it seems too paternalistic for our modern society. Patients are encouraged to take control of their care, and doctors are exhorted to tell their patients "the truth." But some people really don't want to hear their diagnoses — or at least not just yet. Often people guess what is going on but don't want to hear the words or talk about their illness in specific terms. Still others don't want to be told for other personal or cultural reasons.

While this form of communication is not for everyone, it can be very important for some. If you are one of those folks, you might focus on the

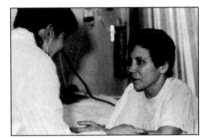

effects that your illness is having on your life (too tired to go shopping, lack of appetite, etc.) without discussing the effects of the illness on your organs and body chemistry. You can ask your doctor what you can expect in terms of daily life without listening to a recitation of medical facts. And you can certainly change your mind and ask questions later if you want to talk about specifics.

You should know that most doctors, and many family members, are uncomfortable with this method of living with illness, even if you prefer it. You may have to insist that this is the way you want to handle things. You may have to insist more than once. If this is your choice, however, it is likely to have been your choice before. Family, friends, and doctors may be uncomfortable, but not totally surprised. Your choice, then, may be a source of puzzlement without being a source of friction.

When you are hesitant to ask questions

Some people are shy about asking "too many" questions. Many people are hesitant about asking some questions, but not others. Usually, your doctor has heard your questions before, no matter how silly, embarrassing, or far-fetched they sound to you. At some point, however, you may want to ask a question, but just can't get the words out. At times like those, try the "surrogate approach."

Have your spouse, parent, child, or whoever is close to you ask about the information while you look on tolerantly. This may seem rather devious, but works well if you are uncomfortable with any sign of irritation, real or perceived, from your doctor. Such irritation is often easier for someone else to bear if they are very protective of you or don't feel as dependent on the doctor. Furthermore, your family member may welcome the opportunity to have his or her own questions answered.

The surrogate approach works just as well for gathering other medical information. While you may be just as interested in the details of your care, you may be expending most or all of your energy on getting treatments or managing day-to-day activities. Someone else may have more energy for gathering information, asking questions, keeping track of answers and other details, and running down hard-to-find people. They may also be less troubled or discouraged by brusque replies, impatience, or evasions.

Chapter 7

Controlling pain

Oh, oh, oh! she cried
as the ambulance men lifted
her to the stretcher —
Is this what you call
making me comfortable?

W. C. WILLIAMS
from "The Last Words of My English Grandmother"

You, like many people, may be especially afraid of being in terrible

pain at the end of your life. You — and the people caring for you — should know

that even severe pain can be brought under control. However, to do this, you may

need to rethink some of your ideas about pain and pain medication.

Some people hesitate to take medications because they fear becoming depen-

dent on — or even addicted to — pain relievers. Others are worried that, if they

take medicine "too soon" in the course of their illness, then there will be no medication strong enough later if the pain gets really bad. And still others are afraid that side effects will interfere with their thinking, concentration, or energy level. The fact is, good pain management can usually control your pain throughout the course of your illness without lots of side effects, without addiction, and without keeping you too tired to enjoy the things you want to do.

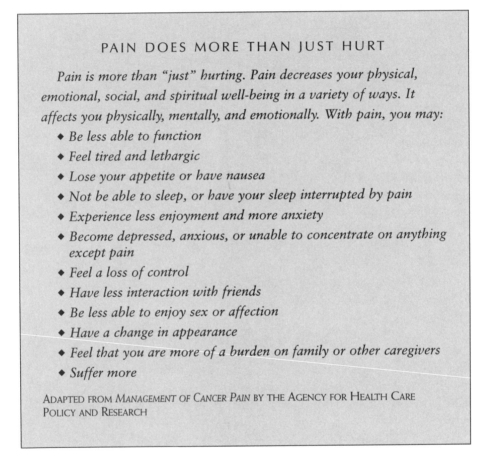

PAIN DOES MORE THAN JUST HURT

Pain is more than "just" hurting. Pain decreases your physical, emotional, social, and spiritual well-being in a variety of ways. It affects you physically, mentally, and emotionally. With pain, you may:

- *Be less able to function*
- *Feel tired and lethargic*
- *Lose your appetite or have nausea*
- *Not be able to sleep, or have your sleep interrupted by pain*
- *Experience less enjoyment and more anxiety*
- *Become depressed, anxious, or unable to concentrate on anything except pain*
- *Feel a loss of control*
- *Have less interaction with friends*
- *Be less able to enjoy sex or affection*
- *Have a change in appearance*
- *Feel that you are more of a burden on family or other caregivers*
- *Suffer more*

ADAPTED FROM *MANAGEMENT OF CANCER PAIN* BY THE AGENCY FOR HEALTH CARE POLICY AND RESEARCH

Types of pain

The only way your doctors will know about your pain is if you tell them. How you describe your pain will guide your doctors' plans to relieve your pain. Understanding and using these descriptions may help you get the relief you need more quickly. There are different types of pain, and you may experience none, one, or several of them depending on the diseases you have.

To choose the best treatment for pain, doctors usually classify pain according to *duration, cause* or *location, pattern,* and *severity.*

Your doctor will ask about the *duration* of your pain.

Acute pain is usually sudden or caused by a specific event such as surgery or injury. It lasts for hours or days and may cause increased heart rate, increased blood pressure, and anxiety.

Chronic pain may exist for months or years, often from diseases such as arthritis and cancer. Chronic pain rarely causes changes in heart rate or blood pressure but can cause loss of appetite, sleep disturbances, and depression. Many patients have trouble labeling chronic pain as "pain" at all. Instead, they use terms such as "discomfort," "ache," or "troubles." This is fine, as long as patient, family, and caregivers all understand one another. Many people with chronic pain don't look like they are in pain — it has gone on too long.

Your doctor will ask about the *location* of your pain.

You can locate pain which occurs in bones and muscles. It is usually described as sharp, aching, throbbing, or pressure.

Some pain comes from internal organs. It is usually spread out and not easy to locate in one place. Internal pain may be gnawing or cramping, or it may be sharp, aching, or throbbing, depending on what internal organ is the cause of the pain.

Pain sometimes comes from diseases affecting the nerves. These are the same nerves that help us know when things are hot, cold, sharp, or dull. Neuropathic pain is really a variation of these sensations — burning, tingling, shooting, and stabbing.

Some pain does not have an easily identified source. Such pain is very real — just because you can't quite describe it doesn't mean it is "all in your head."

All pain is part *physical* and part *psychological*. The physical part is the irritated tissues and nerves. The psychological part is how pain affects the rest of your life. And, just as pain affects your appetite, sleep, mood, social activities, and sense of well-being, these things affect your pain.

Your doctor will ask about the *pattern* of the pain you feel.

Try to recognize the pattern of your pain. It will help the physician decide which types of pain medicine are right for you: long-acting, short-acting, or a combination of the two. Do you have pain all the time? Even if your pain relief is good most of the time, does pain occasionally come unpredictably and intermittently? If so, you have what

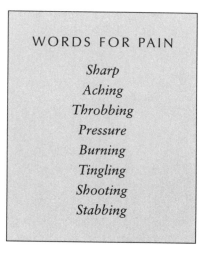

WORDS FOR PAIN

Sharp

Aching

Throbbing

Pressure

Burning

Tingling

Shooting

Stabbing

doctors would call **breakthrough** pain. Does it occur predictably when you do certain activities, like taking a bath, changing wound dressings, getting out of bed, or traveling? If so, you have what they would call **incident** pain. Does the pain increase just before the next dose of medication is due? Doctors call this pattern *"end of dose"* pain. The pattern of your pain may be like one or more of these, or it may have its own pattern. It is important to describe all your pains for your doctor.

Your doctor will ask how *severe* the pain is.

Pain is often described as ***none, moderate, severe,*** or ***excruciating.*** Pain can also be measured on various scales (including picking a number between 0, for none, and 10, for excruciating). YOU are the only one who can determine the severity of your pain. How much pain anyone else has in similar circumstances is not important in figuring out what you need. However, you might feel comfort knowing that others have been through similar experiences and have found ways to cope. You might find some people to talk with about severity of pain, medications, or activities that affect pain in order to share experiences — just don't expect that things will be the same for you.

People experience pain differently and need different doses of medicine to relieve pain. Using more or less medicine than someone else doesn't reflect on your character or ability to tolerate pain. While some people, including doctors, may express surprise at your medications, it is usually because they do not understand one of the most important rules of pain control: *The right dose of pain medicine is the dose that relieves the pain.*

Choosing the right pain medicine

You may have already taken non-prescription, *over-the-counter* medicines: *aspirin, acetaminophen* (Tylenol™), *ibuprofen* (Advil™, Motrin™, etc.), or similar medications. These are the same medications your doctor is likely to suggest for mild pain.

"What if over-the-counter medicines aren't helping anymore?"

If these medications are not relieving your pain, *tell your doctor.* The doctor needs to know that you are in pain, where the pain is located and how it feels, what medications you have tried and in what doses. Your doctor will probably add a medication called an **opioid** (sometimes called a "narcotic").

> COMMON OPIOIDS
>
> Codeine
> Oxycodone
> Hydrocodone
> Morphine
> Hydromorphone
> Fentanyl
> *(but avoid meperidine)*

These medications are often given in pills that also contain aspirin or acetaminophen. These combinations of medicines have a *synergistic effect* — that is, they work together to relieve pain better than either drug could do alone.

For example, people with cancer that has spread to their bones (bone metastases) might try a *non-steroidal anti-inflammatory agent* (ibuprofen or similar drug) in addition to an opioid. However, these drugs have many side effects and patients should always check with their doctor before taking them. People with a history of stomach ulcers, internal bleeding, or liver or kidney disease are especially prone to side effects.

"I am taking opioids. Should I keep taking the medicine I used to take, too?"

If your doctor writes a prescription for a pain medication, ask if you should continue to take your over-the-counter medications. *Do not continue to take over-the-counter medications unless your doctor tells you that it is safe to do so.*

If these opioids or combination medications do not relieve your pain, or if you are having severe pain, other opioids should be prescribed. Although there are many such medications, the commonly used ones include *morphine, oxycodone, hydromorphone, methadone,* and *fentanyl.* One older opioid called meperidine (Demerol™) has too many side effects and too short a period of activity and should rarely be used. If your doctor prescribes any opioid, *ask if you should add an over-the-counter medicine to your schedule.*

Different ways to take pain medicine

Pain medicine can be taken in a number of ways. Most of the time, you will take pain medicine *orally*, by mouth, as pills or liquids. Over-the-counter medicines are usually taken regularly every 4 to 8 hours, depending on the medication. Opioids are usually taken regularly by mouth every 4 to 12 hours. Morphine, hydromorphone, and oxycodone are available in long-acting forms that may be taken every 8 to 24 hours. Doses of opioids for breakthrough pain may be taken as often as every 30 minutes, depending on the dose and the specific medicine. Be sure you know your schedule for taking medications. Write it down and review it with your doctor.

> *I knew I was free in a way I'd never felt before. . . . The pain was still unquestionably in me; but . . . it seemed contained and watched from a distance.*
>
> REYNOLDS PRICE
> *from* A Whole New Life

"My mother is in severe pain and cannot swallow the pills we have for her."

For pain that is difficult to control, or for patients who are having trouble swallowing, various options are available. Pain medicine can be given *subcutaneously*, through a thin catheter attached to a very small needle placed just under the skin. A small battery-operated pump (PCA pump or CADD pump) can deliver injections continuously or on a regular schedule and allow patients to take extra doses for breakthrough pain.

Patients having trouble swallowing for a short period of time may be given *rectal* medications. This is especially useful if swallowing becomes difficult or a pump malfunctions and it is the middle of the night. Most oral medications, but not all, can be given rectally with good results. However, many people would not want rectal medications for a long period of time. Rectal medications are not very useful for patients having diarrhea.

Some people treat their pain with a *transdermal* ("across the skin") patch. The opioid fentanyl is the only one you can get in a patch right now. The patch is placed on the chest or back and changed every three days. The patch is an effective method of controlling pain because it keeps the dosage at a fairly constant level. But, because it takes medicine in the patch 12 to 18 hours to reach a useful level in the bloodstream, a quicker acting (oral, sublingual, rectal, or injectable) medication must be used during the first few days of wearing a patch and should be available to treat breakthrough pain.

Finally, many medications can be administered *intravenously* (IV), through a catheter in a vein. While this works in a hospital setting when an IV may be placed for other reasons, it may also be used at home. Some people will have had "permanent" catheters placed in order to give other medications. These are easy to use for pain medications, but patient and family have to learn some routines to use in caring for the catheter.

Pain medications can also be given by injections into muscle or into the space around the spinal cord. There is always a reasonably convenient and effective way to take pain medications.

Doses of pain medicine

Over-the-counter medications are taken in the same doses as recommended on the label. When medications such as aspirin, acetaminophen (Tylenol™), ibupro-fen (Advil™, Motrin™, etc.) are included in prescription medications, the total dose of these should still not exceed the maximum recommended daily dose on the over-the-counter labels, so be sure to ask your doctor or pharmacist what the maximum dose would be.

"What is the usual dose of morphine? Isn't mine too high?"

The right amount of opioid medica-tion is the amount that relieves your pain with minimal or tolerable side effects. There is *no usual dose*. Some people need small doses of opioids, while others need much larger doses. The amount of medicine that you need for pain relief is not related to how well you tolerate pain or how well you are coping with your disease. It is not a weakness to take large doses of medi-cine if that is what you need to relieve your pain.

Just as there is no usual dose, there is *no maximum dose* of opioids. This is unlike over-the-counter medications, which DO have a maximum dose (and have serious side effects if you take too much). For opioids, you increase the dose if your pain increases. Also, there is no ceiling effect — no point when increasing the dose won't work anymore to reduce the pain. Some people worry that they will get so used to the medication that it will not relieve their pain anymore. There is always a dose which will overcome any tendency of the body to be "used to" opioid drugs.

> ## DYING WELL
>
> *It was pain, raw and unyielding that drove him to ask for help.*
>
> *"Oh my God, I can't take this. I can't do this. I don't want to die like this. It's so dark, so horrible, it hurts so bad."*
>
> *The nurse drew up the morphine. "It's a beast, clawing at you, but we're going to take care of that beast right now."*
>
> *The needle pierced his skin, and in ninety seconds he relaxed and said "You mean it, don't you?"*
>
> *"Mean what?"*
>
> *"You'll be here."*
>
> NEW YORK TIMES MAGAZINE, JULY 6, 1997, PAUL WILKES

"My husband says he won't take more pain medication — he feels like he's giving in to his disease."

Some people do not want to take medication for pain because they feel that doing so is giving in to their disease. Remember, though, that living well is often the best revenge. Trying to ignore your pain will not make your disease go away. Ignoring pain will only make you even more aware of your disease, and will detract from the time you have left. Treating your pain will keep your disease from controlling your life more than it already does.

Some people look at the amount of pain they are in as a measuring stick. They judge whether their disease is getting worse by how much pain they are having. Although pain may worsen as some diseases worsen, it is not a reliable indicator of disease activity. Sometimes a small injury or change hurts a great deal. Some people have a lot of pain with less disease; others have little pain with advanced disease.

A few rules about pain management

There are some general rules that are helpful to know.

If you have more pain after having had no pain on a stable dose of an opioid, your regular dose will generally need to be increased by at least one-half (50%). For example, if you are taking 10 milligrams (mg) of morphine every four hours, your doctor will usually need to increase your dose to 15 mg every four hours to get pain relief again. This is just as true if you were taking 100 mg every four hours; the new dose is likely to be about 150 mg.

*The dose of medication needed to treat **breakthrough pain** is determined by the dose of pain medicine that you take regularly.* The breakthrough dose is usually equivalent to one to two hours' worth of your regular dose. So, your break-through dose should increase as your regularly scheduled dose increases. This is **NOT** because you are taking too much medicine. It is because the breakthrough dose has to be calculated as a percentage of the regular dose. Again, the person taking 10 mg every four hours will need 3–5 mg for breakthrough pain, and the person taking 100 mg will need 30–50 mg. These larger doses often cause some anxiety for professionals who are not used to using them. Talk to your doctor about the dose of medicine you should take for breakthrough pain, and have your doctor talk with people in your family or care team who need to understand how the dosing works.

*Because **incident pain** is predictable, the best treatment is to take a dose of med-ication before starting the activity that produces pain.* The dose may or may not be the same as your breakthrough pain dose. Work with your doctor and use your own experience to determine what dose best prevents pain before specific activities.

*You can treat **end of dose** failure in one of two ways, depending on your medicine and your medication schedule.* You can *increase the dose* of medicine, or you can *decrease the amount of time* between doses. Also, if you are using pills that are not long-acting, you might switch to long-acting versions that "smooth out" the tran-sition time between doses. Talk with your doctor about the best choice for you.

The amount of medicine that you take will be very different depending on the route used. If you switch from morphine tablets to injections, for example, the dosage usually needs to be cut to about one-third.

It is usually better to take one kind of opioid at a time, although you will need to take two if one is a transdermal patch. Taking only one opioid limits the side effects and makes it easier to calculate dose changes. However, there may be times when you need to change opioids. When this happens, your doctor may prescribe a slightly lower dose than the "*equivalent dose*" to your previous opioid. This is because equivalent doses are not exact and because your body may need less of an opioid that it is not used to having. Use your breakthrough medication for pain while you and your doctor adjust your new medicine.

Opioids are really very safe drugs; used as described, they are very unlikely to speed up dying even if you end up taking very large doses. Some people feel that opioids must kill — they are so often in use at the end of life. But this is not the case. They provide a great deal of comfort and are quite safe when used appropriately.

How often to take pain medicine

Usually, you must take opioids around the clock to relieve and prevent pain. Some people try not to take opioids too often for fear that they will become addicted to the medicine. But waiting until you "need the medicine" or "can't stand the pain anymore" is NOT an effective way to take opioids. First, it means that you will have much more pain. Second, when your pain becomes extreme, it will take more medicine to relieve your pain. To get good pain relief with the least amount of medicine, take your medications, especially opioids, on schedule. Try to prevent pain rather than to have to treat it.

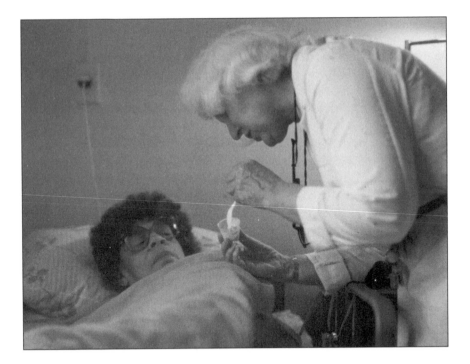

Fear of addiction

Many people are worried about addiction to pain medicine. Unfortunately, as our society has battled illegal drug use, people have become discouraged from taking legal medications when they really need them. But you should not "just say no" to good pain relief. And you will not become an addict by taking your medicine as prescribed.

Addiction is a psychological disorder of drug craving and compulsive drug use when taking drugs is harmful to the user. Addiction is really very rare in people who take opioids for illness. It is NOT the same as taking medicine because you have pain. It is not the same as tolerance or physical dependence, either.

Tolerance means that increasing doses of an opioid are needed to maintain the effects of the medicine. In treating pain with opioids, tolerance is a useful feature. It allows most side effects to wear off a few days after a dose is increased. *Physical dependence* means that the body becomes used to having an opioid present. Physical dependence happens to everyone who uses opioids for more than a few days, but all it means is that opioids should never be stopped suddenly. They should be weaned over a few days if they are going to be stopped. If they are stopped suddenly, you may have **withdrawal** — a very uncomfortable flu-like syndrome including muscle aches, nausea, diarrhea, and sometimes vomiting or even muscle spasms. If a person suddenly cannot take opioids by mouth, the weaning needs to be done by some other route (by rectal suppository or intravenous infusion, for example).

> *"That's just pain," she said. "It goes eventually. And when it's gone, there's no lasting memory. Not the worst of it, anyway. It fades. Our minds aren't made to hold on to the particulars of pain the way we do bliss. It's a gift God gives us, a sign of His care for us."*
>
> CHARLES FRAZIER
> *from* Cold Mountain

Side effects of pain medications

Opioids do have side effects; the most troublesome is **constipation**. Almost everyone needs stool softeners and laxatives to prevent constipation. You may also need an occasional enema (see also *Constipation*, Chapter 8). Keep in mind that you will **NOT** develop tolerance to the constipating effects of opioids. As you increase the amount of your dose of pain medication, you should increase your stool softeners and laxatives.

Opioids can cause **drowsiness**. Usually, however, your doctor can prescribe a dose of medication that will relieve your pain without causing confusion or excess sleepiness. Do not be alarmed by increased drowsiness for a day or two after increasing your dose of medicine. Some of your drowsiness may be from not sleeping well because of your pain. You may be exhausted and need to "catch up" on your sleep. Or you may need a few days to develop tolerance to the drowsiness, which will then lessen. Very sick people can have somewhat diminished response times even when they are not feeling drowsy. However, if you generally feel well and you are taking a stable dose of medications, you probably can drive safely. Talk with your doctor before you drive a car or do anything else that might be dangerous if you were slowed in response to an emergency.

If your drowsiness does not go away in two or three days, ask your doctor if another medication might be responsible or if you might benefit from taking a stimulant to counteract the sedating effects of the opioid. **Remember that patients should not have to accept sedation or coma in order to be comfortable unless they are very weak and near death, when the tradeoff is often welcome.** If you are much stronger and active, there is probably something more that could be done for your pain.

RELIEVING PAIN IN OTHER WAYS

Although pain medications are useful, there are other methods that help to relieve pain effectively, often in addition to pain medications. Most are pretty harmless, so feel free to try them out and see if some work for you. These include:

- *Heat and cold*
- *Massage*
- *Electrical stimulation (TENS unit)*
- *Exercise*
- *Meditation*
- *Relaxation*
- *Imagery*
- *Acupuncture/acupressure*
- *Hypnosis*
- *Peer support groups*
- *Pastoral and spiritual support*

Some people experience *confusion* or *delirium* when they take certain opioids. This usually limits the use of the specific opioid to a few doses because no one wants to take a chance that the confusion will continue or get worse. This is not the same thing as an *allergy*, although people are often told to say they are allergic to the medication to avoid it being given to them again. Allergies to opioids are actually very rare. However, just because someone becomes confused taking one opioid does not mean that he cannot try a different opioid. Usually there is a dose of opioid which avoids this problem, at least most of the time.

If taking an opioid causes *nausea*, then you should consider trying another opioid or taking an *anti-emetic*, which is a medication that stops nausea. Often the nausea disappears as tolerance develops. Do not let an easily controlled side effect such as nausea keep you from taking your pain medicine.

A few people taking high doses of opioids develop *muscle twitching* (myoclonus). This occurs mostly when a person is in and out of consciousness prior to death. When that is the case, the tremors and twitching are more likely to bother family, friends, and staff than they are to bother the person having them. If, however, you are having myoclonus that interferes with your activities, then a muscle relaxant or change in medication may be helpful.

If you have lung disease or congestive heart failure, you may experience both pain and shortness of breath. Conveniently, opioids are used to relieve the feeling of breathlessness that people with heart and lung disease often experience. Nevertheless, extra care should be used when treating your pain with opioids. When you are very close to death, the opioids that provide comfort by relieving severe pain could cause you to breathe a little less effectively and therefore slightly hasten your death. If this tradeoff is acceptable to you, you should make it clear to your doctors and nurses that being comfortable is more important to you than living a little longer.

> *. . . he was moribund and screaming . . . I had no morphine . . . I finally instinctively sat down on the bed and took him in my arms, and the screaming stopped . . . He died peacefully in my arms a few hours later. It was not the pleurisy that caused the screaming, but loneliness.*
>
> ARCHIE COCHRAN
> from "One Man's Medicine"

More medications that relieve pain

Pain that starts in the nerves themselves, "neuropathic pain," is best treated with *antidepressants* and *anticonvulsants*, often in combination with opioids. These are often used in doses lower than the doses used to treat depression or seizures. However, if someone has neuropathic pain and also has depression or seizures, these medications may be prescribed in traditional doses to treat both conditions at the same time.

Steroids (prednisone, dexamethasone, and others) also help relieve pain when used with opioids. The steroids reduce inflammation that can exert pressure on an already painful area. They also reduce *cerebral edema* (fluid in the brain tissues) associated with tumors or metastases in the brain, thus improving pain and some neurological symptoms. Steroids can also improve appetite and overall sense of well-being. Side effects of steroids usually depend on the dose and how long someone takes them. Most of the short-term side effects, such as elevated blood sugar, swelling of the legs and arms from fluid, difficulty sleeping, and confusion, can be managed. Because steroids can cause stomach ulcers, your doctor might prescribe an anti-ulcer medication whenever steroids are taken.

Finally, when pain is coming from a specific place, but is difficult to manage with the the usual medicines, *nerve blocks* may be performed, usually by an anesthesiologist. A nerve block is performed by injecting the area of the nerve with an anesthetic to keep the nerve from transmitting painful impulses. This is just like anesthesia for dental procedures, but it can be longer lasting. Other nerve blocks can be performed by placing a catheter in one of the spaces around the spinal cord and instilling small amounts of opioids and anesthetics. If such a catheter is placed, a pump may be used to deliver small quantities of medicine continuously to maintain pain relief.

In summary, pain can almost always be managed well enough so you can be comfortable and life can be meaningful. If pain gets to be overwhelming, usually it is because available treatments are not being used well.

Managing other symptoms

Although I arrived with an initial resistance to continual contact with the dying patient, the actual experience was quite different from what I had expected. Instead of a terminal care or "death house" environment with cachetic, narcotized, bedridden, depressed patients, I found an active community of patients, staff, families and children of staff and patients.

Dr. Leonard M. Liegner

Various symptoms cause trouble at the end of life. Many can be alleviated most, if not all, of the time.

"I feel very short of breath, as if I just can't breathe."

Depending on why you are short of breath, various procedures may ease your breathing. Fluid that collects around the lungs can be drained through a needle. You may get relief from changing position, being propped up on pillows, using oxygen, or shrinking a tumor with radiation or steroids.

If you have mild, persistent shortness of breath that can't be treated directly, you may breathe easier with a regular, low dose of opioids. Opioids include morphine, oxycodone, hydromorphone, and similar drugs. Although they are frequently prescribed for pain relief, they also ease the feeling of being short of breath. Taking opioids at bedtime can help you sleep comfortably and prevent you from waking up fighting to breathe. Some patients get the same sort of relief from drugs commonly used for anxiety.

They changed my oxygen mask and within minutes my breathing began to clear — a strange sensation, like removing thick cobwebs one by one.

TIM BROOKES
from Catching My Breath

Frank James, a 67-year-old retired bricklayer with severe emphysema, called his doctor's office to see when Dr. Miller would stop by. Ever since Frank got so short of breath that a doctor's office visit was exhausting, Dr. Miller had been stopping by every month or so to check on him at home. They had a firm understanding that Mr. James would never again be put on a ventilator. Mr. James' sister, Clara, lived with him and had agreed to page Dr. Miller if there was a sudden change or a bad episode. Thus, Mr. James was startled to hear the receptionist: "Mr. James, Dr. Miller has had a health problem of his own. He's arranged for a new doctor, Dr. Winchester, to take over his practice until his own health gets straightened out." As his anxiety mounted, Mr. James felt his breathing getting hard and motioned to Clara to take the phone. She arranged for Dr. Winchester to come by a few days later.

After examining him and talking generally, Dr. Winchester said, "I see from Dr. Miller's notes that you have firmly decided not to go back to the hospital for shortness of breath."

Mr. James: "That's right. My time is close. This life is okay, but it's not great. When the angels come by next time, I'm going along."

Dr. Winchester: "What will you do?"

Mr. James: "I was supposed to page Doc Miller. What am I to do without him?"

Dr. Winchester: "When you get really short of breath again, do you want to have a drug to make you sleepy? You know that might mean you'd die more quickly."

Mr. James: "Yeah. But that's what Doc Miller promised."

Dr. Winchester: "Let's see what I can do. I don't live nearby like

Dr. Miller. I can't be as sure that you can reach me quickly, and I have two other doctors covering for me after hours."

After some investigation, it turned out that the local hospice could ensure a quick response. Clara was comfortable with working with the hospice team to get Mr. James the medication he would need. By the time Dr. Winchester talked with them the next day, Mr. James and his sister were reassured that they had a good plan, a caring doctor, and the opportunity to live fully in the time remaining. Clara called her son and her prayer group to tell them the good news.

Some doctors really resist using opioids for shortness of breath. If your doctor is concerned, you might share this book and encourage a look at texts on symptom management. You might also try just a low dose for a few days (or a few bedtimes). You may be able to try the drugs out in a situation where someone can monitor any tendency to breathe less well, such as when you are in a hospital or having a family member or a hospice or homecare nurse check on you after four and eight hours. A trial run with close checking might be reassuring enough to you and your doctor.

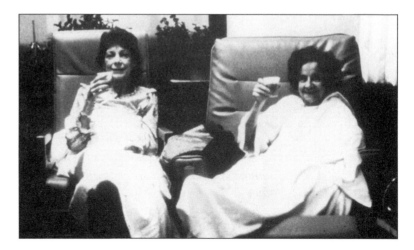

Shortness of breath is a common symptom for people who are dying. Some, however, have illnesses that make it likely that they will die with much more severe or sudden shortness of breath that does not respond to treatment to remove its cause. People with chronic heart or lung disease require more aggressive treatment to relieve the distress. Some illnesses, such as emphysema, are more likely than others to make you feel as if you just can't catch your breath. You may be afraid that you will feel as if you are suffocating — but you should *not* feel this way, no matter how you die. This is the emergency situation that you must be prepared for if your end of life is likely to include shortness of breath.

Most hospice physicians agree that patients suffering in this way should be given an opioid drug, usually morphine, to relieve shortness of breath, even if the patient becomes unconscious. If you have an illness likely to cause shortness of breath, you should talk frankly with your doctor about what he or she is willing to make available. Having specific plans in place can help ease your worries and make it more likely that your symptoms will be treated. Making arrangements while you are short of breath just doesn't work well! If you are likely to experience severe shortness of breath at the end of your life, make sure that your doctors and nurses will treat your shortness of breath aggressively, even if it may lead to unconsciousness or hasten your death somewhat. You may need to keep the medication in your home and have a way to have it administered relatively quickly. If your doctor and nurses are not comfortable with such a plan, you should try to get a palliative care or hospice consultant, or even consider looking for another care team.

MOUTH DRYNESS

Mouth dryness can be very uncomfortable. Here are some ways to relieve it:

- *Use commercial products or liquid vitamin E to ease chapped lips.*
- *Use mouth swabs moistened with water or suck on hard, sugar-free candy to relieve your dry mouth. Some new chewing gums designed especially to deal with dry mouth might help. Ask your pharmacist for a pack.*
- *Brush your teeth or use mouth sponges to clean your teeth, mouth, and tongue.*
- *Use only alcohol-free or low-alcohol formula mouthwashes. Alcohol and petroleum-based products can be very drying and should be used with care, if at all.*

"I just can't eat."

Digestive system problems are common in very sick persons. Some of these problems are related to symptoms of disease. Others are related to medications. All are best prevented, or treated early, rather than letting them get to the point of making you uncomfortable.

Nausea/vomiting: You may have nausea or vomiting because of certain medications, constipation, or bowel obstruction. Your medication may be the cause; ask your doctor about changing your medicines, or adding an *anti-emetic*, an anti-nausea drug. Constipation can cause nausea and vomiting, so treat it promptly (see below). Sometimes an imbalance in blood chemistry is the problem, so your doctor may need to check some blood tests.

Many people find that they have no appetite, and that forcing oneself to eat is not pleasant. Usually you are best advised to follow your body's instructions. Try small amounts of particularly appealing food. Also, recognize that food is often important for its symbolism (of home, friends, and traditions) and its bringing people together socially, rather than for its nutrition. Unless particular foods or salt make you sick, when you are close to the end of life, eat what you want, not what someone thinks you should.

The dying need but little, dear, —
A glass of water's all,
A flower's unobtrusive face
To punctuate the wall,

A fan, perhaps, a friend's regret,
And certainly that one
No color in the rainbow
Perceives when you are gone.

EMILY DICKINSON

Constipation: Constipation is commonplace and very uncomfortable. With limited intake, little activity, and effects of medications, it is no wonder that your bowels may be sluggish. You may also experience abdominal cramping from constipation. Talk to your doctor or nurses about using stool softeners, laxatives, and enemas to relieve constipation, especially if you are taking opioids. Always try to prevent constipation. Relief of constipation can improve your comfort, often even during late stages of dying.

Bowel obstruction: Your bowels can get blocked sometimes, especially in abdominal cancer. If you might have many months to live, doctors will advise surgery. However, if you are close to the end of life, you can stay quite comfortable without surgery by using medications to slow bowel contractions and other means to prevent stomach overfilling, as needed. A little pathway may open up, perhaps with some help from steroids, so that fluids can be absorbed normally. Although bowel obstruction may be a final complication before death, dying this way can be made quite comfortable (see Chapter 11 on forgoing nutrition and hydration).

> *Mr. Horace Black came to an inpatient hospice with widespread cancer and a stomach obstruction. He had a plastic tube suctioning his stomach, hooked to a vacuum pump. He was quiet and resigned. He had almost no family left, only a sister living in a nursing home nearby.*
>
> *The hospice nurse asked him if he'd like to try going without the suction tube. He couldn't believe that this might be possible and talked with*

the doctor, who said it might actually be preferable to get rid of the tube. The worst that might happen would be some vomiting (and the tube could be replaced if he wanted it back). In fact, if he wanted, he could take a little food and drink.

A few hours later, after some additional medications and with the tube gone, Mr. Black sipped a little fresh orange juice. Then this very reserved man called his sister and was overheard to say, tears running down his cheeks, "Rose, I'm alive again! Either that or I'm already in heaven! I'm free of that awful sound, and I'm actually tasting juice. Life is so sweet!"

Things went well for him. He had little appetite but enjoyed small tastes of favorite foods. He died peacefully ten days later.

"What are bed sores and how can I prevent them?"

When you are very sick, you are prone to have skin breakdown wherever the weight of your body presses into the bed. You are at greatest risk if you move very little or you are in bed or in a chair for a long time, especially if you also have been losing weight. Ordinary pressure on the skin as you sit or move across sheets may be enough to tear or break down your skin. It is worth a great deal of effort to keep skin well-protected; skin breakdown is uncomfortable, a major indignity, and a major expense.

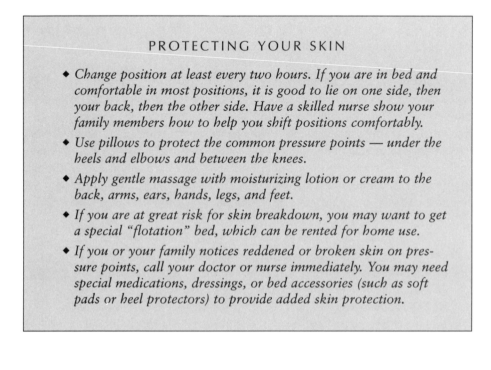

PROTECTING YOUR SKIN

- *Change position at least every two hours. If you are in bed and comfortable in most positions, it is good to lie on one side, then your back, then the other side. Have a skilled nurse show your family members how to help you shift positions comfortably.*
- *Use pillows to protect the common pressure points — under the heels and elbows and between the knees.*
- *Apply gentle massage with moisturizing lotion or cream to the back, arms, ears, hands, legs, and feet.*
- *If you are at great risk for skin breakdown, you may want to get a special "flotation" bed, which can be rented for home use.*
- *If you or your family notices reddened or broken skin on pressure points, call your doctor or nurse immediately. You may need special medications, dressings, or bed accessories (such as soft pads or heel protectors) to provide added skin protection.*

"I want to stay awake; there's so much yet to do."

Fatigue accompanies most fatal illnesses. Sometimes this tired, weak feeling comes from the disease. Other times, medicine can make you sleepy or slow down your thinking. It is certainly reasonable to try to save energy for the things that really matter to you. It is often not essential to make a trip to the physician's office or to continue a medication or exercise that is no longer helping, especially if doing so saps energy you need for something else. Sometimes it is worthwhile to try a stimulant — caffeine or a stimulant pill. Talk with your doctor about trying out something like that if your fatigue seems to be the major block to your enjoying your family or some other activity.

"Some people are so depressed, but I'm just so anxious."

Depression: While it is natural for you to feel sad as you contemplate the end of your life, this is different from true depression. If you have no interest in what is going on, see only the bleak side of life, take no pleasure in things that you usually enjoy, or seem to feel no emotions at all, then you may be suffering from a reversible depression. It is important for you or your family to talk to your doctor so that depression can be diagnosed and treated. Treatment is often effective, even in the last weeks of life. Not only will you feel better, but your family will feel better knowing you enjoyed the time you spent with them.

Anxiety: Anxiety is more than normal worrying; anxiety is feeling so worried and fearful that it interferes with any pleasurable time. If you typically feel anxiety during periods of stress, you may be more likely to feel anxiety now. The kinds of maneuvers that have helped you in the past will probably help you now. These may include reassurance, medications, and channeling your worry into productive endeavors.

Some people have greater anxiety because they feel uninformed or overwhelmed. If you are feeling this way, it is very important that you tell your doctor and family that you might do better if you had more information or more help. Good communication is probably the most important remedy for anxiety of this nature.

"Should I be worried about getting confused or just being 'out of it'?"

When you are very ill, it is easy to become confused. Confusion may be caused by a new medicine, a minor infection, or even a change in living arrangements. If this happens to you, your family should offer you soothing reassurance, perhaps

reminding you where you are and what is going on around you. Your doctor should be called in case it is helpful to adjust medications or prescribe antibiotics.

Sometimes the visions and experiences that the dying person has are comforting and meaningful: seeing family who have died before, for example. You and your family may be grateful for these experiences. If you are quite frightened or upset, however, you may feel better if your doctor orders a mild sedative or if someone can stay with you at all times. Medications are often quite effective, even at low doses.

Roughly half of dying persons are unconscious for most of their last few days. This common "drifting off" while asleep is a peaceful way to die, especially if you and your family are at peace and all plans are made. Some people contend that a dying person is often still able to hear. While this is unproven, your family can talk to you and say their goodbyes, assuming that, in some way, you can hear them.

"Remind me — can anything good happen?"

A list like this can make you feel a little overwhelmed, even though each symptom can be treated. As you have read elsewhere in this book, it is just not enough to have good symptom management. Good dying is not just avoiding bad experiences. Living well with a fatal illness involves having experiences that matter — having the chance to grow spiritually, getting to say some farewells and to feel the love of those who care about you, even just getting to see the flowers bloom one last time. You will have more chance at this if you are comfortable and confident of your doctors and nurses, of course. But you can often pursue these uniquely human "good works," even when symptoms are troubling, or when you are at odds with your care team. When you know that time may be short, every hour counts.

Chapter 9

Learning about specific illnesses

"I told my son, 'Spencer, I hope every mosquito that bites me this summer dies from the chemotherapy.' He quickly replied, 'Either that, Mom, or there are going to be a lot of bald-headed mosquitoes at Hide-A-Way Lake this summer.'"

DODY SHALL
7-year breast cancer survivor

Regardless of your illness, you are likely to share many concerns with others who face life-threatening disease, including the fears, worries, and needs for information and support that accompany this critical time in your life. Your particular illness will shape some of what you can expect to happen, and even how much can be predicted. It helps to know that doctors often can give only very general guidance on how long you will live, and what problems are likely to arise. Like birth, death is not always predictable or logical. Nevertheless, you should press your doctor, and often a knowledgeable nurse, to tell you the best and worst that your illness is likely to cause.

Organizations devoted to a particular illness can provide you with helpful information and resources, often connecting you to support groups based in your own community. Only a few, though, are prepared to deal with the problems that illnesses cause close to the end of life. We have included some of the addresses, phone numbers, and Internet web sites in Chapter 17. The Internet, which can be reached through terminals at many public libraries, offers an overwhelming amount of information. Be cautious in relying on some of the information posted in newsgroups or on bulletin boards; some of it will be no more reliable than advice you might get from a random person sitting with you on a bus. Check it out with your nurse or doctor before you trust it. One reliable source of information is the federal government's site, healthfinder (http://www.health finder.gov/), which screens sites before adding links to them.

How long do I have?

Regardless of your disease, you will want to understand your prognosis — that is, the probable course of the disease. This conversation first occurs after the initial diagnostic testing or surgery has taken place. However, discussion of prognosis should remain an ongoing consideration during any treatment planning, including when there is evidence of advanced disease. You and your doctor will often find it hard to confront these issues. It is always easier to "put it off until the next visit."

This conversation might be easier if you include it in nearly every encounter. Try out something like this: "I understand that we are always pretty uncertain when looking at the future, but what I understand now about how this disease is likely to go is that I am likely to live with it for some months before it starts taking its toll, and that then I will probably have just a few months left. Is there any-

---

QUESTIONS WORTH SEEKING ANSWERS TO

◆ *What might the "story" of the rest of my life be like (complications, needs, time frame)? Specifically, how am I likely to die?*

◆ *What are the best outcomes that I might reasonably hope for?*

◆ *What are the worst outcomes that I might reasonably have to deal with?*

◆ *Thinking about the more serious or disruptive problems that my medical and personal situation might cause, what can be done to plan ahead to manage them?*

◆ *How will this illness and its treatment affect me and my family?*

---

thing else you can tell me now? Is it reasonable to think that I will still be able to travel to be with my children this Christmas?"

Some days, you really just won't want to deal with the future. Even then, you can help the conversation next time by saying something like this: "With all the worries of the last few weeks, I can't really bear to think of things getting worse. Still, next time I see you, I would appreciate an update on how I'm doing and what problems are likely to arise, given how my disease is progressing and how I feel." By doing this, you create an opening that will make it easier for either of you to bring up the subject next time.

What follows in this chapter are summaries of important issues likely to arise in each of a series of common illnesses causing death. These thumbnail sketches are incomplete, but they give you enough information to guide you in knowing what issues to pursue for yourself. The topics we present are:

♦ heart disease
♦ cancer
♦ obstructive lung disease
♦ kidney failure
♦ liver failure
♦ HIV/AIDS
♦ dementia
♦ frailty of advanced old age

Heart disease

More Americans will die from diseases of the heart and the circulatory system than from any other cause. For most, the death will seem sudden, even if the person has been ill for some time. Most people with serious heart and blood vessel disease have episodes of serious illness — heart attacks or heart failure, for example — and then long periods of "nothing changing."

By the time you realize that heart disease might well be the cause of your death, you will already have heard about improving diet and exercise, stopping smoking, and controlling blood pressure and fats in the blood. However, you are not particularly likely to have heard from a doctor about how your disease is likely to affect you over time. Many doctors haven't really thought about it — they work on the problem you have right now and get you "back on your feet," then don't think much about how your life is going until you are sick again.

I stepped from plank to plank
So slow and cautiously;
The stars about my head I felt,
About my feet the sea.

I knew not but the next
Would be my final inch, —
This gave me that precarious gait
Some call experience.

EMILY DICKINSON

This leads to all kinds of misfortunes for many people with bad heart disease. No one ever warns them that they might live a long time, or might be gone rather suddenly. You will think that you will get a decent warning of when your time is at hand, just like your Aunt Bertha with breast cancer or cousin Harry with kidney failure. Not so. You may become too short of breath to walk stairs, or you may stay relatively well. Either way, you are likely to end up dying within a few days of being quite stable in your "ordinary" health.

Society has not really taken the opportunity to think about what it would be to live well with the high risk of sudden death. Certainly, you are not likely to want to stop all treatment — ongoing treatment and treatments of bad episodes keep you pretty comfortable and functional. On the other hand, you probably would like to avoid dying on a ventilator in intensive care. And you want that decent opportunity to say your farewells and make peace with your life.

Serious heart disease is a signal that you really should make plans in advance for the kinds of sudden events that can be emergencies. Your family needs to know whether you want the emergency rescue team called, whether you want resuscitation tried, and whether you want intensive care stopped if it seems that you have lost the ability to live outside of a hospital or nursing home. You should write down instructions for your family and put them in obvious places in your home (e.g., on the refrigerator or telephone). Also be sure your instructions are filed in your doctor's medical records and your records at the local hospital.

Dying with heart disease requires that you say "farewell" in a "can't be sure" mode. Rather than the final farewells that movies portray as people die of violence or cancer, you need to draw people together and to finish your life work in a way that acknowledges that you might still live a long time, or you might not. Perhaps you can make a video for the grandchildren; that is an enduring gift. Or you could write some letters and put them with your will. Most people respond pretty well to an open acknowledgment of the uncertainty of the situation. Perhaps you can call a brother whom you have not seen in some time and say:

"My doctor says that I just won't know when my time is up. I would really like to see you and have some time to talk. It won't be like farewells — maybe I'll still be around for a decade. But, just in case I'm not so lucky ... can you find an opportunity to come visit for a few days in the next few months? Hearing that I have a bad heart really makes me see things differently. I would like to spend some time with you."

People with heart disease generally do not have serious problems with pain, but you may well be troubled with fatigue and have little tolerance for exercise. Some people do have chest pain, but that can usually be eased with drugs. At the end, you might have serious shortness of breath.

One major decision that you should make in advance, if possible, will be whether to use a machine that will take over breathing (a ventilator or respirator). Sometimes, the odds of that working are so low that the doctor will advise against it. Sometimes the ventilator might well work in relieving the shortness of breath, but you may be too weak to live without the ventilator. You deserve the chance to talk this over with your doctor and to make plans. You will find more discussion about ventilator use and decision-making in Chapter 11.

Because these decisions are difficult, you really need a doctor you can trust, who has the skills necessary both to rescue you from episodes of shortness of breath and to help you when death will be the outcome. Especially, you need to ask the doctor explicitly whether he or she will be willing to use opioids or other drugs to ensure that you will not feel a sense of suffocation if there ever is a time when you stop a ventilator or choose not to use it. If the doctor is not willing or has never faced such a situation, you might do well to find another doctor, or at least a good hospice program with a nurse who will stand by you. You also need to be sure that your family is aware of your decisions and will support them.

You need to move as much treatment as you can into your home (including into a nursing home, if that is where you live). To do this you need (1) to have a scale to take your weight every day (and a way to get changes treated quickly), (2) to have key medications on "standby" (for pain, shortness of breath, and weight gain) so your doctor can have you take them right after a telephone conversation, (3) to have a decision made among you and those who are around you as to whether you will go to the hospital in an emergency, and (4) whether to have resuscitation attempted.

Severe heart disease once killed people quickly. Now, most of us will live a long time after onset. A few will even get a chance to try a transplant. If you might be one, you will need to do even more thorough planning — both for survival through transplant and the more likely event of dying before transplant is attempted.

Usually with heart disease, death will be rather sudden when it finally happens. To have dying unfold in the way you want, you really must plan ahead. You need to make key decisions in advance and you need to ensure that you have a capable and experienced doctor and care team.

Cancer

Early in the course of dealing with cancer, treatments aim mostly at cure or at least a substantial prolongation of life. With these goals, it is certainly worth going through a lot of discomfort. However, when cancer recurs or spreads despite treatment, then the cancer is likely to cause death eventually. The benefits of further treatment aimed at modifying the cancer must always be weighed against the burdens those treatments will cause. Usually, a time comes when all of the available treatments to change the course of the cancer offer nothing worthwhile. Through all of this, treatments are always appropriate when they enhance comfort, improve your functioning, and support families. Even when there is "nothing more to do" about the cancer growth, there's "lots to do" to maintain comfort and give you the chance to do the things that are meaningful to you and your family.

Lord, You've sent both
And may have come yourself. I will sit down, bearing up under
The death of light very well, and we will all
Have a drink. Two or three, maybe.
I see now the delights

Of being let "come home"
From the hospital
Night!
I don't have all the time
in the world, but I have all night.
I have space for me and my house,
And I have cancer and whiskey
in a lovely relation.

JAMES DICKEY
from "The Cancer Match"

Doctors use all kinds of terms for cancer — malignancy, carcinoma, lymphoma, tumor, and so on. Most people just see cancer as a word for a bad disease that can act like a parasite and destroy the body. About one-quarter of Americans will die from cancer. Compared to some other life-threatening diseases, cancer more often can be "managed." The time course is more well-understood, and most people are still able to take care of themselves and stay mentally alert until close to the end. For most people, with most cancers, pain is a real concern — but it can be controlled.

The term "cancer" refers to many diseases, each with its own distinctive characteristics. What is common to all is that some cell undergoes changes that allow it to grow in an abnormal fashion, multiplying uncontrollably. The continuing growth of these deviant cells leads to the development of a mass or growth called a tumor. Two unique characteristics of cancer cells create its life-threatening nature. First, cancer cells may spread to adjacent areas and invade normal tissues and organs, depriving them of nutrition and competing for space. Second, these cells may travel to a distant part of the body where they begin the development of another tumor, called a *metastasis*. The most common sites of metastatic spread are the bones, lungs, liver, brain, and central nervous system.

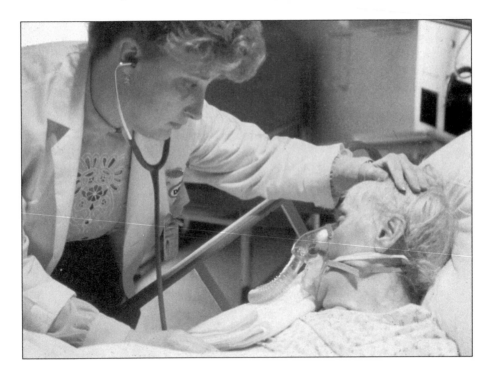

The most common signs and symptoms of advanced cancer are weakness, loss of appetite, loss of weight, pain, nausea, constipation, sleepiness or confusion, and shortness of breath. Pain is the most important symptom to plan for. Make sure that your doctor and your other caregivers are good at preventing and treating pain. Be sure also that your doctor and care team are experienced and comfortable in treating shortness of breath. Most serious symptoms in cancer are predictable, and prevention or rapid treatment works well. Thus, it is worthwhile to get your doctor to think with you about how to prevent or treat likely or very disruptive complications.

Some types of cancer — certain lymphomas, leukemias, and breast and prostate cancers — are characterized by a chronic nature. Long-term management using a combination of surgeries, medications, and radiation slows the progression of these diseases and alleviates symptoms. People live for many years with some of these illnesses.

The tongues of dying men

Enforce attention like deep harmony.

WILLIAM SHAKESPEARE
from King Richard II

When treatments won't really change the time course of the cancer, you still need comfort care, or what doctors call palliation, the relief of symptoms that interfere with your quality of life. In fact, you should aim to live well throughout the course of your illness, pursuing those personal goals that you can achieve while remaining comfortable at all times.

Treatment planning, how you and your doctor plan to manage and treat your disease, must be updated throughout the entire course of the disease. Cancer is often unpredictable. Furthermore, someone with advanced cancer who is receiving supportive and comfort care may need quite intrusive and technologically advanced treatment for specific emergencies, such as a broken bone, seizures, or tumors that compress the spinal cord. Occasionally, individuals who have not yet become debilitated can benefit from a short course of chemotherapy or radiation to reduce the size of a troublesome tumor. At all times, the benefits of any treatment must be weighed against its burdens. You don't want to be subjected to treatments that are worse than the disease!

Cancer has a special place in our culture, as a particularly evil menace. You may feel that way, or you may tell yourself, "I had to die sometime, and this is not the worst thing that could have happened." Sometimes having brochures from the American Cancer Society, the National Cancer Information Center, or other resources helps. You should know whether there are any implications of your having this cancer for your family — some cancers tend to run in families and some do not (and some are still unclear). You also should know whether anything you did contributed to the illness. You might want to consider how you will respond to insensitive people who blame you for your situation, something that often happens to smokers who develop lung cancer. Many people with cancer find it helpful to meet with others with their disease, perhaps in a support group, in order to hear how others deal with the challenges they confront.

Lung disease: emphysema and chronic bronchitis

Lung disease is also known as chronic obstructive pulmonary disease (COPD), or as emphysema or chronic bronchitis. They are progressive and irreversible diseases that affect the ability to breathe in oxygen and breathe out carbon dioxide. Common symptoms of lung disease are:

- cough with phlegm
- shortness of breath with any exercise
- wheezing

Often, someone with lung disease will experience these symptoms for ten years or more before they become so bad that activities of daily living become difficult. Most people with lung disease find their difficulty breathing to be the most troublesome symptom. As the disease becomes severe, walking even short distances may be impossible, and breathing may become difficult when resting or lying flat. While there is no cure for the underlying disease, there are various methods available to treat shortness of breath.

Often, you will have oxygen at home, which can be used most of the time and as needed to help alleviate the difficulty breathing. The amount of time you spend using oxygen can be increased as the disease progresses. Various drugs dilate, or open, the air passages and make breathing easier. People with lung disease often find these drugs give temporary relief to their shortness of breath, loosening mucus and aiding in the production of sputum, which relieves blockage of the air passages. These drugs do have side effects and may not be right for everyone with lung disease. Also, family caregivers can be taught a technique known as *chest physiotherapy*, in which they tap on the back of the person and turn them in specific positions to help bring up phlegm and clear the lungs to help prevent bronchitis and pneumonia.

As the lung disease becomes more advanced, you might not have enough oxygen circulating, a condition that doctors call *hypoxia*. Also, you might not blow out enough carbon dioxide as you breathe, which doctors call *hypercapnia*. Together, these two effects lead to the feeling of shortness of breath and sometimes to decreased alertness. These problems with breathing can lead to confusion, strange behavior, tremors in the hands, and seizures. Physicians can provide oxygen therapy, medications to reduce shortness of breath, anti-seizure medications, and medications to decrease the tremor.

Persons with lung disease can also become very anxious because of their difficulty breathing. This anxiety actually makes breathing more difficult. Medication can be given to reduce anxiety until the breathing improves, and meditation or guided imagery often helps you regain control.

People with lung disease may also experience pain. Often, pain is located in the chest as a result of coughing and excessive use of the chest muscles for breathing. At times, persons with lung disease cough so violently that they can fracture a rib. Medication or injections can usually ease these pains.

There are times when it will be important to call your doctor right away. Alert your doctor if you:

- develop a fever
- cough more frequently than usual
- produce more sputum or see a change in sputum color to a green or rusty brown color
- experience increased chest pain on breathing

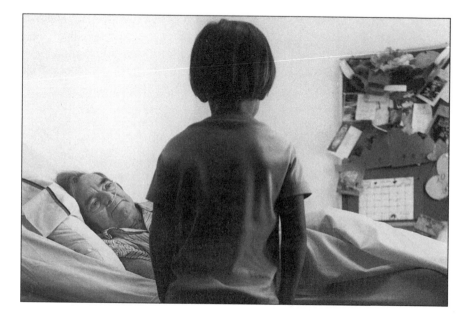

These worsening or changing symptoms may be signs of a sudden worsening of lung disease. Especially during winter months, you will be more susceptible to infections, including bronchitis and pneumonia, which are the most common cause of setbacks. People whose lung disease has become worse because of infection can be treated with antibiotics and possibly a short course of steroids.

Depending on your symptoms, you may benefit from hospitalization and aggressive treatments such as ventilator assistance. One alternative to intubation and ventilation that is available for people with lung disease who are very short of breath is called "CPAP," or continuous positive airway pressure. With this treatment, patients are fitted with a tight air mask and oxygen is given at a continuous pressure that forces the airways to stay open so the oxygen can get into the lungs. For some people, using the CPAP can be enough to get over a period of difficult breathing, and CPAP causes less discomfort than the ventilator. Some people use it every night.

Because of the nature of the disease, it is very difficult for physicians to tell how close people with lung disease are to death. Lung disease can usually involve several emergency episodes in which a person will be acutely ill, requiring "rescue" care to try to keep him alive. The underlying ability of the lungs to function will slowly but steadily decline, and the disease will eventually lead to death. Because of this certainty and the fact that you are usually in no condition to talk during a bad spell, you need to make plans with your family members and physicians about ventilator support. You should read the discussion in Chapter 11 about how to make decisions concerning various medical treatments.

People with lung disease and their family members need time to think about the illness, the prognosis, and options for treatments. If no discussion occurs until you are admitted to the hospital for an acute episode, you will be too ill and decision making will fall on your family or doctor. Not only does this place a large burden on the family or doctor, but it also can lead to decisions that you would not have wanted. Further, you should talk with your doctor and your family about your preferences for hospitalization and ventilators regularly, because you may well find that your priorities and preferences change.

At 67, Mr. Smith had lived with COPD for 20 years. His family brought him into the hospital one night because he was having difficulty breathing. This was Mr. Smith's third hospital admission in six months. On his second admission, Mr. Smith had been put on the ventilator and had successfully gotten off and returned home. While he was

at home, Mr. Smith told his son that he didn't want to be on the ventilator again, even if he became unable to breathe on his own.

On this admission, Mr. Smith arrived at the hospital gasping for breath, feverish, and nauseated. He was found to have pneumonia causing a sudden worsening of his COPD. Mr. Smith was too breathless to talk to his doctors but could understand what was said to him. Based on his wishes and discussion with his family, it was decided not to use machines to help Mr. Smith breathe. He was treated with small doses of intravenous morphine and oxygen until he was comfortable and lightly sleeping. The following morning, Mr. Smith was comatose, his breathing very shallow, and his air exchange poor. The son knew that his father would die soon, and he stayed by the bedside. Mr. Smith passed away quietly a few hours later.

You may choose not to use cardiopulmonary resuscitation (CPR — attempting to restart the person's heart if it stops beating). As the lungs become more and more damaged, the benefits of CPR and ventilation decrease until they are no longer beneficial at all, but you need to decide when you will have reached that point (see Chapter 11).

A few people will get lung transplants, and some of those will work well for many years. For most, though, serious lung disease will eventually cause death. With the knowledge that lung disease has become advanced, and after multiple hospitalizations, you may determine that quality of life is of primary importance and elect to stay at home even when symptoms worsen. Health care providers can help with home care or hospice, with visiting nurses, oxygen and other breathing treatments at home, antibiotic therapy, and medication to relieve anxiety, pain, and difficulty breathing.

Both you and your family may find it better to be in the comfort of familiar surroundings with adequate treatment for relief of symptoms, knowing that the disease is not curable and hospitalization will not alter the ultimate prognosis. Alternatively, you may decide to try the hospital, but to stop if you are not doing well. Either way, plans need to be made with your family and physician to handle symptoms and events that may occur near death. For example, doctors can prescribe various treatments for shortness of breath; medication can be kept on hand for pain and to relieve anxiety and help with sleep; and drying agents can be prescribed if you have a lot of secretions.

Toward the very end of life, you may become less and less alert and may stop eating and drinking. You may become confused, may not recognize loved ones, and may become agitated and restless. Usually any such symptoms last only a short time, but you really need to have a doctor or hospice that knows how to handle shortness of breath as part of dying. They have to be willing to give opioids to relieve shortness of breath if that is what you need.

Kidney failure

Loss of kidney function leads to serious illness, affecting many aspects of physical well-being. The kidneys filter by-products of body chemistry and adjust the amount of liquid in the bloodstream. Many people have progressively diminished kidney (sometimes called "renal") function as they grow old, but usually this slow decline can be managed with diet and drugs. When the kidneys fail completely, you cannot live for long unless you have dialysis or a kidney transplant. A transplant that works relieves the person of kidney failure. However, transplants are not always available, appropriate, or successful. Dialysis is the name for the process of artificially replacing the main functions of the kidneys. Hemodialysis refers to filtering the blood through a machine; peritoneal dialysis refers to using fluid exchanges through the abdomen. Either procedure can be used to sustain life for years, but they do burden you and your caregiver, and each procedure has complications.

"The first time I saw the kidney machine I thought it looked like a big washing machine."

S. HAYWOOD

Sometimes a person whose kidneys no longer work decides not to continue or even not to start dialysis and to let death come from kidney (renal) failure. If you are considering this option, you need to know what is likely to happen. Usually, dying from kidney failure is fairly gentle and most symptoms can be suppressed. The characteristics of your renal failure and your other medical problems help to predict which symptoms may arise.

As the by-products of the body's chemistry accumulate in renal failure, these substances cause an array of symptoms. You almost always lose energy and become sleepy and lethargic, but you may find it hard to sleep at night. Over time, the typical patient just slips into deeper and deeper sleep and gradually loses consciousness completely. However, early on, mild confusion and disorientation are common, and usually require only reassurance as treatment. Sometimes, though, upsetting hallucinations or agitation arise. These can be treated very quickly with tranquilizers and anti-anxiety drugs. Certain minerals in the bloodstream can also accumulate and cause twitching of muscles, tremors and shakes, and even seizures. The tremors are usually of no importance to your comfort, but their onset can signal a need to prevent seizures. Medications to prevent or treat seizures are usually quite effective. Some patients develop mild or more severe itching before they become too sleepy to notice. This can be treated with creams, massage, erythropoietin, and antihistamines. Sometimes a fine white powdery substance covers the skin, but it is not the cause of itching and is of no importance. Appetite decreases very early, again to no one's surprise. The accumulation of acids in the bloodstream causes rapid, shallow breathing; this is not an uncomfortable feeling, and the rapid breathing is not changed by oxygen.

Many people with kidney failure pass very little or no urine. If you pass little urine, without dialysis you have to be careful to avoid problems with salt and water overload. Restricting your fluid intake to less than one quart of liquid a day will keep you from having much trouble. Fluid overload results in swelling of the body (edema), particularly of the legs and the abdomen. The excess fluid can also cause congestion of the lungs and the heart, leading to rapid breathing and shortness of breath. Sitting upright helps relieve the breathing difficulties, at least for a while, as it shifts the fluid away from the chest and toward the legs; it may be impossible for persons in this condition to lie flat. Oxygen and morphine may also ease any feelings of struggling to breathe.

It is important to know that persons with some urine output have lived surprisingly long times after stopping dialysis — sometimes for months. People with no urine output are likely to die within a week or two. If this is your choice, or the choice of someone you love, try to be sure that you have a doctor and nurse who are familiar with the problems that might arise and that medications to treat those problems are readily at hand, especially if you are in a nursing home or at home. In such situations, having a knowledgeable and experienced hospice team involved is often worth exploring, as they will make it their business to get you any urgently needed medications. You probably will have a kidney specialist by this point, and that doctor may be a real help both in making decisions and in keeping you comfortable. So, on the whole, when you have to die, allowing kidney failure to take its course is not generally a hard way to go. In years past, before dialysis, kidney failure had a reputation of being a gentle death.

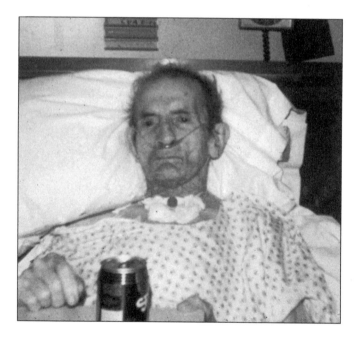

Liver failure

Liver failure results in impairment of many functions we take for granted. Liver failure mostly arises slowly, over many years, but its progression is usually unnoticed. It can happen from infections, cancer, alcohol or other toxic substances, and genetic causes. Often, when symptoms first appear, already very little liver function is left. Much of the treatment of liver failure is focused upon salvaging whatever liver function is left and avoiding overtaxing the liver. Some few with liver failure will qualify for, and successfully get, liver transplantation. Most, though, will eventually die from the progression of the liver disease, though some, with careful attention to avoiding further stress on the liver, may live for years.

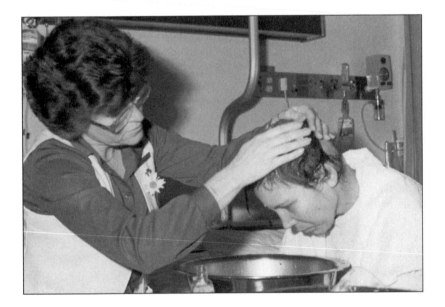

The liver has a multitude of functions: it helps digest food, filters and eliminates certain toxic chemicals in the blood, makes essential proteins, and maintains the level of energy-making compounds in the bloodstream. People with advanced liver failure are jaundiced because *bilirubin* accumulates in the skin, turning it yellow. The whites of the eyes become bright yellow-orange. Jaundice itself is not painful, but the abnormalities can cause quite troubling itching of the skin. Since certain compounds are not being put into the gut by the liver, bowel movements change from brown to chalky yellow-white. These brown compounds showing up in the urine make it appear quite dark.

With liver failure you may:

◆ Feel weak, slow, and lethargic
◆ Experience muscle tremors and twitches, and, in some cases, seizures

- Feel quite itchy.
- Become confused, sleepy, or lapse into a coma.
- Have trouble with bleeding
- Get a swollen belly and swollen legs

Often, you can delay the onset of confusion by keeping the bowel motion very rapid; for example, with a laxative called lactulose. Sometimes the itching of the skin responds to drugs that bind up some of the toxic chemicals. Nausea and vomiting, when they occur, usually can be suppressed with anti-emetic drugs.

Many people with liver failure get a very swollen abdomen because fluids that usually pass through the liver cannot do so. Fluid in the belly (called "*ascites*") can stretch the skin tight enough to be uncomfortable or can press against the lungs, making it necessary to remove part of the fluid with a needle. Because the liver is not making the proteins needed in the blood, fluid often seeps out of the bloodstream into the tissues, causing generalized swelling (edema). This swelling affects the belly, legs and arms, and sometimes the face. Elevation of the legs, diuretic medications, and fluid and salt restriction may help these symptoms.

We sometimes congratulate ourselves at the moment of waking from a troubled dream; it may be so the moment after death.

NATHANIEL HAWTHORNE
from The American Notebooks

Bleeding is fairly common, because the failed liver is no longer able to make essential clotting substances. For example, there may be oozing from the gums when teeth are brushed and large bruises may appear on the skin. In some cases, bleeding becomes the life-threatening event, usually with bleeding into the stomach. Treatments for this kind of severe bleeding may include interventions to block the blood vessels and transfusions of clotting proteins and of blood.

Unlike some illnesses where there is a particular treatment to consider stopping, such as a ventilator or dialysis, most liver failure patients will not have a single clear issue for decision. Nevertheless, you can decide to forgo any further transfusions if bleeding occurs, and to stop any other aggressive treatment that might sustain your life when complications arise. You should decide about resuscitation and hospitalization. Mostly, living with liver failure is the challenge. Dying from liver failure usually includes the fairly rapid onset of confusion and coma, and thus is a merciful end. Having plans in place in advance for medical treatment decisions and for saying good-bye to friends and family is important to do.

HIV/AIDS

At one time, AIDS was a quick death sentence. Then there was a time when it was a rapidly progressive chronic disease with various difficult pathways through the end of life. Recently, the course of AIDS has changed again. With new drug regimens, many people are living for much longer, and how the usual person will die is again unclear. It still seems likely that persons with AIDS will probably die of AIDS, but often this will happen only after many years of living with the HIV infection. The very last phase is likely to include infections, tumors, or mental confusion. If you want, you can take a strong hand in shaping what treatments will and will not be used when AIDS becomes far advanced.

"There are many who believe that this disease is God's vengeance, but I believe it was sent to teach people how to love and understand and have compassion for each other. I have learned more about love, selflessness and human understanding from the people I have met in this great adventure in the world of AIDS than I ever did in the cutthroat, competitive world in which I spent my life."

ANTHONY PERKINS
Actor

AIDS has become a "high-tech" disease. The medication regimes and machinery involved are difficult even for experienced health care professionals to manage. You will be well-served to seek out doctors and teams who have lots of experience with AIDS patients, since they will be right up to date on the best information as it becomes available. They also will be familiar with your needs and the challenges you face. Even if you are in a rural area or otherwise can't have an experienced team as your primary source of care, you might well find an experienced team in a nearby city to consult occasionally.

Because HIV infection is (incorrectly) thought of as being dangerous to people nearby, because people with advanced AIDS are often remarkably ill in appearance, and because many people with AIDS have few anchors in social and family life, you may have to rely on paid caregivers and non-family volunteers more than most people affected by chronic disease in old age. You would do well to connect with family, even if they have been distant. Often, "buddy" programs in the community can really help. Most people with

AIDS will live a long time, but you will probably be very sick from time to time, and will have long periods when you have limited energy. You will do better if you have some connections to friends and family.

AIDS has affected mostly people who are relatively young. Thus, you are not as likely as retired persons to have substantial financial resources and permanent housing. Yet, you may still have young children and family caregivers who are younger, too, and must work. And treating AIDS is very expensive. Almost everyone with AIDS needs to consult knowledgeable and experienced social workers who can help to secure qualified support services for you and your family. Likewise, plans must be made for the care of any dependent children, some of whom may have been infected as well. Social workers are helpful here, too.

The situation may seem quite overwhelming. Caregivers often doubt their ability to meet the physical and psychological needs of AIDS patients. Yet, astonishing networks commonly are created, and caregivers ordinarily feel useful and positive about their work.

Caregivers may worry about becoming infected. This is really exceedingly unlikely if everyone learns a system called *universal precautions* and uses it consistently, even when it seems a little silly or a little troublesome.

Bereavement seems harder for AIDS patients and their families. Many victims (and their caregivers) are younger and frequently must deal with the losses of friends and family members who have also died of AIDS. Caregivers who are HIV-positive are being asked to confront their own futures every time they care for a loved one with advanced AIDS. For them, anticipatory grieving may be much more intense.

Not many years ago, it was very awkward to deal with death certificates with "AIDS" as the cause of death, and it was often even difficult to get funeral services. Now, you and your family are much less likely to run into these problems, but you still would do well to inquire and plan ahead. Preplanning funerals and handling of the body, and arranging things having to do with the care of dependent children and financial estates, is especially important for many people with AIDS. Many of these things are much easier to do when the person dying can still sign legal papers and make decisions. It is often a great burden to family and friends to have to handle everything through the courts and official channels.

Remember, you often can't avoid feeling angry, and you will need to grieve. The situation is tragic. The intensity of your feelings is a reflection of the intensity of the situation. Just be sure to reach out for support, and to try to express your appreciation when support is offered.

Patients with AIDS frequently take many medications. These regimes can themselves cause symptoms. Because of the unpredictable nature of the disease, it is sometimes hard to know which medications provide comfort or suppress the illness and which ones are ineffective and cause problems. Active aggressive treatment often continues right up until death. When you can't keep track of why you are taking certain medicines, you may need to review them all with your doctor or nurse and see if some can be stopped or their timing can be simplified.

Depression or depressive symptoms are very common among people with AIDS. You should know the warning signs of these disorders and seek help if they occur. The desire to commit suicide can itself be a symptom of depression. So, any decisions about euthanasia or assisted suicide should be delayed until a physician can make an evaluation and treat underlying psychiatric disorders.

HIV/AIDS sometimes causes dementia or confusion. Again, it is important to use health care providers who are familiar with the management of AIDS and with these psychiatric disorders.

Physicians try to evaluate symptoms and treatments by keeping in mind "the big picture." You should do the same. Will the medication or test significantly enhance your quality of life or enable you to do something important? Is the treatment or test being used to prevent a symptom or to extend life? How does the medication make you feel? Remember, how you live is more important than the numbers on the laboratory reports. And how you die is less important than how you live right up to the end.

Dementia

More than one-fourth of those who live into old age will have some dementia, most often because of Alzheimer's disease or strokes. Dementia poses the most difficult questions for most people, future patients and caregivers alike. Persons with dementia die from an array of different complications, but mostly these are somewhat treatable. Yet, the treatments are frightening, even if only because they may require that the person leave familiar surroundings. And the life saved, at least at the end, seems so limited that it is often not clear exactly what should be included in "good care."

Everyone agrees that good care requires keeping the person clean, providing food and warmth, trying to keep him or her safe, and attending to things that cause pain. However, at some point, persons with dementia often stop eating enough to get by. Should they be fed with tubes? Some feel that such feeding is essential, even if it requires placing a tube in the stomach surgically to avoid having to restrain the person's hands. Patients often pull out a tube placed through the nose, but a surgically placed tube can be hidden under a dressing. Others feel it is really an affront to drag out the end of the person's life when he or

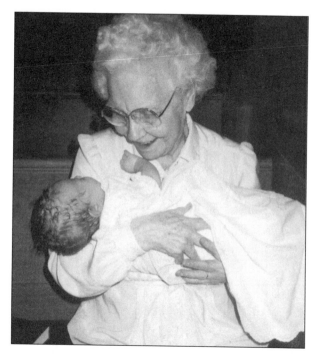

she can have so little awareness or enjoyment. The courts have ruled, over and over, that using artificial nutrition or hydration is a treatment decision just like chemotherapy or surgery, and that families and doctors can choose to use or to forgo this kind of treatment.

How do people die who choose not to be fed artificially? What evidence we have indicates that they do not die more quickly, and that they do not feel thirsty or hungry. Their dying without tube feeding, though, tends to have less struggling with restraints (which are often used to keep feeding tubes in place) and less trouble with an excess of fluids in the lungs, which causes shortness of breath. Without tube feeding, they probably lose a little more weight and might be at more risk of infections or skin problems, but these effects are also unproven.

Mostly, people treated with or without feeding tubes end up sleeping away most of the last few weeks, and nothing very dramatic happens.

If you find it quite perplexing to sort out whether a family member should have artificial nutrition, consider these things:

- Is he uncomfortable now?
- Could I tell if he were uncomfortable now or later?
- Would the situation be clearer if we tried tube feeding for a week or two?
- What do I think he would advise if he could have foreseen this?
- If the tube feeding were not readily available, would family members have wanted to seek it out?

If you are clear about what you want, or feel that you might want to have all options available, be sure that your doctor, home care help, and nursing home (if appropriate) all agree. It can be very difficult to get a patient out of a nursing home or into the care of a new doctor if family and professional caregivers disagree about whether the patient can go without artificial feeding.

The same kinds of questions come up about the use of antibiotics and surgeries, and even about hospitalizations. These treatments somehow are usually a little easier to turn down once the patient is quite demented. Still, family members need to have given the issues some thought and need to have forged a relationship with providers willing to follow the family's choice. You might also find it helpful to read the general discussion about deciding to forgo treatment in Chapter 11.

Dementia poses special problems for finding meaning. Usually the patient is living just in the moment, and issues of meaning and spirituality are beyond his or her capabilities. The family, if they are providing care, are often quite stressed, often worn out. Enduring in the face of these challenges can be victory enough, but support groups, spiritual counseling, and recourse to one's faith often enable a sense of accomplishment in getting through a very difficult time.

While some changes have to be accepted through such adjustments in our own images and ideals, others can be resisted, met more actively, influenced for better or worse. A major challenge in taking care of demented people is telling the difference between the two kinds of change.

JAMES AND HILDE LINDEMANN NELSON
from Alzheimer's: Answers to Hard Questions for Families

Dying while very old

When you are very old and dying, you may have different concerns than would a younger person. You may find your wishes about care near the end of life are in conflict with those of your family members or friends. You may find that you have come to feel comfortable with the thought of death, especially if

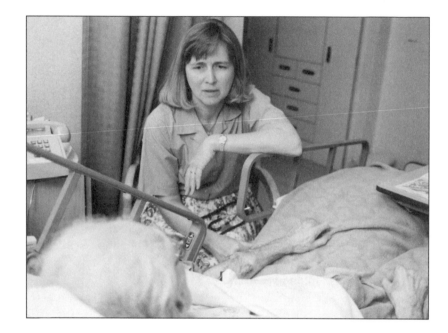

your spouse and close friends have passed away. Younger relatives and friends may wish to seek out new medical treatments for your disease, while you may be more content to put off dealing with medical things and put comfort first. Your son or daughter, for instance, may wish to try every treatment to keep you alive, in part because that seems to be what it takes to be a good child. Even older adult children must grapple with what it will mean to be motherless or fatherless.

Conversely, you may find yourself alone. You may no longer have family and friends alive and may count on acquaintances for caregiving support. As you become more weak with your illnesses and age, you may find that you feel isolated from your community. Your routine may change. Instead of going to the supermarket on Mondays, a club event on Wednesdays, and church or synagogue over the weekend, you can only muster the energy to make all the arrangements for a trip to the doctor's office every month. Make sure you communicate your needs to members of your community. People from church or other organizations to which you belong may feel awkward dropping in uninvited but would be pleased to help you with a chore if asked.

You may wish to maintain your independence for as long as possible and avoid asking others to help. However, making connections now can prove valuable should your strength diminish. Also, having many supports decreases your chance of becoming isolated. Ask neighbors to call you before they head to the grocery store so that they can pick up small items for you. You may even ask for a non-essential item, such as candy, so that you can look forward to a visit (and give some of the candy to the child who does the delivery). More advice is given in Chapter 5.

Advance planning is fairly obvious but often ignored. You really need to have plans in place for what to do if you are suddenly very sick and likely to die. Will your doctor come to your home? Is there a point when the various illnesses are enough to make hospice available to you? Can you have a skilled nurse who will come? Will you go to a nursing home at some point? There are a lot of uncertainties, and many of the possibilities will seem pretty troubling. However, remember that few will actually happen, and that it is better that they work out in the way you want, rather than for some unknown emergency room doctor to be deciding your fate. If you are having trouble answering these questions, you can find more guidance in Chapter 10.

Your physical appearance is probably still very important to you. Ask a neighbor to take you for haircuts or manicures. Having someone talking and making you look better will uplift your spirits.

While you may enjoy getting dressed for outings, take care not to over- or underdress. Pay attention to the weather and use layers accordingly. You may feel inappropriate if you do not wear a suit to events where you usually do so, but it would be unwise to wear one in 95-degree weather. As you age, your natural thermostat does not work as well as it used to and you could overheat. Also, numerous medications could make your blood pressure drop — and make you feel quite dizzy if you stand up quickly. Similarly, you should prepare for cold weather by always having a sweater or jacket available.

You may or may not have been in the habit of routine exercise. While you may no longer be able to take long walks, you need to do some exercises of the upper or lower body in order to maintain some muscle strength. This routine is important to prevent dependence on others. You may be more motivated to exercise if you do it with music. Playing the same song every time you exercise will help to establish a routine.

> ### SIMPLE EXERCISE PROGRAM
>
> *Ten arm circles forward (in the evening, do these backward)*
>
> *Ten leg lifts (sit in a chair, lift leg up, straightening knee)*
>
> *Ten shoulder stretches (use fingers to crawl up wall above your head)*

As you age, your senses of taste and smell diminish, so that you will find it more difficult than a younger person to enjoy food. Much to your surprise, you may find that you enjoy adding strong flavors — vinegar, hot spices, aromatic spices, and pepper. Also, you may have dentures and find it difficult to chew certain foods, such as meats. Supplemental protein drinks, cheeses, eggs, or peanut butter can be good substitutes. Multigrain crackers eaten with the peanut butter or cheese may decrease the likelihood of constipation. Do not concern yourself with eating a low-cholesterol diet. You should eat what tastes good, even if it is ice cream.

Vegetable juice or vegetable soup may be easier to digest than cooked vegetables. If possible, take a multivitamin with minerals each day. If, however, these pills are too large to swallow, have a family member cut them in half, or get the liquid or chewable forms made for children (and have your doctor or nurse help figure out how much to take).

You may find salty foods, such as crackers or nuts, more tasty than others. Do not restrict these if they taste good unless you have certain illnesses such as congestive heart failure or hypertension and your health care provider has recommended decreasing the salt in your diet. Be sure to ask the health care provider about whether dietary restrictions still apply. Your doctor may have told you years ago to be careful about salt intake or cholesterol in your diet, but the situation may be different as you age. For instance, your mild high blood pressure and subsequent need for salt restriction may disappear because you have lost weight.

When your appetite is poor, the thought of a large meal may worsen it. If a neighbor or friend brings over a large meal, or if you receive it from a community service agency such as Meals on Wheels, dish a third of the meal onto a dinner plate and eat only that amount. Save the rest for another time. Unlike a child who is eating to grow, you are eating just to enjoy yourself and to give yourself energy to manage the things you want to do each day.

Like other elders, you may be living with more than one illness or condition. You may suffer from osteoporosis and osteoarthritis as well as a new-found

> *"But our machines have now been running 70 or 80 years, and we must expect that, worn as they are, here a pivot, there a wheel, now a pinion, next a spring, will be giving way; and however we may tinker them up for a while, all will at length surcease motion."*
>
> THOMAS JEFFERSON
> *from a letter to John Adams, July 5, 1814*

cancer. You may have coped fairly well with these chronic diseases but find yourself overwhelmed by the prospect of dealing with another illness. Also, you may be concerned that treatments and medications may interact. This is a valid concern. Be sure to inform your doctors and nurses about how you cope with your other illnesses.

Many elderly persons have some urinary incontinence. This, unfortunately, can worsen with many medications and some medical treatments. For instance, radiation or surgery done to treat prostate cancer usually worsens urinary incontinence. Do not give up your life because of this condition. Some persons with urinary incontinence dislike going out of the house for fear of having an accident. This further isolates them from their community. Try out all the new pads and underwear that can really keep you secure. Also, discuss this condition with your health care provider and ask if certain medications are still needed. For instance, diuretics, which are often used to treat hypertension, can worsen incontinence. Ask if they are still necessary. There are medical and surgical treatments for incontinence, but often patients are reluctant to discuss the condition.

If you are elderly, you may be the last remaining member of your generation or at least the last person living in your house. As you get your affairs in order, it is, of course, important to make a will, but it is also necessary to give certain loved items to friends or members of your family. Don't assume that your only great-grandchild will find the antique doll in your closet and keep it for her own. If you have a strong opinion about who gets what, write it down. You don't want family members squabbling. You may enjoy giving the gift while you are still alive!

As an older person, you may have strong religious convictions. You may regret not getting out to your place of worship as often as you used to. You may miss both the spiritual and the fellowship aspects of the services. Communicate with church, synagogue, or mosque leaders and ask if the services can be brought to you. Ask them to tape the services so that you may listen. Tell them that you would like a few members of the choir to come over and sing. Ask the pastor for a reprint of his or her sermon. Try to stay connected with the congregation.

Getting to live to old age is probably the supreme accomplishment of our society. Once, very few had the chance, but now most will. However, we do not yet have the social arrangements that ensure that you can live comfortably and meaningfully in your eighties and nineties and beyond. You and your family will have to confront some social arrangements directly and find what will work best for you, your illnesses, your family situation, and your finances. It seems to help to keep the spiritual issues in mind, rather than letting medical problems and practical arrangements take over all of your attention. Push yourself and your family, at least a little, to enjoy some time doing things for one another, telling stories, voicing love and forgiveness, and so on. Those will be the shared experiences that get you through hard times, and those will be the times that your family and friends will remember with fondness.

Chapter 10

Planning ahead

*I slept in a bed
in a room with paintings
on the walls, and
planned another day
just like this day.
But one day, I know,
it will be otherwise.*

JANE KENYON
from "Otherwise"

Most of us do not plan for serious illness and death. And many of us feel that if we don't talk about bad things, they won't happen to us. However, talking, planning, and being better prepared for the end of life can let you live fully and more comfortably in your final days. Have you thought about the care you want during a severe illness or as you are dying? Have you talked with your family about plans to ensure you will get the care that you want? When you are very sick, you are likely to have some times when you cannot say what you want done. By deciding some things ahead of time, you can have a say in your care.

How can you get started? First, think in very general terms. Do you want every possible treatment tried, even when it involves mechanical support for body functions, or even when it is not likely to work? Do you want to die at home, even if doing that means not having a way to get some treatments? Have you talked with your family about the kind of care you want? Does your physician know how you feel? Many of us don't take the time to figure out our wishes and hopes for the end of our lives. Others write living wills, but don't tell anyone what they really want that document to accomplish. These conversations are an important part of living and dying well with a serious illness.

"Why should I make plans now?"

Discussions about what kinds of treatment you want at the end of life are likely to be most useful if you plan long before decisions have to be made. You might

call this *"what if?"* planning. *What if* I should become too sick to eat except through a tube? *What if* my doctors say I will have only a short time to live? *What if* I can't talk or write or signal my thoughts? Who do I trust to make important treatment decisions for me? This *"what if?"* planning, though uncomfortable at first, will help you feel more in control. It also can be a very special gift to family and loved ones, who can be spared the burden of making choices without knowing what is most important to you.

Many of the choices you will make about the end of life will involve medical treatments. But these decisions are not likely to be the most important ones. Your ideas and hopes about the end of your life — being with your family, or making peace with God, for example — are the more meaningful ones. Your values and beliefs should guide medical choices whenever possible — not the other way around.

One way to approach these kinds of choices is to consider the questions on a **values history questionnaire** like the one on page 122. These are not questions that you may have seen on a living will. Your answers will not be simple "yes's"

WORDS OFTEN USED IN ADVANCE PLANNING

ADVANCE CARE PLANNING: *Determining and documenting your goals and wishes for specific treatments based on your medical condition and personal preferences. Clinical care is shaped by your choices, even if you become unable to make decisions for yourself. By anticipating emergencies, crisis decision-making is decreased.*

ADVANCE DIRECTIVE: *Any statement made by a competent individual about preferences for future treatment if that person is unable to make decisions at the time. "Advance directive" is often used to describe the two forms which most states recognize as legally important — the living will and the health care proxy (or durable power of attorney).*

FORGOING LIFE-SUSTAINING TREATMENT: *Choosing not to have specific treatments that would have been expected to extend your life. This can be done by withholding one or more treatments, which is a choice not to start the life-sustaining treatment. It can also be done by withdrawing a treatment once it is started.*

HEALTH CARE PROXY: *A method of giving another person legal power to make medical decisions when you no longer can. The written form used to appoint the proxy is often called a "durable power of attorney" for health care decision-making.*

LAST WILL AND TESTAMENT: *A legal document to determine what will be done with your money, property, and other possessions after you die. If you do not write a "will," the laws of the state will determine how your wealth is passed along to family members.*

LIVING WILL: *A document that indicates an individual's written instructions for treatment to be used when that individual becomes unable to express his or her wishes for health care treatment. Often it's a preprinted form.*

PHYSICIAN-ASSISTED SUICIDE: *A sequence of events in which a physician hastens a patient's death by providing the necessary means (drugs) or information to enable someone to take his or her own life.*

or "no's." While this questionnaire may look complicated, it can help you to talk about your wishes with someone who may have to make decisions for you when you cannot. Filling out a questionnaire like this will help you think about how you hope things will be. Your answers will also be a useful way to get started talking with your family.

A VALUES HISTORY QUESTIONNAIRE

1. What do you value most about your life? (For example: living a long life, living an active life, enjoying the company of family and friends, etc.)

2. How do you feel about death and dying? (Do you fear death and dying? Have you experienced the loss of a loved one? Did that person's illness or medical treatment influence your thinking about death and dying?)

3. Do you believe life should always be preserved as long as possible?

4. If not, what kinds of mental or physical conditions would make you think that life-prolonging treatment should no longer be used? Being:

   • unaware of my life and surroundings

   • unable to appreciate and continue the important relationships in my life

   • unable to think well enough to make everyday decisions

   • in severe pain or discomfort

5. Could you imagine reasons for temporarily accepting medical treatment for the conditions you described?

6. How much pain and risk would you be willing to accept if your chances of recovery from an illness or an injury were good (50-50 or better)?

7. What if your chances of recovery were poor (less than 1 in 10)?

8. Would your approach to accepting or rejecting care depend on how old you were at the time of treatment? Why?

9. Do you hold any religious or moral views about medicine or particular medical treatments?

10. Should financial considerations influence decisions about your medical care?

11. What other beliefs or values do you hold that should be considered by those making medical care decisions for you if you become unable to speak for yourself?

12. Most people have heard of difficult end-of-life situations involving family members or neighbors or people in the news. Have you had any reactions to those situations?

ADAPTED FROM THE VERMONT ETHICS NETWORK

Talking with your family is very important — and can be very hard. The people who love you most will often find it difficult to talk about your serious illness and eventual death. But if they need to make any decisions on your behalf, knowing what is most important to you can guide and comfort them. At the very least, give them your answers to the questions in the values history questionnaire. Sit down and talk about it with one or two people at a time, or send them letters. If you can arrange a family meeting, talk to your whole family AND give them a copy of your completed values history questionnaire. And be sure to discuss your answers specifically with whomever will be speaking for you when you cannot — your *surrogate* or *proxy decision maker*.

If you have signed a standard living will, you may think that you do not need the values history questionnaire. Advance directives, such as living wills, are legally endorsed documents and the values history questionnaire is not. However, despite the precise legal language, living wills are often difficult to interpret. Conventional living wills include words such as "terminal," "extraordinary," and "heroic" that mean different things to different people at different stages of disease. Thus, your answers to the values history questionnaire can be useful to your proxy, who needs to understand what you mean in your advance directive, taking into account your stage of disease and overall condition. You are often best advised to complete a values history *and* a legally endorsed advance directive.

"How can I be sure my choices will be followed?"

First and foremost, tell your family and doctor what is important to you and write it down. From a legal perspective, it is better to write down what you want than to trust that everyone will remember what you said. A written statement gives your choices clarity, visibility, and validity. Be as precise as you can, both about what treatments you want and about what you hold dear, so that everyone will remember what you said.

Remember, too, that you can always change your mind. Your choices may change with your experiences. For example, people often choose aggressive care at the start of an illness, but then change their minds when the disease is not responding to treatment. It makes sense that your choices about your care might change as your condition changes.

Preparing advance directives and talking about how you and your family plan to cope with serious illness and death can help to make the end of life a time of comfort and dignity — not a time of hurried choices. (See also Chapter 5 on how to get the help you need.)

"What else matters with advance directives?"

Written advance directives are often unavailable or can't be found when important decisions need to be made. What happens to patients who are at home

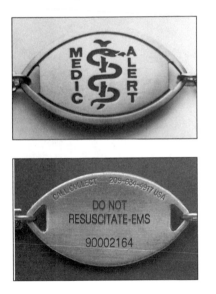

when emergency treatment becomes necessary, but have an advance directive in their hospital medical records?

Emergency medical teams will try cardiopulmonary resuscitation (CPR) on all people found to be in cardiac arrest. This response may not coincide with the wishes of people who are seriously ill. In an effort to give patients control of this situation, many states have ways to advise emergency medical technicians (EMTs) about your directives. Some states issue bracelets, indicating a person's wish not to be resuscitated if he or she is found unconscious by emergency personnel. In other states, emergency medical technicians now look for "do-not-resuscitate" (DNR) forms in prominent areas in the home, such as on the refrigerator or next to a person's bed. Similar to living wills, DNR forms allow individuals to document preferences for care. Ask your doctor or call your local emergency medical services organization to find out about local policies.

"I had a living will in Ohio and now I'm in Florida. Do I need a new one?"

You have done a lot just thinking through the issues and writing down your instructions. Probably, doing that will be enough to guide your family and doctors. However, you should still rewrite your advance directive if you move to another state. Some states have said exactly which types of advance directives the law will recognize as binding. State laws differ. Some states will recognize the laws of the state in which the directive was executed. So, if you move or cross state lines for health care, find out about this issue.

QUESTIONS TO ASK YOUR DOCTOR
TO HELP YOU PLAN AHEAD

- *What symptoms am I likely to have as my disease progresses?*
- *What medications or other treatments should I have at home in case of sudden symptoms? How do I use them?*
- *How can hospice help me?*
- *Who do I call in case of emergencies? You? 911? Hospice nurse? What about after normal office hours?*
- *I do not want to have CPR or a breathing machine. How do I make that known in cases of emergency?*
- *Can I get an in-home Do Not Resuscitate order in this state? How? What can I do instead of going to the hospital in an emergency?*
- *What assisted living facilities, nursing homes, or hospitals do you routinely visit to take care of patients?*

"What about planning for where to live when I am more disabled?"

Most life-threatening illnesses can cause worsening disability. You are wise to make plans for how you will cope with disability. Those plans might require fixing up a first floor room as a bedroom or putting grab bars in the shower. They might require thinking through whether a family member might move in, or whether to convert a room to accommodate someone who could stay overnight. If you see the possibility of a nursing home in your future, visit several while you are still "in the driver's seat." You will learn a great deal about which one will suit you best and how to live well there. As you see more disability coming your way, it is a good idea to talk with an experienced social worker or home care nurse — someone who has "been there" with lots of other people. Their suggestions will be very helpful in making sure that you can live where you most want to be for as long as possible.

"What about planning my finances?"

If you have only modest wealth and income, you and your family need to know what care is covered by Medicaid. Your best source of information is likely to be an experienced social worker. If, however, you have some property and savings, you really need to do some planning. This usually requires the help of a lawyer, though it may not cost much if things are pretty uncomplicated. The lawyer will help you think through your goals, both the goals you have while you are still living and those for after you have died. The kinds of arrangements that you can make are quite varied and sometimes complicated, but they are also often effective in securing good care while you need it, financial security for your spouse, and a legacy for others. Doing good financial planning takes some time, so try not to put this off until death is very close.

"Why do I need someone to speak for me?"

Your doctors should always know who to turn to for decisions when you cannot decide for yourself. If you have no close family — or your family doesn't work together very well — it is important to figure out who should be your "voice," and to involve that person in treatment decisions all along throughout your illness.

You can write your decision into a "durable power of attorney" or "health care power of attorney." This gives another person authority to make decisions if

you become unable to do so. These designations are considered "durable" because they remain in effect even if you become unable to make decisions for yourself. Most people appoint a close friend or family member. If you don't have anyone, a minister or lawyer may serve. Make sure the person you choose will support you in the way that you want, understands your treatment choices, and knows what you value.

Giving someone else this authority is often more important than writing down preferences. Naming an advocate makes it easier for your choices to be recognized and followed. Otherwise, you risk having decisions made contrary to your wishes or by people you would not have chosen. This predicament also burdens those who love you by forcing them to make decisions without any clear guidance. Remember that these documents are only in effect when you actually lose decision-making ability, and not before. Many people fear that these documents will override spoken wishes if they still have decision-making abilities, but this is not the case.

Durable power of attorney forms do not give explicit guidance to the proxy about what decisions to make. Many states have developed forms that combine the intent of the durable power of attorney (to have an advocate) and the intent of the living will (to state your choices for treatment at the end of life). These combination forms will probably be more effective than either of the two used individually.

"My mother had a living will but the doctor ignored it. Is this common?"

Some people assume that advance directives have not been as effective as they could be because doctors often ignore them. This is not true; in fact, doctors usually follow clearly stated directives. Directives aren't "followed" when they are too vague to indicate exactly what should be done. Many standard forms use the phrase "no heroic means" to describe the treatment the patient does not want. Just what does this phrase mean? What might be "heroic means" to one person may be ordinary to another. The classification often depends  on your illness. Such imprecise and vague language doesn't really give much direction unless other conversations have made the meaning clear. Advance planning helps doctors know what you want, instead of having to guess.

"Is it legal to refuse life-sustaining treatment?"

Every American has the right to choose not to have any particular medical treatment. How do courts define "medical treatment?" When people become unable to breathe on their own, or unable to eat solid foods or drink liquids, they are sometimes put on a respirator to assist breathing or are given nutrients through tubes. Courts have defined these as "medical treatments" and have ruled that patients and families may decline to use them. Some people may consider it invasive or unnatural to have tubes inserted or to be hooked up to machinery. Others believe that if something can be done to extend their lives, they want it to be done. These are personal decisions that we have the right to make for ourselves (see also Chapter 12).

"What else should I plan for?"

At the start of this chapter, we noted that doctors and others on the health care team will focus on medical treatment decisions. You, however, should have a very different agenda much of the time. Often, you will find it rewarding to make plans about who you want to see, what you want to do now, what should happen near the time of death, and what should happen after death. These plans are all too easy to put off if you spend too much time and energy on thinking about medical treatment. If you find you have a great deal of anxiety over a specific medical treatment issue (resuscitation, for example), stop and ask your doctor whether this is really likely to matter much. Often, the honest answer is that the treatment won't make much difference (and the struggle is really over a symbol). Remember, enjoying *this* day is always important. Making plans for the people you cherish may be much more rewarding and important than anguishing over medical treatment decisions.

WHAT MIGHT YOU PLAN?

- *To enjoy nature and be in touch with the spiritual*
- *To leave some record for future generations*
- *To heal old wounds*
- *To share time with those you love*
- *To have the funeral or memorial you would like*
- *To have your last days at home (and therefore have what you need available there)*

"All of this is sort of depressing, isn't it?"

Most of us would agree that we don't enjoy making decisions about dying. Yet, doing so allows you to feel more confident that you will have some control over how you live, even when very sick. Your loved ones will also feel more secure because they know what you want. Think through your choices for treatment at the end of life, then give this gift to your family. Don't force others to guess about your wishes when they are facing an emergency.

Chapter 11

Forgoing medical treatment

If I'm lucky, I'll be wired every which way
in a hospital bed. Tubes running into
my nose. But try not to be scared of me, friends!
I'm telling you right now that this is okay.
It's little enough to ask for at the end.
Someone, I hope, will have phoned everyone
to say, "Come quick, he's failing!"
And they will come. And there will be time for me
to bid goodbye to each of my loved ones. . . .

RAYMOND CARVER
from "My Death"

Not everyone would agree with this poet's sentiments, and especially if the person dying were to be "wired every which way" for months and months. How, though, do you decide what is "just the right amount" of treatment?

Many treatments are started because there is still some real chance that the patient will improve. Even if the patient is dying, some treatments may be used in hopes of improving comfort. So artificial life support may become an issue for discussion or decision, even if you have plans not to use such treatments when you are "terminal" or the situation is "hopeless."

Artificial nutrition ("tube feeding"), intravenous (IV) hydration, antibiotics, and breathing machines are usually put in place because there is the expectation — or the hope — that a patient is going to recover from a temporary setback. Deciding to use these treatments in the course of a serious, chronic illness demands careful consideration. Once treatments have begun, it can be hard to decide to stop. You need to know, though, that you can stop treatment whenever you firmly decide to do so. Here's an approach to thinking about the issues.

> *"On one hand, you're the doctor, and you want to provide hope," he said. "On the other hand, you can inflict a great amount of harm. There's a great potential to cause even more pain with pointless treatments."*
>
> DR. DAVID MINTZER
> *from* Final Choices: Seeking the Good Death
> *by Michael Vitez*

Thinking about the issues

As with all medical treatments, the benefits and burdens should be balanced against each other when deciding whether or not to continue tube feedings, IVs, or ventilator breathing. The burdens imposed by these artificial treatments should not be ignored just because the treatments are keeping someone alive.

Artificial treatments are often very effective. Many people are alive because they had a spell of sickness and a machine — to provide nutrition, water, or air — got them through. Indeed, when there is any doubt about whether a treatment will improve comfort or quality of life, a *time-limited trial* is often very useful. Trying a treatment for a reasonable period of time allows you to see if there is a benefit to using the treatment. The key is to define the time limit before starting the treatment, so that everyone is expecting a reassessment then.

Some people worry that once they start a treatment, they will not be able to stop it. Legally and ethically, not starting and stopping are seen as equal actions. If a treatment is not improving comfort or quality of life, then there is no reason to continue it.

Tube feedings, IVs, and breathing machines are obviously not the same thing as eating, drinking, and breathing naturally. Not only are they mechanical and not responsive to our feelings of hunger, thirst, and breathlessness, but they also are troubling, uncomfortable, and efficient — just what human contact is not.

The way we talk of these treatments makes it easy to forget that they are, in fact, medical procedures. We talk about "feeding" patients — but the patients are not chewing, swallowing, or tasting through feeding tubes. We also discuss how patients are "breathing" on ventilators, making it easy to forget that the machine is doing most, or all, of the breathing for them. The words can be misleading because they can make these machines seem almost natural.

There is no question that feeding tubes, for example, help thousands of people recover from or live with what otherwise might be a terminal condition. Sometimes people who suffer a stroke cannot swallow at first, and a tube is inserted to provide hydration and nutrition. Often these patients can learn to eat again, and the tube is eventually removed. Sometimes a patient with throat cancer might not be able to swallow after successful treatment of the disease. He or she may have a feeding tube and still carry on otherwise normal activities. Few would question whether feeding tubes are appropriate in cases like these. But there are many cases where feeding tubes and IVs are more of a burden to the patient than a benefit.

Stopping treatment

Sometimes people feel that if they stop a treatment such as a feeding tube or breathing machine, then they will have "killed" their loved one. Again, the law does not see stopping these procedures as raising any questions of homicide or suicide. You are under no legal obligation as an adult to take any medical care (unless your disease is a risk to others). The natural progression of the disease is what prevents you from eating, drinking, or breathing normally. Stopping treatments that replace these natural functions only allows the disease to follow its natural course. Even if these treatments have been in place for months or years, it is all right to stop them and allow death to occur.

SOME POTENTIAL BENEFITS OF NOT USING TUBE FEEDINGS AND IVs NEAR DEATH

Effect on the Body	Benefit
Less fluid in the lungs	*Easier to breathe*
Less fluid in the throat	*Less need for suctioning*
Less pressure on tumors	*Less pain*
Less frequent urination	*Less risk of skin breakdown and bed sores*
Increase in the body's natural pain-relieving hormones	*Increased comfort and less pain*

Mr. Gordon was a 99-year-old concentration camp survivor with stomach cancer, admitted to an inpatient hospice for end-of-life care. Mrs. Gordon, 94 years old, stayed with him day and night, and often wondered aloud how she would live without him. As the days passed, Mr. Gordon ate less and less, despite his wife cajoling him to "eat to keep up your strength." Still, Mr. and Mrs. Gordon had agreed that he did not want a feeding tube, as that would not do anything to cure or treat his cancer.

When Mr. Gordon became comatose, his daughter and grandson were called from their home hundreds of miles away. Mr. Gordon's grandson stayed with him for a while, then left the room and tearfully insisted that the doctor put in a feeding tube to "give him a few more days." The doctor explained that tube feeding might give Mr. Gordon "a few more days" but would more likely cause pain from having the tube in place, diarrhea from liquid feedings that Mr. Gordon's stomach and intestines could no longer tolerate, and shortness of breath from fluid buildup.

Mr. Gordon's grandson admitted that he was not ready for his grandfather to die. He found it hard to believe that artificial feedings would not strengthen Mr. Gordon. Mr. Gordon's daughter reminded her son of how peaceful Mr. Gordon looked. She compared that to having pain, diarrhea, and shortness of breath. Although Mr. Gordon's grandson still did not want his grandfather to die, he did not want him to have pain or other discomfort. No feeding tube was placed. Mr. Gordon died the next day, peacefully, surrounded by his family.

Time-limited trials

If death is not expected in hours to days, you and your family may consider a time-limited trial of artificial nutrition (food) and hydration (liquid) to see if it improves your comfort, alertness, or energy. To give tube feedings for a short period of time, a tube is usually threaded through the nose into the stomach. For longer periods of tube feedings, tubes may be placed through the abdomen directly into the stomach. This is a surgical procedure performed by gastroenterologists or surgeons, depending on the patient's other medical problems. Intravenous (IV) catheters are usually placed in the veins of the arm or hand to give artificial hydration. If IVs are going to be used for nutrition as well as hydration, they usually must be placed in the large veins of the arms, neck, chest, or groin.

You and your family should agree in advance with your doctor about what you hope to accomplish from trying tube feedings or IV fluid. You should also determine, in advance, how long to wait to see if you are feeling any better before removing the tubes.

When food seems like love

In all cultures and throughout all history, offering food has been a sign of caring and hospitality. Our mothers made sure we were well fed. Most people enjoy eating with family and friends, especially on special occasions. In most religions, food is part of sacred rituals. It is no wonder, then, when someone we love is unable to eat and drink naturally, that we feel compelled to "feed" them in some way. It seems to be basic caring.

But as death approaches, you will not "keep up your strength" by forcing yourself to eat when it makes you uncomfortable. If eating is a social event for you, or providing food is one of the common ways of expressing caring in your family, your loss of appetite may be distressing to you and your loved ones. You might enjoy small amounts of home-cooked food — dishes that mean something special to you. However, you should also know that a decrease in appetite is natural, and eating less may increase, rather than decrease, comfort.

Since most dying persons are more comfortable without eating or drinking at the end of life, forcing food or liquids is usually not beneficial, especially if restraints, intravenous lines, or hospitalization would be required. Not forcing someone to eat or drink is *not* letting him "starve to death."

The truth is, for those who are dying, the time comes when it might be more compassionate, caring, even natural, to allow dehydration to occur. Forcing tube feedings and IVs on dying patients can make the last days of their lives more uncomfortable.

The benefits of dehydration at the end of life

The evidence from medical research and experiences of clinicians suggests that dying people are often more comfortable without artificial hydration, whether provided by a feeding tube or IV. Until this generation, everyone who died a natural death died without artificially supplied fluids. The stopping of eating and drinking has always been part of the last phase of a terminal condition. Only recently have people been afraid that not providing food and fluid through a tube would cause someone to "starve to death." There is no medical or clinical evidence that not using a feeding tube or IV leads to a more painful death. In fact, the research says just the opposite.

The main burden associated with dehydration at the end of life is a dry mouth. Very few dying people feel any thirst. Good mouth care, ice chips, or moistened sponge swabs relieve any discomfort from a dry mouth.

Tube feeding and the dementia patient

Increased difficulty with eating and swallowing is one of the signs that an Alzheimer's patient has moved into the final stages of the disease. He or she may tend to choke on food and drink and, therefore, run the risk of a respiratory infection. He or she may lose interest in food or forget how to swallow. These signs mark the end of a very long and sad disease process. By this point, the patient is totally dependent on others for care, incontinent, unable to recognize family or to speak intelligibly, and failing to thrive.

Some may choose to treat the reduction in food and fluid intake with a feeding tube. Family, doctors, or nurses may say they do not want the patient to "starve" to death. Providing tube feeding is certainly an acceptable way to provide care.

However, the patient isn't feeling any hunger. The dying is part of a very tragic disease, and the inability to eat is an expected part of its last stages. Inserting a tube will not stop the progression of the fatal disease — dementia — and it might prolong or speed up the dying process. Since dying without hydration is often quite comfortable, many choose to allow the patient to experience a natural and peaceful death without artificial feeding. The patient takes whatever he or she can tolerate by spoon feeding and drinking. Sips of water and ice chips are enough to relieve a dry mouth. Thus, many choose to forgo tube feeding. This decision poses the kind of perplexing situation that may become more clear as society has more experience with it.

Artificial feeding and the permanently unconscious patient

Many people can be supported with artificial feeding even though they are not conscious. Some stroke patients may never again respond to any stimuli. Some young people have suffered head trauma and become permanently unconscious. Two well-known court cases involved Karen Ann Quinlan and Nancy Cruzan, who both lived for years supported by feeding tubes though they were never aware of their surroundings. These patients are said to be in a *persistent vegetative state*. Are we obligated to keep such patients alive even though there is no hope of their recovery to a conscious state? If we do choose to withdraw the tube feeding, would these patients experience a painful death? Would we be "killing the patient?"

The courts and medical practice have ruled it acceptable to withhold or withdraw tube feeding from such patients. This is not taking an action to kill the patient; rather, it is allowing a natural death to occur. Again, all the advantages of dehydration in any dying patient will benefit these patients in their last days. They will die a very comfortable and peaceful death.

The real struggle for the families of these patients is an emotional and spiritual one. Can we let go? Are we continuing the artificial feeding for others or for the patient? If the patient could choose, would he or she withdraw treatment and allow a natural, peaceful death?

Choosing to stop eating and drinking

> *The patient was 42 years old and had been suffering from a slowly disabling neurological disease for ten years. He had concluded that the burden of living had become so great that he was ready to die. He had a loving wife, a large, caring family, and even continued to work as a consultant out of his home. He was confined to his wheelchair or to bed. He was totally dependent on others for all of his care. He took large doses of drugs just to be able to get out of bed in the morning and keep his vital systems going. He experienced regular infections and occasional hospitalizations. He was a man of deep faith and regularly worshiped with his congregation. He knew his disease was terminal and that his condition would only get worse.*
>
> *He rejected the idea of suicide for moral reasons as well as the burden it would place on his family. He chose to stop all his medications and let the disease run its natural course as quickly as possible. Over the weeks following this treatment plan, he became weaker and more frail. His heart and other vital systems were failing. Six days before his death he stopped eating and drank only sips of water. He was fully conscious during his last days. He had pushed his body to its physical limits and knew that to refuse to eat and drink would allow his death to come more quickly. He died peacefully in the night, his wife sleeping at his side.*

> *My own belief is that the use of heroic and experimental medical technology is often a moral outrage, showing callous disrespect for the sacredness of human life and pathetic inability to face the reality of human death.*
>
> PEGGY STINSON
> from The Long Dying of Baby Andrew

Occasionally patients do make a deliberate choice to stop taking in food and fluids, and they may actually say they are doing this to speed up the dying process. These are people in the last stages of a terminal disease. They do not suffer from a mental illness or other condition that has affected their reasoning. They are not "suicidal" in the usual sense of the word. They have concluded that the burden of living has gotten so great that they want to die.

This choice is usually disturbing to family members and to medical personnel. In such instances, the family and caregivers need to be sure that the patient is not suffering from depression or pain. Perhaps these conditions could be adequately managed; and, once under control, the patient may no longer want to hasten death. It is very important to consider carefully whether the conditions that the patient feels are too great a burden can be relieved. These burdens may be emotional issues like discord in the family, or spiritual issues like a need to feel forgiven.

After the emotional, spiritual, and symptom management issues have been adequately addressed, the patient may still refuse to eat. If this happens, it usually is in the very last days of the course of the disease. Just as a patient can refuse surgery or chemotherapy that might prolong life, a patient also can refuse to eat. However, finally, the patient's decision binds everyone else.

Of all the wonders that I yet have heard,

It seems to me most strange that men should fear;

Seeing that death, a necessary end,

Will come when it will come.

WILLIAM SHAKESPEARE
from Julius Caesar

Decisions about ventilators

Ventilators push air and oxygen into the lungs and often save lives. Even so, people with very serious diseases may prefer not to have a ventilator or to have one removed. Reasons not to use a ventilator include:

- Ventilators may interfere with your ability to speak and swallow.
- Ventilators do not reverse the disease process itself.
- Ventilators are uncomfortable.
- If you are very sick, it can be hard to recover enough to come off the ventilator.
- You may require extra sedation.
- You may need many blood tests and X rays to monitor your condition.

These are all things to consider when deciding whether or not to try a ventilator. Reasons to try a ventilator may be your degree of disability, or the level of discomfort you have. At the same time, you may be very anxious about going on a ventilator.

As with feeding tubes, you can tell your doctor you want a time-limited trial on a ventilator. For one or two weeks, a ventilator can be hooked up through your nose or mouth. For a longer period, you would need a tracheostomy (a hole in your throat) to insert the tube.

Ask your doctor how comfortable he or she is in removing the ventilator. Can your doctor keep you comfortable as the ventilator is removed? Does your doctor have experience with using medications for sedation, so you won't ever feel short of breath? Can you go home or stay at home? Be sure your doctor will do what you want.

As with other decisions you will make at the end of life, this one is complex because of the emotional issues raised by stopping a ventilator. Nevertheless, you can choose to forgo all use or to have a time-limited trial with a planned withdrawal.

Decisions about resuscitation

When a person's circulation stops, death occurs. If someone's heart stops, he or she will die unless circulation is restarted quickly. Since a person's sudden collapse must be addressed so quickly, many people are trained to make the efforts needed to restart circulation right away. And, usually, treatment is what people in the community would want.

However, when you are seriously ill, you may find this procedure — called *cardiopulmonary resuscitation* — to be worthless or even deeply disturbing. While you may be grateful for the time you have, or at least willing to endure whatever time you have, you might not want someone to disrupt your time of death with a flurry of activity that is doomed to have little effect.

Once you have decided against trying resuscitation, how can you prevent people from trying anyway? You need to have a clear discussion with your doctor and those near you to be sure that everyone understands that you really don't want resuscitation tried. It is rarely successful in those who are very sick, and life after resuscitation is often short and uncomfortable. Therefore, deciding against resuscitation is quite reasonable. However, since resuscitation has to be started right away, there is a presumption in favor of using it whenever the situation is unclear. It is up to you and your doctor to see to it that your plans are clear!

At home, you will have less risk that resuscitation might be tried, unless someone panics and calls the emergency medical system. As mentioned in Chapter 10, there are usually ways to ensure that the emergency crew will follow your wishes, but you have to know the procedures in your area and follow them.

In a hospital, you should ask for a "do not attempt resuscitation" order. If possible, ask your doctor to phone this order ahead of your admission. When you arrive at the emergency room or the admissions desk, ask to be sure that an order is in place as soon as possible. When you get to a hospital room, ask your nurse and any doctors who see you to be sure that your order is in place. Most hospitals have some way to identify patients who have requested "do not attempt resuscitation" orders — a bracelet, perhaps. Ask about the process and be sure it is followed.

In a nursing home, the situation may be parallel to a hospital, or more may be entrusted to your main nurse. Ask how you can be sure that no one will misunderstand what you want. In a nursing home, you need to be clear about whether you should be sent to a hospital if you become quite ill. If you decide that you would want to go to a hospital only to relieve symptoms, or not at all, be sure to make that clear as well as your intentions about resuscitation.

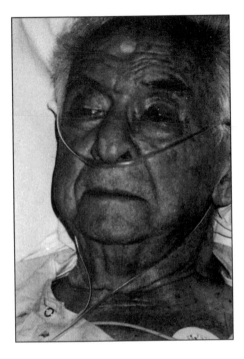

The many meanings of "DNR"

Deciding whether or not you want a DNR order sounds so simple. And yet, this decision causes much anxiety for families and health care providers. Why? Because these decisions are often put off until the patient is too sick to make them. And making the decision means acknowledging that you are likely to die. To hospital staff, the DNR decision is a sign that things are pretty bad.

Yet it is important that this decision be made. Without a written order, doctors and nurses will attempt resuscitation. Nurses and doctors who are likely to have to try the resuscitation are reasonably upset over the prospects of having to do such brutal procedures without any real chance of success. So, if you are the patient or a family member, you have some real control in this situation. First, figure out whether you really want resuscitation tried, on the basis of its chances of success and how you prefer to die. Then, if you want no resuscitation but you don't want to be counted as one who has given up, insist that the doctor write an order that makes that clear. State clearly what you do and do not want done. Then the doctor can make clear in the record that you want no resuscitation but you do want diagnosis and treatment for anything else that comes up.

Other decisions to forgo treatments

This advice holds true for almost any treatment. You need to know what it will accomplish and what burdens it will cause. You often will want to try it out before deciding that it is not "worth it" for you. This holds true for simple treatments like antibiotics or insulin, for routine treatments like tube feeding, and for dramatic treatments like ventilators or chemotherapy. The principles are the same, and the need for a compassionate and knowledgeable doctor is also constant.

Chapter 12

Hastening death

If, following the quality-of-life, take-me-out-and-shoot-me principle, we end up using assisted suicide to preempt the infirmities of old age and terminal illness, how well equipped will we be to encounter infirmity elsewhere? How to become fluent in help if we have banished helplessness from our vocabulary?

RAND RICHARDS COOPER
from "The Dignity of Helplessness"

Many people are so afraid of dying in pain, of becoming helpless and dependent on others, that they want to kill themselves rather than wait for disease to take its course. People are afraid of dying alone or being attached to life support in a hospital. Some fear running up huge medical bills that will bankrupt their families. And many fear the loss of dignity that comes with being very ill and dying.

When the picture is so bleak, no wonder we want to change it quickly. No wonder people want to take control over the end of life. As a society, we praise independence and freedom; if we have been in control for most of our lives, losing control at the end seems almost unbearable.

But are suicide and euthanasia truly options? Do they provide a way out of pain and suffering?

Your answers to these questions depend on how you feel about the controversial issue of physician-assisted suicide or physician administration of a lethal injection. In the abstract, these are good subjects for debate. But when you are dying, or watching someone you love die, the issue hits home and you may feel simply overwhelmed, helpless, and afraid. Thinking about hastening death, before it becomes an urgent question in your own life, can help you to understand your current options and to discuss your fears with your family or health care team.

People sometimes think that if they are being cared for by hospice, they will be able to ask for a lethal injection or an overdose of pills. However, hospice does not offer such assistance. Instead, hospice is an alternative to the technologically driven death in a hospital that so many dread.

Many people are afraid that they must be willing to hasten their death if they want to have good symptom relief. Good symptom management, however, very rarely shortens life, and even then only by a few hours (see Chapter 7).

SUICIDE OR PHYSICIAN-ASSISTED SUICIDE: WHAT'S THE DIFFERENCE?

SUICIDE *is taking your own life by your own hand and in your own way. You do not ask or expect others to help you.*

PHYSICIAN-ASSISTED SUICIDE *means that you ask a doctor to write a lethal prescription, which you will take. Without the doctor's help, you cannot take your own life.*

EUTHANASIA *is the act of killing someone who otherwise would suffer terribly from an incurable disease. This is sometimes called "mercy killing."*

Considering suicide: When you just can't face another day

Living with a chronic illness and the knowledge that you are dying is hard to do. You may feel cheated, betrayed by your own body and the world. You sometimes feel that your doctor is just not doing enough, or that a cure should still be possible. Being treated for serious illness can be expensive, uncomfortable, and disheartening. Being sick requires many sacrifices and changes. Often, you have to ask others to do things you once did for yourself. Some days, you may feel so full of despair that the idea of just dying now seems like a reasonable alternative. In fact, attempts at suicide are often tied to clinical depression, a disease that makes people feel sad, unworthy, guilty, and overwhelmed. Depression is not the same as feeling sad: it is having no positive or hopeful feelings and often just no energy to care.

Many dying people who focus on suicide are depressed. Many others have alcohol and drug abuse problems. Many older people who commit suicide not only are depressed but suffer from long-term physical disabilities as well. Still others

> *I am too tired*
> *To move on, or to mind the paths traveled.*
> *Where I find moonlight and gentle breezes,*
> *I shall unload, lay down, and rest in peace.*
>
> HELEN CHEN
> *from "Reflections in the Dusk"*

are depressed because of medication they take to treat diseases (such as hypertension). Most of the depression that leads patients to consider suicide can be treated effectively with medication and therapy. Most dying people are not depressed, and most who are depressed can be helped (often within days or a few weeks).

Being depressed is like wearing blinders or trying to read in the dark. Your perspective is just not what it should be. You may not even be able to remember times when you were happy and felt that life was worth living. You may feel that you have been depressed for years. It is certainly a time when the future seems irrelevant and bleak.

Many health care professionals can diagnose and treat depression, though you should know that depression is often overlooked. It can help for you to ask: "Is this depression that makes me feel so low?" Your doctor should talk to you about your symptoms and find a treatment. You can also get help by calling a local or national suicide prevention hotline or finding a community mental health center. These hotlines offer confidential help from trained and friendly volunteers who will listen to your troubles and lead you to resources. By asking for help, you open the door to support and hope. Getting help for depression can give you time to think about your life more clearly. Often you will come up with adequate options for the fear and loss of control you feel.

Your doctor might recommend that you join a support group, such as a breast cancer or stroke group, or even a depression or "12-step program" in your community. Talking to others who share your experience and concerns can take a weight off your mind. Sharing your feelings — and just being with other human beings — is a powerful way to heal.

You may find that you are not, in fact, depressed, and you may continue to feel that dying is just taking too long. If so, you should consider not only the other issues discussed in the rest of this chapter, but also the possibilities of hastening death by stopping treatments. Ordinarily, people who are very sick can stop a medication, can forgo artificial nutrition and hydration, and can accept sedating levels of drugs. These are not so definitive, or confrontative, as suicide or euthanasia, and they are usually fairly effective in avoiding prolonged dying (see Chapter 11).

"I want to spare my family."

If you are terribly sick and in pain, it is understandable that you might want to "get it over with." You might feel that dying quickly will spare your loved ones the burden and pain of suffering. Such feelings are common, given the emotional and financial toll of living with a life-threatening disease. While the burdens of care can be overwhelming to family, it is also true that caring for another human being often enriches us, making us more compassionate and kind, or showing us strengths we did not know we had.

No matter how you die, your family will suffer. In the depths of your despair, you may not envision the effect a decision for suicide or lethal injection would have on them. Suicide can devastate its survivors. Spouses and children ordinarily feel responsible for not relieving your emotional pain. They are often angry at being cheated out of a chance to talk to you and help you. The guilty feelings last for years, marking their future relationships. Religious beliefs might lead others to judge you very harshly, and your family may bear the brunt of such judgment.

If you ask your family if they feel burdened or overwhelmed, they might say they are. But they are also likely to say they'll do anything for you, and put aside your worries. In fairness to the people you love, talk to them. Tell them you think suicide may be the best option. Very often, they won't agree and their perspective may help you see both more valued ways to continue to live and less destructive or dangerous ways to hasten death (see Chapter 11 on forgoing treatment).

"I want to be sure to die comfortably. Wouldn't suicide be a guarantee?"

Some of us want everything possible done to keep us alive. Others want to die when nature decides it is time, and we do not seek or want aggressive or curative care. No matter how you envision your death, no matter what you do to prolong your life, you should be able to rely upon your health care team to give you the pain relief and emotional support you need to die comfortably. Each of us will define an "acceptable dying" in our own way, but you

> *But be glad for me if I can die in the presence of friends and family. If this happens, believe me I came out ahead. I didn't lose this one.*
>
> RAYMOND CARVER
> *from "My Death"*

should each feel that you will have the basics: that you will not have severe physical symptoms, that your family will have help in providing care, and that you will have the support needed to be at peace with yourself. The information provided throughout this book will help you to shape a good death for yourself, without having to undertake suicide or to ask for euthanasia.

Nevertheless, you might not be able to find a health care arrangement that inspires trust, or maybe you just don't want to take any chances. Then you should know that suicide attempts — even physician-assisted suicide — can fail. Sometimes the dose of pills is not enough, or you vomit some of the medication, or some other complication arises. Then you risk brain damage without having succeeded at causing death. This prospect may lead you to seek a doctor's help in giving a lethal injection. However, you are exceedingly unlikely to find a doctor who will comply. Although patients can accumulate pills on their own, the doctor's involvement in prescribing or giving a lethal injection is illegal, and it carries such severe penalties that few will even talk about it.

Thus, trying to control the hour of your death is an uncertain proposition. Most people find it better to get good, reliable care.

"Don't the laws now allow physician-assisted suicide?"

Physician-assisted suicide is illegal in every state except Oregon. In 1997, the U.S. Supreme Court issued rulings on physician-assisted suicide and sent the issue back to the states to decide. The Court decided that it could not identify a right to request a physician's help in dying. Therefore, the merits of state laws that bar physician-assisted suicide are appropriate for the states to decide.

At the same time, the Court reaffirmed that Americans do have the right to refuse or end life-sustaining treatment, such as ventilators and feeding tubes. The Court pointed out that there is a difference between letting someone die and helping someone to die. Refusing treatment lets your disease run its natural course. Having someone's help in suicide, the court ruled, is different.

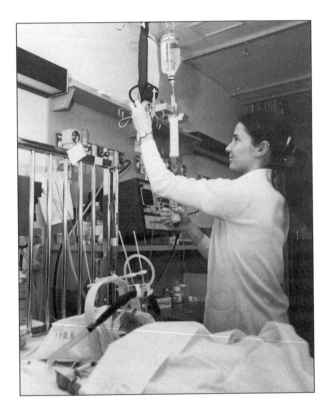

The Court also emphasized the importance of pain control for dying people. The court's ruling may well have created a right to pain and symptom management — at least keeping the states from erecting barriers. Many doctors are hesitant to prescribe opioids (also called narcotics) because they fear the state will revoke their license or their prescribing privileges. The court's ruling will probably weaken this concern.

In reality, should you try to hoard pills to overdose, you are not likely to be prosecuted. And certainly talking about suicide is not against the law.

Unless you live in Oregon (where physician-assisted suicide is legal), any action taken by a doctor — deliberately prescribing pills, giving a lethal injection, or even being present at your suicide — is illegal.

"What about Oregon?"

In 1997, Oregon voters reasserted their desire to make physician-assisted suicide legal. Oregon's law requires that the patient be "capable" to make the choice and that he or she make this choice voluntarily, without pressure from family or health care providers. It is not yet clear how these troubling characteristics will be interpreted in the law.

The Oregon law includes a two-week waiting period to ensure that a patient has really considered suicide and definitely wants to die. This safeguard actually limits the usefulness of physician-assisted suicide, because people who might seek it are often very near death.

In its first six months, there have been two publicized suicides under Oregon's law, and fewer than ten have been reported confidentially to the state. This relatively low number might stem from Oregon having invested substantially in improving end-of-life care generally. Although their improved end-of-life care is available to all, the physician-assisted suicide statute is available only to long-term Oregon residents. You cannot move to Oregon at the end of your life simply to end it.

"What are some of the arguments against legalizing physician-assisted suicide?"

Legalizing physician-assisted suicide is a part of the debate about improving end-of-life care. It can't be seen as a quick and easy way to protect patients from inadequate care arrangements. Too many people still suffer needlessly, often because doctors and families just do not know how to serve people who are dying. Many suffer because doctors fail to provide adequate medication for pain. To legalize physician-assisted suicide, some believe, would make real reform, such as better pain control, less likely. Without those reforms, patients end up with no prospects to live well while dying. In this scenario, making suicide an option is not offering a genuine choice.

Many people fear that physician-assisted suicide will create a climate in which some people are more deliberately pressured into committing suicide. The very old, the very poor, or minorities and other vulnerable populations might be encouraged to hasten death, rather than to "burden" their families or the health care system. Again, this is not a genuine choice, but a social issue, one that stems from how our society cares for its elders and for the poor, and whether minority groups can get good health care. In either case, making suicide available does not solve the underlying social problem. Even for those who have adequate financial and social resources, having physician-assisted suicide available could create a troubling new situation. Seriously ill and disabled persons could feel that they had to justify a choice to stay alive. They could feel that suicide is, in some sense, "expected" by family or friends. As a society, we have never asked people to justify their being alive, and it seems likely that asking them to do so would run risks of being quite difficult or demeaning.

Finally the safeguards built into the proposed statutes will be very difficult to implement. "Terminal illness," "competent" patients, and "voluntary action" are each very ambiguous categories. Waiting times and restrictions on the help available are likely to create tragic situations that push public opinion toward loosening restrictions.

A 1997 study conducted by the American Medical Association (AMA) found that more than half of Americans believe physician-assisted suicide should be legal. However, when people are told about alternatives to the technological treatments so many of us fear, and about the availability of pain control and hospice care, their support for physician-assisted suicide goes down to under one-fifth. This study seems to show that when people are informed about all of their end-of-life choices, they are less likely to opt for suicide.

"What arguments support physician-assisted suicide?"

Supporters of physician-assisted suicide believe that this is fundamentally an individual choice, and one that should not be limited by laws. They believe that individuals have the right to make life-and-death decisions for themselves without government interference.

Supporters of legalization are responding to the fear of being in terrible pain and agony, of being hooked up to life-support equipment, and of becoming a financial or emotional drain on their families. They fear becoming dependent on others or having a very poor quality of life. Sadly, our current health care system and its practices leave people suffering unreasonably and unnecessarily at the end of life. Too often, people suffer from avoidable pain and other symptoms in their final days. And such suffering can occur even with good care. People advocate for more reliable physician-assisted suicide to guard against these possibilities.

Sometimes just having a means to suicide limits anxiety and allows the patient to enjoy life more fully. And making physician assistance legal might make it easier to monitor and regulate.

Of course, dying people and their families have every reason to consider the policy questions of legalizing physician-assisted suicide. However, most are constrained to live within the law as it is now.

"I don't trust doctors."

If you are fortunate, you will have doctors, nurses, and others who are easy to trust. Maybe you've known them for years, or maybe you have needed them urgently and they have always come through. But you may feel uncertain. You may have no regular doctor or nurse, or you may have needed help badly at some time and they let you down, or you may have heard stories of bad care. What can you do?

First, trust and confidence don't usually arise immediately. Talking about your fears and being well-informed are helpful. With serious illness, there are some special fears worth noting. First, morphine and other opioid medicines are very useful and very safe. When your doctor starts using them, death may still be far off, and using these medications usually prolongs life. Higher doses of morphine or other opioids may well be needed near death, but there is no evidence that using enough to stop suffering also causes death (see Chapter 7).

Second, despite the current changes in health care, doctors are still well-protected from the costs of your care. Some people have come to fear that new health payment arrangements make doctors prone to resenting patients whose needs lead to big bills. If you are worried about this in your situation, try to talk with your doctor or with a social worker or chaplain. Perhaps they can show you that the care your doctor is recommending is the same as doctors generally recommend for people with better insurance. Perhaps they can help by talking frankly about the limits that your financial situation does create.

Finally, though, it is reassuring to know that the conflicts over expensive care have mostly been about particularly high-cost procedures, which are very rarely an issue for people who face serious and eventually fatal illness. For most care,

> *In our system, it is easier to get open heart surgery than Meals on Wheels, easier to get antibiotics than eyeglasses, and certainly easier to get emergency care aimed at rescue than to get sustaining, supportive care. It would be so easy to encourage dying persons to be dead rather than to find them services. If it were easy to get good care, the question of whether one should be able to choose to be killed would be troubling and important. But it is not easy to get good care. . . . Accepting a responsibility to work to change the shortcomings of the present system argues against reducing the pressures for change by removing the sufferers through death.*
>
> JOANNE LYNN
> from "Travels in the Valley of the Shadow"

doctors and nurses seem generally to be providing about the same care to rich and poor, and to persons of different social and ethnic groups. Remember, doctors and nurses are people who chose a career in serving the sick.

"Outside of Oregon, is there any physician-assisted suicide?"

The most extreme example of physician-assisted suicide is the work of Jack Kevorkian, M.D., a retired and unlicensed pathologist who has helped dozens of people die. Kevorkian has been tried for murder but not convicted. Public opinion about what he does varies. Those who find him an outrage point out that he has no ability to deliver good care and no long-standing relationship with those

he helps to die. Also, some of those whom he has helped to die have not had life-threatening illnesses. Because he has no real relationship with the individuals, he is not able to assess them for depression, or to try to treat their symptoms.

In another example, Timothy Quill, M.D., has written about the help he gave to his long-term patient, "Diane." He provided her with enough medication so that, over time, she would have what she needed to kill herself. Through his ongoing conversations with her, he was aware of her suicidal intentions and believed that her decision was appropriate. His major regret was that he was not with her when she died, for fear of being prosecuted on criminal charges.

Recently a national survey showed that two to three percent of U.S. physicians had complied with a request to prescribe a drug intended for use in suicide. Very few of these drugs were ever taken.

Obviously, however, your main concern when you confront the end of life will be to get excellent care. If you also want to consider the issues in suicide, physician-assisted suicide, or euthanasia, you owe it to yourself to read more and to find some people — doctor, chaplain, counselor, family — who will be willing to talk with you.

Coping with events near death

The last night that she lived,
It was a common night,
Except the dying; this to us
Made nature different.

We noticed smallest things, —
Things overlooked before,
By this great light upon our minds
Italicized, as 't were.

. . .

Emily Dickinson

Earlier generations may have had so much experience with dying that most people knew how to recognize approaching death. When people died at home, families also knew more about how to deal with the practical aspects of the time near death. Now, however, this knowledge is just not commonplace.

Many of us have watched people die only on television or in the movies, neither of which gives a very realistic view of the process. This chapter will give some practical facts and advice to family and friends of people who are near death.

"How will I know when death is getting close?"

Just as doctors usually cannot pinpoint the day when a baby will be born, they cannot predict the exact day or hour when you or your loved one will die. You might need reassurance that it is simply not always possible to know when death is near. Some illnesses make prediction difficult. However, many illnesses have a few hours or a few days when it is evident that death is close. The person dying usually is no longer eating or drinking, except for perhaps a few sips of liquid now and again. The person may be sleepy or confused for much of the time and is usually in bed. If the person is dying from cancer or a progressive failure of an organ, he or she will usually have lost a substantial amount of weight. If life support is being stopped, the physician should be able to tell you what to watch for in order to estimate about how long it will be before death.

The winter after you left us was the longest, coldest, snowiest one that anyone had ever seen in these parts. It seemed fitting, somehow. It makes you feel small. It reminds you, So many things are out of your hands.

SARAH L. DELANEY

from On My Own at 107: Reflections on Life Without Bessie

Many people near death will have cool hands and feet and a persistent purplish discoloration in the parts of the body resting on the bed. Many also will have uneven breathing, sometimes stopping for many seconds and at other times breathing rapidly. This kind of breathing and discoloration can persist for a few days, but these signs usually mean a person will die within a day.

Some people have some jerking motions or even seizures from metabolic abnormalities near death. As disturbing as it may be for others to watch this happen, the dying person is probably not aware of it. The involuntary motions usually do not need treatment because they do not seem to cause problems for the patient.

If the dying person has been taking opioid medicines, these will be continued because ending opioids abruptly can lead to uncomfortable symptoms. If the dying person is no longer able to swallow, opioids can be given by suppository, injection, skin patch, or intravenous infusion.

Probably half of patients develop very noisy breathing near death — which is sometimes called a "death rattle." This is the result of relaxation of the muscles of the throat and does not cause the person to feel as though she is struggling to breathe. In fact, most dying patients are not aware of this noisy breathing. However, if family or caregivers find it unnerving, the doctor or nurse can help reduce the noisy sound, either by giving medication or repositioning the dying person in bed.

"What should family and friends do when death is close?"

You, and your family and friends, will need to answer this question for yourselves. Many patients are frightened of being alone, or just want a loved one nearby to help ease their passage, perhaps holding a hand. A few simply want to be alone. Some family and friends find comfort in reading, reminiscing, saying prayers, or singing. Some just want to be there, sharing the precious time. What any one patient or family member wants may change over time, or as other visitors come and go.

Unless it is absolutely unavoidable, family and friends should not spend much time on medical treatment decisions at this point. It is best to have had any such discussions earlier in the course of a disease, or just to limit the time spent on them now. Sometimes families or patients have to remind the professional staff in a hospital that this is precious time and should not be taken up with issues like drug doses or formal advance directives. Remember, too, that this can be a good time to call on religious support, including the hospital chaplain. Music is very helpful for some patients and families. One elderly lady was comforted by a Gregorian chant tape, another by special harp music. Some prefer gospels or modern music. Most families and patients seem to benefit from some kind of music.

This is a very good time to say farewells and to ask forgiveness, if these things have not already been done. People who visit can say to the dying person that he or she lived well and is loved. Often it seems that dying people can still hear, even when they no longer seem to be awake. So saying things to a person who seems to be asleep is reasonable, and it can be important for those left behind.

Some patients and families have a sequence of people who, one by one, come through to say goodbye. Others have more unplanned visits. Some have religious rituals to follow; others make up their own style as they go.

"Is it important to be there at the moment of death?"

Many people feel that they should be present at the very moment that a dying loved one draws his last breath. However, whether this is important depends on the preferences of the family and friends and the dying person. Trying to be there can be quite wearing, since the exact time of death is so hard to predict. People sometimes keep up a death watch for days and finally have to get some coffee, or some sleep. Often, that is when the person finally dies. Perhaps he was "waiting" and needed to be "on his own" a little in order to let go. Perhaps the timing was just chance.

Important things are rarely said just at the time of death, so it is not likely that survivors will miss hearing something important if they are not there.

On the other hand, a few patients really do say remarkable things in the few days ahead of death — seeing persons long dead, giving comfort to family, or making peace about a long-hidden failing. It is important to patient and family for these things to be shared. Thus, spending some time at the bedside is worthwhile. Families often use this time also to share feelings and perspectives that do not often have the opportunity to be heard. They can begin to sort out new relationships and do some practical planning, too.

Families and patients should give instructions to caregivers in hospitals and nursing homes about who should be called, if possible, when death is close, and who should be called when the person has died.

"How does a family member know that the person has died?"

Usually the patient takes a breath, sighs or shudders, and is dead. Many people have another effort or two at breathing but really are not moving air. A few have movement of limbs or trunk for up to ten minutes after death.

Still, how can a family member know that the person has died? If there is no air moving, the person is dead. There is no urgency to making the determination, so an observer can just sit and watch for a few minutes. Family and friends may want to spend a few minutes crying, praying, or meditating.

Most of us are too unfamiliar with death to be comfortable deciding that it has happened. In a hospital or nursing home, someone who can check with a stethoscope can be summoned. In hospice or regular home care, usually a nurse can come to the home within an hour or so.

If the death is at home, the family really needs to plan ahead so that no one feels any need to call 911 or involve the emergency rescue system. Emergency technicians will often find it difficult to size up the situation quickly, so just when the family needs comfort and time, they instead have to explain themselves to an outsider. Families may find more comfort if they call the doctor's office or the hospice. Often it helps to have spoken to the doctor in advance about this need.

Many people really need to hear someone else say that the person is dead. "Pronouncing" a person dead is important. Even if it is perfectly obvious, family should still be able to ask, "Is he dead?" and hear from someone else that he really is. Again, talk with the doctor about how this will be done.

"What happens then?"

After a death, there are more decisions and activities than most families really expect. Take some time to remember the person who just died, to be in touch with loved ones, to pray, or to do whatever is significant and helpful to the survivors. Within a few hours, usually, the body will be moved to a location that handles dead bodies — a hospital morgue, a funeral home, or a government medical examiner's morgue. If a person expects to die at home, make plans ahead of time with a funeral director.

The next of kin will need to be involved in decisions about autopsy. If the doctor or nurse says there is no need to notify the medical examiner, or if the medical examiner declines to do an autopsy, the next of kin should still consider having an autopsy done. Autopsies help answer questions about what really happened. They also keep doctors and other caregivers "on their toes," since autopsies can turn up shortcomings that would otherwise have been unknown.

The body after an autopsy still looks normal and can be shown in an open casket if that is the family's wish. If the person died in a hospital, usually an autopsy is available free. If

Looking down into my father's
dead face
for the last time
my mother said without
tears, without smiles
without regrets
but with civility
"Good night, Willie Lee, I'll see you
in the morning."
And it was then I knew that the healing
of all our wounds
is forgiveness
that permits a promise
of our return
at the end.

ALICE WALKER
from "Good Night, Willie Lee, I'll See You in the Morning"

the person died in a nursing home or at home, the situation is more complex. Sometimes the doctor can arrange for a free autopsy, sometimes there is a fee (of up to a few thousand dollars, which the family must pay), and sometimes one just cannot find a way to get an autopsy. Obviously, this situation is complicated enough to warrant having considered it in advance whenever possible, especially for deaths at home.

If the death is sudden or unexpected or just at home, the medical examiner must be notified in order to make a determination about whether there will be a required autopsy. Family members have very little authority to stop public officials who want an autopsy because they are concerned with public safety.

> *"I don't want to die in my sleep," you declared. And I said, "Why?" (I'm sure I sounded quite exasperated.) "Well, if I die in my sleep I might miss something."*
>
> SARAH L. DELANEY
> *from* On My Own at 107: Reflections on Life Without Bessie

Family or patient must make the decisions about how the body will be handled. More often now, people are choosing cremation, perhaps because it is much less expensive than traditional burials. Again, planning ahead will help make this transition a smoother one. The dying person and family may have made plans and may even have pre-paid for services.

Otherwise, the family will need to make decisions quickly about caskets, location of burial, services, announcements, and so on. Many have pointed out that this is not a good time in the lives of families to be negotiating costly items. It is all too easy to spend more than is really warranted by family or patient preferences. There are now federal and state regulations which generally require that funeral home directors give customers notice about the costs of services, about which services are actually legally required, and about the full range of casket prices. Finding a funeral home director who is both reasonable and kind is well worth some time, as that person can make the first week or two after death so much easier on the survivors. Some people will have joined a memorial society, a private association that helps members with low-cost funerals and memorials. Also, remember that Social Security, veterans' benefits, and other benefits may be available to help with funeral costs.

So many families are overwhelmed with the number of issues that arise just after death. Their experience leads to a reminder to consider these issues in advance whenever possible. It may seem terribly uncomfortable to be arranging a funeral with the person still alive. However, this is becoming the usual way that families proceed. It certainly helps ensure that reasonably prudent choices are

made and that the family has fewer serious disruptions in the emotionally difficult times just after the death. Here is a short checklist that might help:

WHO NEEDS TO BE NOTIFIED, AND HOW? Will some need travel tickets?
Bear in mind that airlines and some other travel services give discounts to
people who are traveling for such emergencies, but the traveler will usually
need a letter from a doctor or an official death notice. Consider asking the
professional caregivers to help with giving notice to a few family and friends.
Think about setting up plans so that those notified in turn call others.

WHO WILL PROVIDE FUNERAL SERVICES OR THE EQUIVALENT? Will
this be a cremation or a burial? If cremation, families may seek out a service
that provides transportation for the body and delivery of the ashes without
many other services. If the body is cremated, the ashes can be scattered in a
special place, buried in a graveyard, or kept in a special vessel or urn.
Consider also whether the body is going to have to be moved across state
lines. If so, the family will often need to have a funeral director in the city
where death occurred and a funeral director in the city where the burial will
occur. International or long distance transportation of a body is complicated
and requires help of the U.S. Embassy abroad and skilled funeral directors at
each end of the trip.

WHAT KIND OF MEMORIAL SERVICE WILL THERE BE? If it is to be in a
church or synagogue or other public building, speak to someone there to find
out what will need to be arranged.

DID THE PERSON HAVE CLOTHING IN WHICH HE OR SHE WANTED TO
BE BURIED? Making plans like this ahead of time is often quite meaningful.

DO YOU HAVE SOMETHING YOU FEEL IS APPROPRIATE TO WEAR TO A
FUNERAL? People discover that their wardrobe has nothing that seems appropriate. One certainly need not wear black any more in most religious traditions, but it still often seems that one should be somber and conservative.

ARE THERE ANY RINGS, JEWELS, OR SPECIAL MEMENTOS TO BE
PLACED WITH THE BODY? Some people like to leave a wedding ring, others choose to remove it. Some like to slip a letter or note in the casket, or to
place a favorite picture or blanket.

ARE THERE DEPENDENT PERSONS WHO NEED IMMEDIATE ATTEN-
TION? Children and disabled or elderly dependents may be left adrift for
daily care if a caregiving relative dies suddenly. Caregivers and more dis-

tant family need to consider this possibility, especially with the elderly person left at home who may not be known to health care personnel or even to neighbors.

ARE THERE PROPERTY MATTERS NEEDING IMMEDIATE ATTENTION? Sometimes there is real urgency to get rent or taxes paid, house or car made secure, animals fed, and so on.

HOW MANY DEATH CERTIFICATES WILL BE NEEDED? Even for small and uncomplicated estates, people often find they need two dozen. Funeral directors can help, but families should get many more than they think they need, because it is often more costly and troublesome to get them later.

WHO WILL ARRANGE A DEATH NOTICE OR OBITUARY IN THE RIGHT NEWSPAPER(S)? Often, funeral directors will help make these arrangements for or with the family. Consider the need to call places where the person used to live. Get the phone numbers and even a written draft of what needs to be said. Families often find that they need a little time to get dates and sequences of life events just right.

IS THERE A WILL? If not, should one be written before the person dies? A will is almost always helpful in settling the estate, and it is astonishing how much estate even people of modest means will have (a car, a few stocks, a savings account, a debt owed or a debt to pay, and so on). If a will exists, does the person still affirm it? Where is it? How will it be read after the death?

SHOULD CHARITABLE DONATIONS IN LIEU OF FLOWERS BE ENCOURAGED? If donations, to what cause or charity?

WILL THERE BE AN OPEN OR CLOSED CASKET? If closed, will there be a private time for family to have it open? Is there a picture appropriate to have at the service?

WHERE WILL THE BURIAL BE? Who owns the plot? What permissions and notices are needed?

IS ORGAN DONATION APPROPRIATE AND DESIRED? Organ donation (heart, kidney, lung, liver, etc.) can be arranged in advance or at the time of death. Tissue donation (bone, cornea, etc.) can often be arranged even hours after death. Donations are essential to the well-being of others and can fulfill a dying person's wishes.

WHAT WILL BE ENTERED AS THE CAUSE OF DEATH? Usually the doctor decides this, but if many factors contributed to causing death or if the main cause is embarrassing, family members could talk with the doctor and negotiate a resolution.

"Can family keep some information out of the obituary?"

People often do not realize that there are two ways to announce a person's death — a death notice, which is a paid listing in a newspaper, and an obituary, which is a news story. Families purchase death notices, in which they can say whatever they please, as long as it is appropriate in length and taste. Many newspapers will take information for death notices or obituaries only from funeral directors, unless the family comes in person and brings a copy of a death certificate. This safeguard is meant to limit the unfortunate experience of false death notices.

Obituaries are technically news stories, and the family has little control over them. Usually, the newspaper decides for itself whether to carry the obituary, and it often has a formula for what is and is not included. Family will have little control over whether the obituary states the cause of death or the circumstances, or whether unfortunate aspects of the person's life are characterized.

"How long can one wait before burial or cremation?"

In some traditions, burial should be very prompt, within one day. In others, a few days are allowed for family and friends to gather. In modern America, refrigeration (and embalming, when it is chosen) helps to make it reasonable to wait for a few days. In some traditions, a prolonged time of praying with the body present is considered optimal, and these practices are causing some friction with public authorities. The usual funeral and burial occurs well within a week. However, more often now, burial or cremation proceeds within a few days, but a more thoughtfully planned memorial is held a few weeks or months later.

"Can family know what was learned in an autopsy before burial or cremation?"

People also do not realize that it often takes two months after the death to complete an autopsy. A preliminary set of findings is available shortly after the body leaves the morgue, but real understanding usually requires making microscopic examination of various tissues, and that takes more than a month. Often, family members have to remind the doctor or pathologist that they want the autopsy results. Sometimes, the best way to get them is to set a meeting time specifically for this purpose. Even when done with great sensitivity, this will be a little cold and jarring, so it might be wise to bring along a trusted friend or counselor.

"How does a family follow religious and other important traditions?"

Families need to know their own traditions and to express their needs, or to use facilities that are familiar with those traditions. Again, planning ahead will be

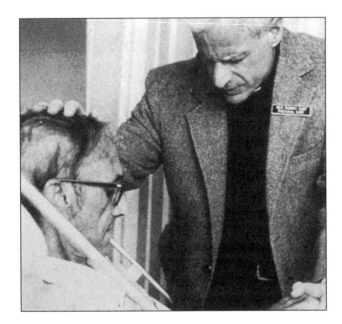

of great comfort. There is rarely any health reason that prevents family from being in contact with a dead body, so those who are moved to participate in bathing the body or in preparing for burial are more limited by popular squeamishness than by real risks. Those who do help with bathing or dressing the body often find it to have been an important labor of love and a significant milestone in coming to terms with the death. If this is important to a particular family member or friend, be sure that the funeral home director knows the plans and agrees to make it possible. Sometimes, the best time to do these things is in the place where the person died, and that may require agreement from other administrators as well.

Many people in modern times are only vaguely familiar with the rituals of their own traditions. When someone in the family is dying, this is a very good time to re-examine the family's traditions and to explore possibilities with suitable religious leaders. There is much latitude now in how memorials and funerals are handled, so families can be adherent to a particular tradition or can modify it as appropriate.

Music and art are often an important part of memorializing the dead. Families might well want favorite music played, and religious or family pictures displayed.

> *The Bustle in a House*
> *The Morning after Death*
> *Is solemnest of industries*
> *Enacted upon Earth,–*
>
> *The Sweeping up the Heart,*
> *And putting Love away*
> *We shall not want to use again*
> *Until Eternity.*
>
> Emily Dickinson

"What does one do at a 'viewing' or at 'visiting hours'?"

A "viewing" is a time when the body is present and friends and family can come and say last farewells. "Visiting hours" are usually a set time period when friends and family can gather to commiserate and share recollections of the dead person's life. The body may or may not be present at visiting hours, and this time might be at home rather than in a funeral home or religious building. Once, bodies were kept at home and the life of the family continued apace until the body was buried. Now, it is much more common for the body to be in a funeral home. Even with cremations, the visiting hours are often at a funeral home. Families can arrange these things in other ways, but they usually are willing to listen to whatever the funeral home director recommends.

Those who come to see family and say their farewells will usually be expected to sign a guest book, to approach the body if it is present, and to speak, as appropriate, to the closest friends and family. Some traditions are more rigid or more openly emotional, but one can usually see those variations fairly quickly. Usually visitors can count on being forgiven for a certain awkwardness, and being gratefully received in the community of the bereaved. It is hard to offend anyone if you are trying charitably to share in grief.

After funerals, families often invite others to join them at home or at a religious building or restaurant for a shared meal, to talk, remember the dead, and share a sense of fellowship and community.

"Are there things that must be done right after the burial or cremation?"

The law requires only that someone attend to the settling of the financial estate, but religious and family traditions may well make a number of other demands. In some religious traditions, families stay at home and receive visitors or say prayers for a substantial period. In some traditions, too, certain survivors are expected to wear special clothes or to abstain from certain activities for a pre-

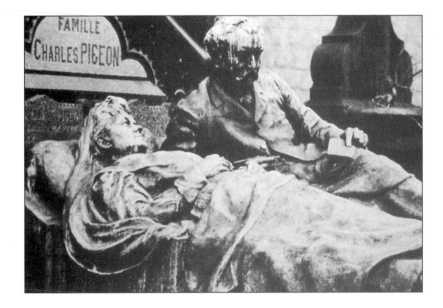

scribed period. Since these mandates are uncommon and vary substantially, family and friends might want to tell others in the death notice or in a handout given at other ceremonies what kind of behavior is expected.

As to the estate, family is well-served when the deceased person leaves behind a will which at least names someone to have the authority to manage these affairs. If there is no will, generally close family will have to go to their county courthouse and get instruction in how to have someone named as "executor." That person will have to report to the court what the person owned and how it was handled. If wealth is passing to a spouse, tax laws are fairly lenient. If wealth is passing to others, however, taxes are often substantial. If the estate is worth much, the family should have a lawyer's advice (in advance of death is much better, of course). Working through the issues in this chapter ahead of death is often quite calming and reassuring, and it is virtually always helpful to the family.

Chapter 14

The dying of children

I'm afraid my baby is going to die. I'm afraid my baby is going to live.

PEGGY STINSON

from The Long Dying of Baby Andrew

Children aren't supposed to die — they are meant to outlive their parents. They are so innocent, and the world can be so cruel. Many parents wish they could take their child's place. Many wonder what they did wrong. Some question their belief in God. Most would do anything to keep their child alive. In this chapter, we address the opportunities and challenges you face as a parent of a very sick child.

If there is a chance for cure, you and your child will want to pursue it. But your child should live, not just exist as long as possible. Your child's life should be comfortable, and it should be a life that both your child and your family value.

But life at all costs is not usually the only goal. This can make it difficult and complicated to make decisions for and with severely ill children.

In the United States, 85,000 children die each year. Some die of problems that are detected at birth, such as birth defects and prematurity. Others die from injuries such as car accidents. Still others die from cancer and rare disorders that may not be detected at birth but that have a progressive course of deterioration. Each of these situations has its unique problems.

Infants

Families have to share in making decisions for seriously ill children. However, an odd set of historical events and court cases in the 1980s led to a series of federal regulations restricting what families could decide for their infants if the decision might allow an earlier death. Called the "Baby Doe regulations," they have confused the medical and legal professions ever since. The latest version of these regulations states that life-sustaining treatment for an infant may be withheld only when one of these conditions is met:

- The infant is chronically and irreversibly comatose.
- Treatment would merely prolong dying.
- Treatment would not be effective in correcting all of the infant's life-threatening conditions.
- Treatment would be futile in terms of the survival of the infant.
- Treatment would be virtually futile in terms of the infant's survival and the treatment itself would thus be inhumane.

Unfortunately, it's hard to know exactly what these regulations mean. You may want more than one opinion. Often neonatologists (doctors who care for newborn and very young babies) do not treat children after they survive to be discharged from the intensive care unit. Therefore, they are often only vaguely aware of the long-term possibilities, the burdens suffered by handicapped babies, and the impact on the family. Thus it falls to the family of a tragically ill baby to gather all the information needed to make the best decisions for the baby and the family. Sometimes nature just takes away any choices and the baby dies despite treatment. But sometimes babies have an astonishing ability to linger if they are given medical support. Parents care deeply and want to do the best they can for their critically ill baby. Here are some ways to help your baby and your family.

Every blade in the field —

Every leaf in the forest —

Lays down its life

in its season

as beautifully

as it was taken up.

HENRY DAVID THOREAU
from a letter to Ralph Waldo Emerson, 1842

Ask if your baby is in pain. Babies can and do feel pain, and they have a stress response to it. Be sure she gets medication that prevents pain whenever she needs it. Even very tiny or very sick babies probably benefit from being sung to and being touched. Ask your nurse how to hold your baby. You may have to learn how to ignore tubes or wires.

Be careful of getting fragments of information about your baby. It helps to have one doctor or nurse who is expected to give you a good overview of your baby's situation at least once every day. Ask questions and don't hesitate to ask for more explanation when the information offered is too complex. Doctors and others should be able to answer all your questions in a way that makes sense to you.

If your baby will not survive, you still can have a "family-centered death." You should be able to have as many of your family and friends with you as you want. Even small children (especially brothers and sisters of the baby) should be allowed to be present. The children ordinarily should be allowed to touch and hold the baby, kiss the baby, have pictures taken of themselves with the baby, preferably with a clock and a calendar nearby so you have a record of the date and time. Children do much better if they are involved. They are much stronger than most people think and do not need to be "protected" from death. In fact, they may suffer a greater loss if they have not been a part of their brother or sister's life and death. Ask for booklets that help you explain to your other children what is happening. Answer questions honestly and be patient if they ask them over and over, even years later. Be sure to include them in the religious ceremonies that are important to your family.

One 3-year-old was asked if she was sad about her baby sister dying. She said, "Yes, but she ain't goin' nowhere; she's staying right here," as she pointed to her heart. Their 18-month-old sister played in the room, climbing on chairs. In the future, she will be able to look at pictures of the three girls together and know she was there, part of the baby's life, a sister forever.

If many people want to visit your baby, you may need to move to an area outside of the ICU. These needs probably can be accommodated. These are, after all, your family's last days with your baby.

Consider making hand- and footprints of your baby, affixing a lock of hair to a piece of paper with a poem or other decorations, or taking pictures of the family holding your baby. These acts will have special meaning, especially if you never got to take your baby home. Many people find that they have not only lost their baby, but their chance to feel like a "Mama" or "Daddy." This grief from not feeling like a parent can be overwhelming, even if you have other children. Pictures and other mementos are tangible evidence of your baby and your loving actions as a parent.

Sudden causes of childhood death

Yesterday your child was normal, healthy, facing a normal future. Suddenly, he is overwhelmingly ill as a result of a car accident, drowning, blood infection, or other problem. Children can pull through often enough that doctors, and parents, hold out hope for a long time. However, you may be faced with the realization that your child is not likely to recover. Now you have to make some decisions about how the very end will be lived. Use what you know about your child to guide you. What did he like to do? What made him happy? What can your family tolerate?

If the child will not be surviving, most people want to try to have a family-centered death. Your entire family should be able to visit at the same time, though perhaps again that will require moving from ICU.

One child, a 14-year-old Pakistani boy, had drowned and was being kept alive until family could gather. His family and community came to honor him and provide a peaceful death, forming a circle around his bed and chanting. Then they drew closer to him (all 35 people in the room, of all ages), crying. When the breathing tube was removed, they poured holy water in his mouth and continued their chants. When he took his last breath 27 minutes later, the whole room looked out the same window and a peaceful hush fell over the crowd.

Fatal chronic illnesses with intact intellect

There is a lot of living to be done after being diagnosed with a chronic and ultimately fatal illness. First and foremost, your child is a child. He needs to do kid things — play, draw, be with friends, be disciplined, have responsibilities, go to school. Sometimes these activities, though the most important to your child, get lost in the intense effort to treat medical problems. Wherever possible, squeeze these activities in.

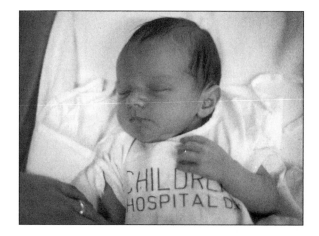

One 16-year-old wanted desperately to graduate from high school. A call to the school by the hospice team resulted in a cap and gown ceremony and graduation party. This same girl wanted to ride on a motorcycle, but needed good pain control to do it. She again was able to accomplish this very personal goal because she was allowed to express it, knew she had a limited lifespan, and had excellent, child-centered caregivers and parents who respected her and her wishes.

Your family has all kinds of needs. Ignoring these needs for the sake of a child who will be ill for a long time can actually harm him. For instance, not taking time to enjoy your marriage can damage the marriage, and the child may lose one of his parents, his pillars of strength. Well siblings need your attention, too. They need to feel loved and valued. Some regularly scheduled, dedicated time with each child fosters goodwill toward the ill child and prevents healthy children from worrying that they no longer matter. Instead of insulating the well children from the ill child, let them help care for their sick sibling. This experience fosters a sense of confidence and value that lasts into adulthood.

Communication

Everyone should try to talk about their feelings and fears about the illness. Open discussion also allows the sharing of anxieties and the accomplishment of important goals.

Penny, a 16-year-old girl with an unresponsive form of leukemia, was doing poorly on her therapy. Her friend, Lindy, a 19-year-old, was

*dying next door of ovarian cancer. Lindy was in a hospice program —
her symptoms of severe vomiting and pain had been brought under
control. She was making a video for her friends and family and asked
Penny to come in for a hug goodbye. Lindy died an hour later, having
left a loving legacy. Penny, though, was never allowed to express her
views. Her family could not bear to contemplate her death. She died a
few weeks later in the ICU after 6 hours of aggressive attempts to
revive her.*

Talking about death does not make it happen, though many people are afraid it
may. Talking about death allows the child to complete important emotional tasks.

Children are sensitive to the needs of their parents, too. They often feel guilty
about financial pressures, marital problems, or causing fear and pain in their families. They may feel that they are bad for having become ill, or that the illness is
a deserved punishment for bad things they have done. You should talk about
your child's fears — and soothe her. Children can be very resilient, and even the
child who is ill often has a lot of strength to share.

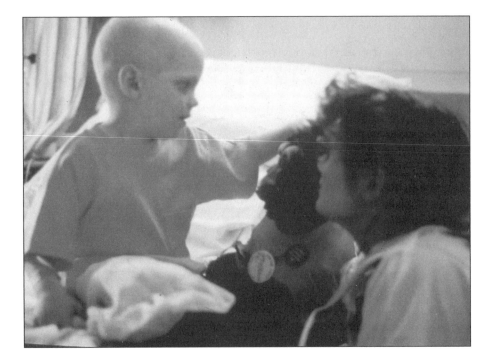

What if your child says, "Daddy, am I going to die?" You first reaction may
be to answer, "Of course not!" But this answer may shake his faith in you. Your
child can be very frightened if he feels you are hiding the truth. "Why do you

ask?" is an answer that lets your child talk about his fears and perceptions. The child may have a new symptom, may have heard of a hospital friend dying, or may just be testing your willingness to talk. Children as young as three years old are often aware that they are dying without having been told. They can often predict their deaths more accurately than their doctors and families can.

Young children have spiritual lives and have important questions to ask. "Why is God doing this? Where am I going? Will I be happy and comfortable after I die?" These questions are best addressed by you, the parents. Answers consistent with your family's beliefs are the most reassuring to your child. Not knowing the answers is okay. Letting your child see your pain is okay. You can comfort each other in your uncertainties and in your love for each other. Chaplains can often be of help, though it is important for the parents to talk with them first.

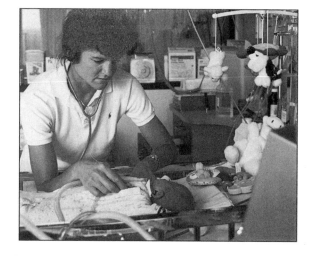

With a few exceptions, the law does not recognize people under the age of 18 as being able to make their own decisions. While they may be immature compared to their peers in many ways, even very young, chronically ill children become especially mature regarding their own health. Parents often see this and feel it. Doctors may not understand the need to consult the child regarding his or her opinion on further treatment. Yet, ask a child-life specialist or a pediatric social worker, and you'll find that the best course includes asking the child. Your child knows what hurts and what she feels is worth continuing to fight for. Deciding medical care for her without her input, even when she is very young, ignores the fact that sometimes continued attempts to cure becomes doing *To* instead of doing *For*. Your child can help you have a better appreciation of her interpretation of what is happening and her suffering. Do not expect your child to make his own decisions about medical treatment either. He may not understand the long-term positive effects of the treatment. Decisions are best made with mutual respect and collaboration between child, parent, and medical team.

When one 9-year-old boy correctly perceived he was dying, his needs were such that he could have gone home. His doctors, however, thought there might still be a slim chance. The child underwent all kinds of tests and treatments. His mother kept asking whether it wasn't time to let him be, but her questions somehow never got answered. The boy was never asked what was important to him. Did he want to go home to his bed or see his classmates one last time? Did he have a special movie he wanted to see? Was there a special friend or relative? He died five days later, in intensive care, monitors still beeping.

Many families want to know what their child's chances of survival are. When they ask their doctors, the answer may be, "Most children with cancer live. But I don't know for your child. It's either life or death — 100% either way." Your response to this should be, "I understand what you are saying, but it is not enough information to allow my child and our family to make the best possible decisions. Can you give me a better idea?"

A person's a person

no matter how small.

Dr. Seuss

For children with cystic fibrosis or other very chronic illnesses, the answer may be, "You never know, you have pulled out so many times before." Yet, when your child is in the hospital more frequently and for longer periods of time, with repeated episodes on the ventilator or in intensive care, chances are getting slimmer. Begin to ask your child, when he feels well, what he wants to do next time he becomes ill. Check in intermittently to see if the goals change as the child becomes more debilitated. Though it is difficult to hear, and difficult not to put your own needs first, you may hear great wisdom if you listen to your chronically ill child.

When treatments are experimental, they are just that. In other words, we don't know at all that they will help. You have to be careful to judge experiments as carefully as you judge your other choices.

At some point, a chronically ill, dying child and the family often benefit from hospice. Be sure to ask about hospice and investigate it long before you need it. If it is a welcoming, life-affirming, knowledgeable program, you may want to use it long before it is clear that death is at hand. Prepare for death even as you hope for life.

Rare disorders

The problem in many childhood terminal conditions is uncertainty. Some children have rare and even undiagnosable problems. There actually may be no statistics the doctor can cite for you. But the doctor, child (when feasible), and parents together, even in these cases, can review the child's course and see when the hospitalizations are becoming more frequent and longer, and when the enjoyment of life for the child seems to be fading. At these times, the goals of care must be revisited. Perhaps going to the hospital is no longer the best choice. Perhaps some medications could be stopped. Perhaps blood tests hurt too much to continue them.

One 3-year-old had a syndrome so rare that only a dozen people were known to have had it. He had been hospitalized only a few days each month. The boy then became more ill, never leaving the hospital for weeks. His mother stayed with him and his older siblings went to live with their grandparents. The family was torn apart by no longer spending any time together. The boy was receiving tests or medications every 30 minutes all night and day, and the mother was a sleepless wreck. Several teams of doctors were working on the child, none checking the schedule of medications and tests of the others. A palliative care nurse noted this and created a more humane schedule, reducing the number of tests and medications and grouping the others together. The child was moved to a room where the whole family could stay day and night. For the first time in 6 weeks, the ill child, his brother, sister, and both parents were together. At the end of 8 weeks, it was becoming obvious that he was not going to live, despite all the aggressive treatments. His family gathered advice from doctors and grandparents and others, and decided to stop. Family and friends gathered for the little one's final day.

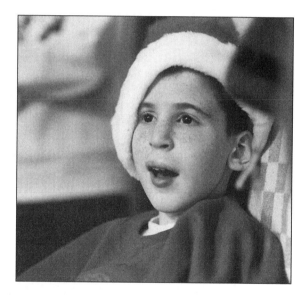

Disorders with impaired consciousness

Caring for children with neurodegenerative disorders is challenging, to say the least. Perhaps nothing is more painful than watching a previously "normal" child deteriorate before your eyes as you stand helplessly by. In these syndromes, a child who had rolled over and perhaps was sitting loses the skills he had learned. Older children, previously able to attend school, become unable to participate and then become progressively more dependent. Some children have their brain function robbed suddenly, in an accident, a fire, or by drowning. These conditions share two problems: an increased likelihood to have and die from pneumonia, and the possibility of the child being so severely impaired that he is unable to feel even hunger, thirst, warmth, or love.

Care is exhausting — financially, emotionally, and physically. Respite care may be available in your area. The social worker probably is the best source of information, but do not be afraid to pull out the phone book or check the World Wide Web. Medicaid may have financial help. Asking friends and relatives to come stay for an afternoon or to allow you to get a full night's sleep is a good idea.

At some point, you will probably question whether recurrent hospitalization is helping or harming your child. It is important to find doctors, nurses, and social workers who can help you decide when you have done as much as you can and can help you through the dying. Allowing a child with severely impaired brain function to die naturally of pneumonia can be a loving gesture. It is the most likely cause of death, whether or not treatment is attempted. Symptoms can be controlled, using morphine if needed for breathing discomfort, with the addition of acetaminophen (Tylenol™) for fever and pain. Morphine does not hasten death, but it does help to ensure comfort.

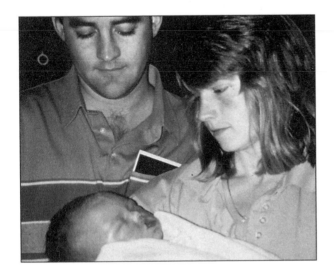

Finally, when a dying child has become so ill as to not feel hunger, there is no need to continue with tube or intravenous feedings. Stopping the feedings can enhance comfort by decreasing the amount of secretions your child is struggling with, decreasing the skin breakdown and hygiene needs, and preventing vomiting (see Chapter 11).

Conclusion

No words can describe what it is like to know that your child is not going to live to be an adult. Your pain can be lessened by concentrating on living fully; being respectful of all involved, including the child, yourself, and the other children in your family; communicating with your child and family openly; re-evaluating goals of medical care at intervals; ensuring excellent symptom control; getting respite when needed; and insisting on informed decision-making. At the time of death and just afterwards, do the important things that make lasting memories of your child and of your family. Most of all, parents need support and help. Losing a child is extraordinarily difficult, and most parents appreciate some help in the journey. You can comfort your child during her lifetime, and heal with your family in the future.

Chapter 15

Dying suddenly

Things can be going along, and then all of a sudden everything is changed.

MADELEINE L'ENGLE

from A Severed Wasp

Death that comes suddenly and unexpectedly is what many people believe they would want, but it turns out to be particularly difficult — certainly for families. Neither the dying person nor the family will ordinarily have been prepared, assuming that there would be time to deal with dying someday — "when it is time." Those left behind may regret not having had the chance to say goodbye. Few people will have had any prior opportunity to say farewells or ask forgiveness, or just to tenderly affirm a bond. Survivors may have many concerns: Did the person suffer? Did he or she have any last words? Could he or she have been spiritually prepared? Survivors may have many unanswered questions about those last minutes or hours. Survivors may have many regrets and questions and no obvious way to answer them.

What can you do to survive sudden death? First, be assured that time does help. Just endure for awhile — the overwhelming sense of unreality, or numbness, or anger will lessen. So will the wild swings of emotion, if that is what you are feeling. You will gradually begin to make good choices, to move forward in your own life. With sudden death, we are especially likely to keep questioning the events that led to death and to feel little sense of a completed life. Some people have found it helpful to act out what would have been said or done, if only you could have been there, or if only you had had a few minutes to talk. Some survivors dream of the person or see him everywhere for awhile. You might take that occurrence as an opportunity to write down what you would say, even to put it in an envelope and tuck it away.

> *"The forces of hate and violence must not be allowed to gain their victory — not just in our society, but in our hearts. Nor must we respond to hate with more hate. This is a time of coming together."*
>
> Rev. Dr. Billy Graham
> *Prayer Service, Oklahoma City*

Sudden death often leaves practical matters in real disarray. There will be children to take care of, or financial matters unsettled, or property to handle. With any luck, there will also be some trustworthy family or friends to help. Share your emotions and check your decisions with someone who is not directly affected by what has happened, if you can. They can tell you if you are making good sense. If you are really on your own, then reach out to some professionals — chaplains, social workers, teachers, professional counselors. Everyone deserves someone to lean on when one is suddenly bereaved. You should also consider continuing with some professional support for awhile. Many people find they need to push themselves into counseling or support groups at first, but later they say that this support turned out to be a lifeline and a great comfort.

Sudden death is not a common way to die now, but it is common enough that it affects almost every family. Sudden death happens in a variety of situations, some of which we discuss.

Violence

When a loved one dies from violence, the survivors commonly experience a nearly overwhelming mix of shock, grief, fear, rage, frustration, and helplessness.

Not only have you lost the person you love, but you have also lost some of your sense that the world can be safe. You may be fearful that the same thing could happen to you, or to someone else you love. You may feel vulnerable and violated. You may experience frustrated rage at the person who did such a terrible thing, or against God, for allowing such persons to exist. You may be angry at the authorities for having so little control. You may take on some of the guilt yourself, thinking that if you had only been there, come sooner, said something differently, this terrible death would not have happened.

Often the survivors of a person who died violently will have to deal with investigators and the press. This can sometimes add an invasion of privacy to your other burdens, but sometimes talking with the press and investigators actually feels helpful — at least someone cares!

If an arrest is made, you hope that justice will be done. But the frustration can be great if the person responsible is unknown or not caught. A long period of time may pass before the person is brought to trial, and there may or may not be a conviction.

People often have savage, vengeful fantasies about the person who murdered or otherwise caused the death of a loved one. This is an understandable part of the grieving process, but the affected person really must reach out to others to avoid acting on this impulse, or acting on an impulse to "take it out on yourself."

Accidents

An accidental death also leaves the survivor feeling shock, grief, and a sense of supreme unfairness. The world may seem much more unpredictable and unsafe. At times, having a clearly identifiable reason for the accident means that some person or agency must bear the blame and guilt of having been careless or thoughtless. You might pursue legal action to ensure that this kind

of accident never happens again, or that the person responsible is punished. This can be a comfort that others will not be hurt, or a source of bitterness that a loved one's death is what it took to make a change.

Of course, sometimes the person most to blame is also the person who most loved the one now dead. If you survive in such a situation, you will need to hear many times that others do not hold you responsible, and that you can forgive yourself. You will need to feel the special love of a family or community to begin to make sense of such an event. Do take every opportunity to reach out to others, and make yourself go for professional counseling in the months following the event.

Natural disasters

Any sudden death makes one feel uncertainty and fear. The world abruptly feels quite unsafe. A natural disaster forces you to feel how small and unprotected we are against the forces of nature. It is no wonder that you may think God picked your own little corner of the world to attack. Added to the loss of a loved one, survivors may have to endure the loss of cherished belongings— even the loss of a whole way of life. You might have to postpone grieving for the dead because of the immediate needs of finding shelter, locating other family members, or dealing with insurance companies.

Survivors of a natural disaster often find comfort in the fellowship of other survivors and in the companionship of community rebuilding. This sense of reconstruction can be the forerunner of healing and the repair of families shattered by the loss of loved ones.

Suicide

Death from suicide often hurts terribly because the person who has died has so completely rejected his or her family and friends. If the suicide comes after serious physical or mental illness, though, you may feel both grief and a sense of relief that a long period of suffering has ended. You may feel really angry toward the person who has died, particularly if she either gave no warning at all or had actually engaged a lot of your time and energy trying to help. Guilt is common; you wonder if there was something more someone could have done.

If the suicide is unexpected, you may wonder if you and others missed a signal or a silent plea for help. You may spend a great deal of time trying to understand what life must have been like, no longer wanting to live. Why didn't he love me enough to stay? Why wasn't my love enough for her to want to stay?

You may feel ashamed, feeling that this reflects shortcomings in you and your family. Some people will hide the actual cause of death from others who may not understand or might judge harshly.

Families that have been affected by suicide should usually avail themselves of help from a mental health professional in the ensuing year. Family members benefit from a nonjudgmental but insightful outsider who can help sort out the conflicts and watch for signs that the survivors might be developing serious problems in coping.

Multiple deaths

When you have to endure the pain of the loss of more than one family member or friend, such as might happen in an accident or a natural disaster, grieving becomes more confusing and complicated. Many people find it so painful that life seems especially hollow. Sometimes a survivor wishes he or she could just die also. It may seem as if the dead persons are in a better place, and that it is the survivors who feel left behind. Sometimes you don't know which person to grieve for first, or most, or you feel guilty over missing one person more than another. The losses are so much that you cannot believe that something this terrible could happen and leave you still living. You will often have lost the family system that was there, and you will often feel disoriented without that familiar structure.

Again, you need an understanding of what happened, friends and family to lean on to hear your grief and to give practical help, and a professional counselor. In these circumstances, you must be gentle with yourself and expect that merely enduring is enough for awhile.

During chronic illness or recuperation

When you believe someone you love still has time to live, despite a severe illness, their sudden death will feel startling. When your loved one was stable just a few days ago, you can feel cheated and angry that you were robbed of the time you thought you would have together. Having already endured the anxiety of the illness and begun to face the eventuality of death, it often seems unfair not to get more warning. It may sound odd, but families of most people who die after years of serious heart failure, and about a quarter of people who die of cancer, say that the person died "suddenly." This is not something that even doctors recognize, so usually no one told you that your loved one might well die suddenly. Nevertheless, the death is not a complete surprise, and your mind will usually have made some adjustments to the eventuality.

You can take some comfort in knowing that the person is spared the worst that the disease can yield. At times, you may be frankly relieved that death came suddenly, particularly when your loved one has been ill for some time and faced a long period of suffering. But this relief can cause guilt, too. Survivors are often afraid that the feeling of relief will seem like happiness that death occurred. It is valuable to realize that our feelings of relief are motivated by love and concern for someone we love. Relief that suffering was avoided does not make the grief less real or wrenching.

Sudden Infant Death Syndrome

The death of a child is a heartrending loss. People might expect their parents or grandparents to die, but no one expects children to die before their parents. When an infant appears healthy, as in the case of SIDS (Sudden Infant Death Syndrome), parents are especially stricken. You fear you did something wrong, or didn't do something that should have been done.

ABOUT SIDS

An enormous amount of research has been done looking into the possible causes of SIDS. To date, only a little is known for sure:

- *SIDS cannot be predicted or prevented.*
- *SIDS is not hereditary.*
- *SIDS has existed through the ages and in all countries.*
- *SIDS is not caused by suffocation.*
- *SIDS infants do not suffer.*
- *SIDS is the most common cause of death among infants aged one week to one year.*
- *SIDS has been associated with low birth weight.*
- *SIDS is more prevalent among some groups, including Native Americans and African-Americans.*
- *SIDS is more prevalent among the poor and less educated.*
- *SIDS is slightly more common in the winter months.*
- *SIDS is sometimes, but not always, preceded by a slight "cold."*

Sometimes the appearance of the baby who has died from SIDS can be confusing. Although some infants look as though they are just sleeping, if some time has passed before it is realized that the baby is dead, blood can pool in the baby's face. To inexperienced eyes, this can look like bruising. It is not surprising, although it is very hurtful, that emergency workers, the police, or even family may think that someone deliberately hurt the baby. Such confusion can lead to terrible misunderstandings or accusations. Sometimes parents believe a sibling, or one's spouse, may have struck the baby.

Even after SIDS is diagnosed, it is natural for parents or other caregivers to wonder if something was done wrong which could have prevented the death. Parents report being plagued with the thought that they should have tried to wake the baby from his nap sooner, or that they should not have slept in on that morning, or that she should have been put down on her tummy, or on her back. We so desperately need to find a reason, a way to comprehend the incomprehensible.

No amount of foresight or care can prevent SIDS. Although SIDS happens most often at night, babies have been known to die in car seats and even while being held. You could not have prevented what happened. Nothing that you or anyone else did, or didn't do, caused your baby's death. Networks of parents who have experienced this loss do seem to help one another a great deal. If you have to endure this loss, be especially gentle with yourself and your spouse. Because this death is unexplainable, it will often cause real strains between a couple. Professional help is probably worth pursuing.

Some special issues — police, autopsy, and organ donation

In addition to the unexpected loss, sudden death often brings with it the need to deal with investigating authorities. Emergency workers, such as the fire department and the police, may have to ask questions. While these people are only doing their jobs, it can be difficult for the family of a loved one who has died to understand, and hard to cooperate. Sometimes the authorities will keep you away from the body of your loved one, either because an investigation is ongoing, or because of the condition of the body. You will eventually get to be left alone and will be able to see the body, but no one may think to tell you so. Many police and emergency services are beginning to consider how to serve survivors better. You might ask if there is a chaplain or someone like that who could accompany you, or you might insist on having a friend or family member along.

Sometimes there is confusion about what exactly did happen. There can be misunderstandings and miscommunications. At times like these, it is worthwhile to keep in mind that some questions may not be able to be answered accurately right away. It is hard to be patient, but it is better to have to wait for a correct answer than get a hurried answer which turns out to be false.

In all cases of sudden death, the medical examiner will be notified and will decide whether an autopsy is required. An autopsy is a special examination of the body that often can determine a great deal about exactly what happened. The body is left looking normal and appropriate for family members to see. Nevertheless, people feel queasy about autopsy. At least in sudden deaths (except per-

haps when there is serious chronic illness as the cause), the decision about autopsy is mostly out of your hands. If you have a strong religious objection, you should voice it, but the medical examiner is generally authorized to ignore your claim if there is any suspicion of foul play.

Sometimes members of the media want to ask questions. It is important to remember that you have a right to refuse to talk to reporters and to request to be left alone. If necessary, enlist the help of the authorities or friends or family members to ensure your privacy.

Among the people waiting to talk to the bereaved family may be medical personnel who want a decision about organ donation. In the case of sudden death, particularly if the death itself takes place in the hospital setting, any undamaged organs of the patient are ideally suited for helping someone else. It can be very difficult in the midst of shock and loss to hear about someone else's needs. If your family member wrote out his or her wishes on a driver's license or an organ donor card, then you can be fairly comfortable in following those choices. If not, you need to know that any decision you make will be supported by the care team.

Sudden death

Many Americans believe that a sudden death is what they would want — preferably a sudden death in advanced old age. However, it is clear that a truly unexpected death is very hard on families and often deprives the dead person of the opportunity to complete a life. Nevertheless, about one-tenth of all dying is truly unexpected, and our community must learn to help support those who are personally touched by sudden tragedy.

Chapter 16

Enduring loss

There is a sort of invisible blanket between the world and me. I find it hard to take in what anyone says. . . . Yet I want the others to be about me. I dread the moments when the house is empty. If only they would take to one another and not to me.

C.S. LEWIS
from A Grief Observed

Grief is one of the most universal human emotions — and one of the most isolating. All the world may love a lover, but few of us know how to honor grief — how to be with a grieving person, or how to handle our own grief. Sometimes grief is overwhelming: how can life possibly go on! Sometimes, though, grief is much less severe. Perhaps life has been so hard that survivors really feel death is a release. Perhaps faith in an afterlife helps. Perhaps the survivor has learned from a prior experience. Grieving is the mark of having been close to another person. The only way to avoid grieving is to avoid having loved.

Each person grieves in her own way, according to her own needs. There is no formula for grief, and no way around it. Like other emotions, grief is simply there, like love, joy, anger, or fear. As with other emotions, we cannot wish grief away, nor can we avoid it. Some of us may try to *ignore* grief, or pretend it does not exist, but eventually we will feel it.

Grief, like death, is hard to discuss. Unlike other emotions that we have grown comfortable expressing or describing, we have no ready words for grief or bereavement. When we're happy, we can say we are on top of the world, flying high, on cloud nine. We can use clichés for anger, too, and say someone has had it up to here, sees red, or blows his top. Grief has no such expression.

But grief has a range of accompanying feelings: anger, loneliness, depression, guilt, relief, sorrow, fear, anxiety. In the midst of grief, we may swing from one emotion to the next, unprepared for the strength of our feelings and uncertain what to make of them.

Grief is a country we all must visit, and it helps to know what it's like there, how others have survived the journey, the maps they followed, the setbacks, and what they learned along the way. This chapter describes the grief that comes with dying. We talk about the changing nature of grief, and how grief can occur many times in the course of an illness, both before and after the death of someone you love. We offer suggestions on how to live through grief, ways to grieve with and for the dying person, and how to cope during difficult times, such as holidays, birthdays, and other anniversary dates. We describe problems that can occur when grief is overwhelming, and where to turn when you need help.

Grieving your own dying

A life-ending illness can give you time to say good-bye to people you love and care about. You have time to make plans for how you want to be cared for at the end of your life, and, perhaps, how you want to be remembered. You may, if you feel well enough, find time to do things you have always wanted to do, or you may wish to resolve old hurts and grievances.

If having a chance to say goodbye is a blessing, it can also be a curse. People who are sick and dying are often afraid and worried. Throughout the course of a life-ending illness, you must pass many milestones, and with each, experience some degree of loss. With loss, in general, comes grief and sadness.

Being very sick and coming to the end of your life, you face a series of changes. Each loss can give rise to grief — the loss of independence, or dreams or abilities now gone.

There are some ways to cope with grief, and to help those you love as they, too, grieve for and with you.

Telling your story

We are all storytellers. For most of our lives, we do just that — tell stories about our day, or something that happened last year, or when we got married or had our first child. Dying is the end of this life's story.

People often find hope and comfort, and a sense of closure, by telling stories about their lives to others. You might ask a close family member, a trusted friend, a health care provider, or a counselor to listen to your story.

Tom was in his mid-thirties when his mother began to die of lung cancer. She began going through old belongings, including linens, old quilts,

---

STARTING POINTS

You might feel uncomfortable trying to tell the story of your life or encouraging a family member to hear it. Perhaps you grew up thinking it was important not to talk too much about yourself. Here are some questions to get you started:

1. *Where were you born? Where did you grow up? What was school like when you were a child?*

2. *What did you like doing? What do you remember about your parents? If your parents were not born in this country, where did they come from? When did they arrive?*

3. *What are some of your earliest memories? Your happiest? Your saddest?*

4. *If you were in the military, where did you serve? What do you remember most?*

5. *If you worked, where was that? What did you do? Did you enjoy it? Do you wish you had done something else?*

6. *If you stayed home and raised children, what was that like? Do you have special memories?*

7. *When did you get married? Where? Did you take a wedding trip or honeymoon?*

8. *Did you travel? Where did you go?*

9. *Who were your best friends? What did you do together?*

10. *What are some of your favorite activities? Can you still do them? If you have a special skill, can you teach it to someone else?*

---

heirloom tablecloths. She wanted to give them to Tom and his wife. Tom was very upset when his mother told him this — he felt she was giving up too soon. It turned out, though, that the linens had stories that went with them. In the end, Tom was glad to have shared this time with his mother, listening to family stories, and hearing things she might not otherwise have mentioned.

... He wants to tell how his son was taken ill, how he suffered, what he said before he died, how he died. ... He wants to describe the funeral, and how he went to the country. ... And he wants to talk about her too. ... Yes, he has plenty to talk about now. His listener ought to sigh and exclaim and lament. ...

ANTON CHEKHOV

from Misery

If you do not want to talk, or don't have someone to talk to, try writing things down. Just jotting down a few sentences each day can help you through this difficult time and might leave a powerful legacy as well. You might try borrowing or buying a cassette recorder. If you feel comfortable in front of the camera, you could even ask someone to videotape parts of your story. Even though it might seem difficult, your story can be a gift to future generations, especially to very young children or grandchildren.

Your story can be short or long; you may not remember all of the details. It does not need to be great literature. It does not have to be told well. Forget the rules you learned long ago in high school English. No matter what stories you tell, both you and your listeners are likely to benefit from the telling, and to feel that living is meaningful because a relationship is strengthened.

People are often surprised to discover that other family members are usually quite interested in their life stories. Older people connect us to the past, to a family history that, left untold, will go unknown. Your story is a way for the people who will survive you to remain connected to you. Their memories can help them through the grief they will feel after your death.

Perhaps you can look at old photographs together and, if you feel like it, label them. If, like many people, you begin going through your possessions, you might ask someone else to help you. Along the way, you may have many stories to share.

Many community education programs, including hospice and other health centers, offer music and art therapy for people who are dying. Such therapy, which can range from painting to drawing to writing "life songs," can be very healing.

Participation does not require any expertise, other than a desire to express yourself. At one program for homeless people who are dying, residents often draw or paint; the paintings now decorate the home and are a way for the dying to be remembered, and to comfort, in a way, those who follow them. Other residents work with a music therapist to compose "lullabies" of their lives. Such creative expression can have a profound and peaceful effect on one's life.

The cycle of grief

Several decades ago, Elisabeth Kübler-Ross described the five stages people often experience when coming to terms with a terminal illness: denial, anger, depression, bargaining, and acceptance. Because these stages portrayed a common response so well, people began to think of the stages as the five stages of grief. Unfortunately, grief does not move along in an orderly fashion, according to a specific order or timeline. Some people may not go from one stage to another. Others find they cycle from anger to acceptance to depression again and again.

Grief is characterized by unexpected changes. People move from one point to another on the circle, then back again, depending on where they are in their lives,

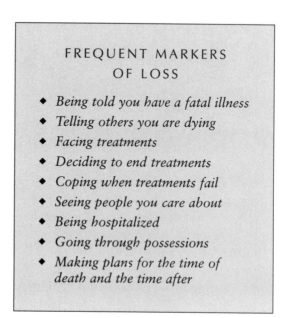

FREQUENT MARKERS
OF LOSS

- *Being told you have a fatal illness*
- *Telling others you are dying*
- *Facing treatments*
- *Deciding to end treatments*
- *Coping when treatments fail*
- *Seeing people you care about*
- *Being hospitalized*
- *Going through possessions*
- *Making plans for the time of death and the time after*

and the events going on around them. New losses may trigger old grief. Unexpected moments may give rise to sadness. One man described bursting into tears on a busy street when a passerby tipped his hat, reminding him of his own late father.

He searched for his accustomed fear of death and could not find it.

LEO TOLSTOY
from The Death of Ivan Ilyich

When you are living with dying, you know how grief feels: lonely, cut-off, isolated, sad, abandoned, angry, or lost. Grief can feel overwhelming, especially in the immediate aftermath of a death. It can begin to feel like a constant part of your life.

Counselors have noticed that people often follow a pattern of grieving:

- ◆ The loss and acceptance of it being real
- ◆ Adjustment to loss
- ◆ Reinvestment in life

At some point, a survivor will find himself or herself gradually reinvesting in life. That investment might be taking care of the survivor's interests, praying or finding meaning each day, or getting up and going to work. Somehow, people do find a way to survive, and eventually to thrive again.

All his life, Gordon wrote poetry, which he shared with friends and family at special events. A distant cousin asked him to tape-record some of his poems, which he did. Now, a decade after Gordon's death, those poems remain, not only as a legacy of his life, but also as a way to capture his voice, his emotions. Gordon wrote this poem about his own approaching death. It was used on a prayer card distributed at his funeral.

As I walk this last trail

And come to the last high pass

I step to the other side

Into the sunshine glow

Waiting there to greet me

Are all the ones I know

Love
Gordie

JULY 1991

"In loving memory of John Gordon Hamilton, 'Gordie.'"

Experiencing grief – family and loved ones

In taking care of a dying loved one, you may experience grief at many points throughout the illness. For instance, there is the grief of first learning about the person's illness, the grief as plans you shared are lost, or as you realize you may be spending your final days together. People often think that they have accomplished their grief and that death will be a simple continuation of a familiar emotion.

Unfortunately, death usually brings a grief all its own. People are sometimes surprised to discover that mourning begins again, and grief appears anew. Often, in the immediate wake of death, we become numb just to survive funerals and memorial services or to take care of a person's estate and belongings. Then, as relatives and friends disperse, we are alone, again, with grief.

The things you decide to do — or not do — are usually perfectly good ways to deal with your own grief. Follow your heart and your mind. They are not likely to lead you in the wrong direction.

Experts on grief and bereavement do recommend a few steps to consider taking as you go through this period of your life:

POSTPONE MAJOR LIFE CHANGES. You may make decisions impulsively that will later prove not to be in your best interest. Impulse spending is only a temporary fix, and geographical changes (such as moving) will not leave grief behind. If you have to make a major life change, talk it over with people you trust and encourage them to counsel you about whether you are thinking clearly.

ASK FOR HELP. Other people may want to offer help but not know how. Ask — the process can be a healing one. If you are widowed and have children at home, you may need help with the practical issues of life, such as child care and survivor benefits.

HOW IT FEELS TO GRIEVE:

Grief, like other emotions, can make its presence known both in body and mind. You may:

- *Lose your appetite*
- *Experience aches and pains*
- *Sleep too long or not enough*
- *Feel depressed, melancholy, hopeless*
- *Feel angry at the world, yourself, or your loved one*
- *Feel guilty for things left unsaid or undone*
- *Feel unable to concentrate*

All of these feelings and sensations are grief's way of making its presence known. These reactions are the normal, human response to loss.

CONSOLATION

Here are a few ways to help survivors through this sad time of life.

- SOLITUDE HELPS. *You may need time to think about your loved one, to remember times you shared, to consider how your life will be now. You may be overwhelmed by your sorrow. You may want to stay in bed and cry or sleep, go for a walk, or sit in a chapel.*

- OTHER PEOPLE HELP. *Friends and family members are likely to empathize with you. Even if they do not know what to say, just being with other people and talking can be supportive. Accept others' invitations to participate in activities — but leave if you feel you need to. Reach out to family or friends when the next hour or day seems unbearable.*

- ACCEPTING SUPPORT HELPS. *Others may want to help by doing things for you. They may want to bring you food or talk on the phone or run errands. Accept these acts of kindness whenever you can.*

- REST AND SLEEP HELP. *Caring for a dying person has been exhausting. You may need time alone simply to regain your physical energy, as well as your emotional and spiritual strength.*

- ROUTINES HELP. *Even though your life may feel turned upside down, try to keep up a routine of healthy eating, occasional physical activity (even a 10-minute walk), and regular sleep.*

- TIME HELPS. *Your life may never be the same again. Whatever your experience with death and dying, you will find that you see the world and your place in it differently. Time lessens some of grief's pain, but it does not diminish your loss or sadness.*

- DREAMS HELP. *Many people dream of the dead person and feel that, in this way, they are with the person again.*

- NATURE HELPS. *Take a walk and focus on something promising in what you see.*

- CREATIVITY HELPS. *You might try writing about your feelings, or creating a special area in your home to honor the memory of your loved one.*

TURN TO OTHERS. Tell others that you are grieving. There is no reason to hide your grief or sadness. Let others know how you are doing.

KEEP YOUR EXPECTATIONS WITHIN REASON. Grief is a major stress in anyone's life. Reduce other stresses, and try to keep your expectations of yourself reasonable. Lower your expectations if you need to.

AVOID THE "SHOULDS" AND "OUGHTS." Most mental health experts encourage grieving people to avoid the "shoulds" of life and focus on what unavoidably must be done and what one would like to do. Feeling that a good person "really should" do more is especially tough on the bereaved.

> **YOU MAY TAKE COMFORT IN:**
>
> - *Telling stories about your life*
> - *Participating in different forms of creative expression, such as art and music*
> - *Keeping a journal*
> - *Seeking spiritual or religious guidance and support*
> - *Sharing your spiritual journey with loved ones*

Living with loss of a loved one

Grief has its own timetable. In general, grief affects daily life for as long as a year. People often feel great sorrow from time to time for many years — but the time between surges usually lengthens as time goes on.

There are few, if any, ways to shorten the period of mourning. Instead, people learn to live with their loss and, in doing so, live through their grief.

Often, one way to cope with loss is to talk to others who have experienced similar losses. Many hospitals and hospices offer grief and bereavement support groups that meet periodically for several months. There you can share experiences, thoughts, and memories. Somehow, the process of talking to others, and sometimes just helping others with their grief, can have a healing effect.

Programs are often tailored to meet specific losses — people whose children have died will have concerns that are quite different from those whose spouses or parents have died. Check that the group you join is likely to be comfortable for you.

A recent Gallup poll showed that people are most likely to turn to friends and family for support, although one-third turn to members of the clergy. Specially trained members of the clergy, called pastoral counselors, may be able to help you with the spiritual and emotional issues that accompany grief. If you are active in a faith community, your religious leader should be able to give you the names of pastoral counselors in your community. Pastoral counselors generally offer services according to a sliding-fee scale.

Music and mourning

For as long as there has been music, there has been music to help people through times of sadness. The origins of most Western music can be found in the Gregorian chants of medieval monks. Sometimes these were written for everyday prayers, but frequently they were written for funeral masses. From those beginnings, a tradition of funeral masses, or requiems, continued in classical music to the present.

Jazz music has long been played at New Orleans funerals. Sad songs are played at first, then happy songs celebrate the deceased and share the joy of his entering a better life. Show tunes, rock and roll, folk songs, and gospel hymns all deal with loved ones dying.

The songs and tunes we hear can serve as a unique companion. In offering comfort, music makes no demands on us at all. When singer and guitarist Eric Clapton's son died, tragically and suddenly, he wrote a song to him called "Tears In Heaven." This beautiful song struck a chord with many people. For those who had lost a child, hearing someone else mourn a similar tragedy helped them to feel less alone in their grief.

No matter the reason, music helps us turn a flood of emotions into something more manageable. With or without lyrics, melodies communicate and interact with our souls. That is why so many cultures use music, and why some songs cross many cultures with ease.

The music people use is as diverse as people can be — from electric guitars to trumpets to choirs; from slow and soft, as in Mozart's "Lacrimosa," to bright and crisp, as in "When the Saints Go Marchin' In." Often people choose to listen to something that was special to the person who has died. This is guaranteed to bring up memories that may be uncomfortable but may also be healing. There may also be special music which has helped before, in other times of struggle, and may help again now.

What makes music so important to those who grieve?

Perhaps listening to music gives us a special time just to think about the people we love. Often our minds are racing too fast, or not moving forward at all, in our initial moments of shock. Having music around gives us a rhythm, a structure around which we can reflect, and grieve. Like a metronome, or deep breathing, it gives a rhythm to our fragmented thoughts.

Music also has the powerful ability to draw out memories obscured by time or emotion. It seems to have a near-magical ability to penetrate through the present day to remind us of other occasions. Sometimes songs and melodies so accurately pinpoint an emotion that they transport the listener to another time and place. In times of grief, this magical quality can recall times and emotions long forgotten because of prolonged illness and strain.

Sometimes in our sadness and shock, we merely feel numb. Certainly this is a protective mechanism, a perfectly normal approach to grief, and nothing to be ashamed of. But sometimes music helps evoke welcome thoughts and feelings.

LISTENING

Grief counselors recommend empathy as the key to helping the bereaved. Sympathetic approaches or those that try to identify with the bereaved may miss the mark. Instead, try to understand the other person's experience without forcing meaning on it. If someone wants to share her stories with you, even stories that you have heard a million times, listening will be a great gift. You will bear witness to her life, to things that gave her pleasure, to her sorrows, fears, regrets. There are a few things to remember as you do this, but most especially:

- *Listen*
- *Do not judge the other person*
- *Show compassion — offer a caress, if it's wanted, or a shoulder to cry on*
- *Be supportive and offer comfort, even if this is simply by being silent*

COURTESY OF ALAN D. WOLFELT, PH.D., OF THE CENTER FOR LOSS AND LIFE TRANSITIONS

Do children grieve?

If few of us know how to honor grief with an adult, or to handle our own losses, how much harder it is to help a child through the process. Children do grieve, deeply and over time. Their experience and expression of grief may be different from an adult's, but it will be no less painful or severe. Like adults, children benefit from attention and love. They may need solitude and companionship, someone to talk to, and someone to cry with. Sharing the reality of what is happening allows children to begin to understand, to cope with, and to integrate the experience of loss into their lives.

Children's understanding of death: what to expect and how to help

Within the first year of life, the infant is able to feel separation and a sense of loss. Creating a warm, safe environment, physical support, holding, hugging, rocking, and reassurances of personal safety ("We'll be here to take care of you.") counteract the confusion and restore some security.

The preschool child, two to five years old, thinks death is temporary and reversible, something like a round trip. "Mommy is dead and will be coming home soon." Death (and illness) may be seen as contagious but also avoidable. Children imagine bogeymen, angels, skeletons, and devils that might take away bad people or those who are too old or too sick or too slow to outrun or outsmart death.

My life closed twice before its close;
it yet remains to see
If Immortality unveil
A third event to me,

So huge, so hopeless to conceive,
As these that twice befell.
Parting if all we know of heaven,
And all we need of hell.

EMILY DICKINSON

The school-age child observes death as the end of bodily life, final and universal. Even though older children and adolescents know it can happen to them, they believe it to be the remotest of possibilities and are prone to challenges and risk-taking behaviors. Children who "grow up with the loss" ordinarily re-examine and re-integrate that loss at each developmental level. When the loss is significant, the grown person will often still revisit her loss at significant milestones in life — marriage, graduations, births, and so forth.

Maturity, of course, does not happen according to fixed age categories. Each child has his or her own timetable.

Very young children may not be able to talk about their grief. Instead, they may show it by acting out, reverting to more babyish behavior, clinging, or withdrawing. Because they have no way to make sense of death and dying, loss of someone close can be quite confusing.

What do you do to comfort a child?

Speak in simple language the child can understand. Ask the child what he thinks, knows, and feels, and respond specifically to those concerns. Don't overwhelm the child with excessive detail and be sure to see how the child is putting it all together.

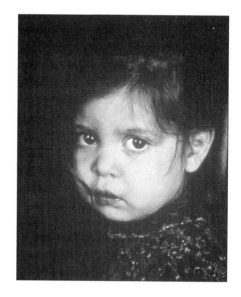

Be honest. Avoid half-truths. Don't tell a child something you will need to correct later on. For example, when the child insists that "Mommy will be back in the spring . . . like the flowers," don't, out of compassion, agree. Instead, you can say something like, "That would be nice, wouldn't it?"

Even the clumsiest statement is better than not discussing the loss at all. Children are quite aware when they are being shut out of a tragic event. They will judge correctly when a topic is taboo in a family setting and close off communication with adults. When this happens, angry outbursts, irritability, and changes in eating and sleeping habits will offer a clue that the child is suffering in his or her own private way. Remember that a child's imagination often creates more frightful images than reality ever could.

Expect expressions of anger — at God, at the lost loved one, at the surviving parent, at the doctors, at anyone in their sight. They can also turn the anger inward on themselves. Because children believe in magic, they sometimes believe that they caused the death because they were "mad" at the parent or other person who died.

Watch children at play. This will offer you valuable clues, particularly with a very young child. One of the many ways children can express their feelings when they cannot express them verbally is by acting them out with dolls or toys. Listen to the stories they make up, in words or in play. You can then encourage memories of the good times and also provide alternative ways of understanding the bad things they remember.

Don't be upset if, after a clear explanation of what happened, children appear to toss it off — seeming cold — and go about their normal activities. It takes time for children to deeply internalize "bad news."

Expect the hard questions to come up eventually, perhaps many months later. Prepare yourself with answers because these questions will express the child's deepest fears. The four central questions are: "Did I cause Papa's (or Grandma's or Grandpa's) death?" "Will I die, too?" "Are you going to die, too?" "If you die, too, who will take care of me?"

Include grieving children in events that precede and follow a death. Help a child to say goodbye in the hospital, to attend the funeral service, and to participate in rituals with the family. They can cope with most situations, provided they are given appropriate choices, are prepared for what to expect, given opportunities to talk it through, and supported emotionally. Simple ceremonies such as lighting a candle next to a photograph; placing a letter, picture, or special memento in a casket; or releasing a helium balloon with a message attached for the person who has died are effective leave-taking gestures.

Allow for the expression of emotions. The child may cry or may not. Adults can let their own tears flow, too. Children will find their own way, but they will look to adults, too, for some examples to follow.

Older children, especially adolescents, may need help to express their grief, especially over the loss of a parent. Adolescence is a difficult enough passage, and grief adds layers of complexity and emotion. Address a teenager's needs early and often, and ask your child's school for help or guidance.

Use books, TV, and movies, too. Many wonderful after-school specials and prime-time programs deal with the death of a parent, grandparent, sibling, or pet: *The Yearling*, *All the Way Home*, and *Death Be Not Proud* are available for rent. Among the many wonderful books written for children is *Badger's Parting Gifts* by Susan Varley. Old Badger dies, leaving a note for his friends: "Gone down the Long Tunnel. Bye Bye, Badger." His friends — the mole, fox, and rabbit — talk about the things each learned from Badger, realizing that he has left them many good memories and abilities. This book can help you talk to a child about an older relative who is dying, or about anyone in the child's life who has died.

Many communities offer special grief programs to provide support for children who are dying or whose parents or siblings have died. Such programs are frequently coordinated through local hospices, religious institutions, and Internet support groups. Some focus on losses through violence, AIDS, or other particular illnesses.

Reinvesting in life after the loss of someone you love

Eventually, those who live on will find ways to become engaged in life again and, like old Badger's friends, will remember good aspects of the time before the illness, or even during the illness. At various points, a survivor will often feel ready to reinvest in life. Someone living without a spouse, for example, might find a new job or hobby. Someone involved in a bereavement or support group might feel ready to share experiences with others. People do discover new loves, interests, and habits.

Survivors often devise their own ways to remember and honor the person who died. Some people create special areas in a home where they arrange items that belonged to their loved one — toys, collections, books, photographs, trinkets — that serve as glad reminders. Perhaps ask members of your worship community to remember the family at special times. Family may visit the graveyard, feeling there a place to talk to the person's spirit. Some plant a tree or garden, install a special stone somewhere, or make donations to a charity. One woman, to honor her late aunt, donated books to a school library, with special bookplates in her aunt's name. Some say prayers on behalf of a loved one, or talk to him or her. There are as many ways to remember those who have died as there are people to remember them.

> *I am especially open to sadness and hilarity since my father died as a child one week ago in this his ninetieth year*
>
> GRACE PALEY
> *from "On Mother's Day"*

It can be very hard to cope with loss during holidays that encourage family togetherness, or on anniversary dates, such as the person's birthday or the anniversary of the death. Again, people often develop rituals or prayers to honor the dead on special days.

As a survivor reinvests in life, he or she may feel pangs of guilt that somehow, by finding pleasure in life, the loved one who died is being forgotten. Try to honor your memories by letting joy enter your life. One mother, writing about the loss of her teenage daughter, states it most eloquently: "The memory does not go away when you start to heal, and living a full life does not deny the emptiness left by loss."

THE SWEATER

Donna Peratino's 80-year-old father was dying of pancreatic cancer. Thin after radiation and chemotherapy, he became very cold and began to wear a sweater. This is Donna's story:

I asked my father about the sweater one day, noting that it belonged to his brother, George, who had died of cancer just over a year before. My father had gotten the sweater from his sister-in-law, who had asked if there was anything he had wanted to remind him of George. Although my father did not need a physical object, he accepted the sweater as a gesture of courtesy to my aunt. George had worn the sweater throughout his own illness and dying.

I asked my father how he felt while wearing the sweater. He said that it made him feel that he was "next in line." I nodded and, after a few moments of quiet, asked if there was a different path for him to choose. I then asked him if, given a choice, which color sweater he would like and what characteristics it would need to have to comfort him and keep him warm.

That afternoon, I returned with a deep blue, cable-knit cardigan that lit up my father's eyes and evoked a sigh when the shopping bag was opened. He tried it on and the new, smaller sweater fit perfectly. His delight and appreciation for this seemingly small act of kindness radiated and touched my soul.

After a few moments, we agreed there was one step left. We had agreed that the new sweater would replace the old one. After my father had reached up to the closet shelf and brought down the carefully folded green sweater, I held it with him as he passed it to me. We paused and I asked him to think of all that his brother had been to him and all they had shared. While my father appreciated the sweater and how it had served George, he was going to let it go. My father and I locked eyes for an all-too-quick instant, and then he raised his open palm, kissed his fingers to his lips, and brought the kiss to the sweater.

This shared moment has brought me great comfort in knowing there were many small, important ways that I contributed to my father's long-term battle, in which he outlived his doctor's prognosis by one year. Throughout this time, he wore the blue sweater as a symbol of his commitment to continue as long as he could, and to move on when it was his time.

After my father's death, my mother hurriedly disposed of his clothes as a way of coping with the reminders of all she had lost. Slacks, shirts, ties, and tuxedo were all gathered and donated to charity — except one piece that found its way to the third drawer of my dresser.

Chapter 17

Additional resources

Don't assume that it's too late to get involved.

MORRIE SCHWARTZ
from Tuesdays with Morrie

⧉⧉ This book contains a wide array of information to help you as you face

serious illness. Although it answers many of your questions and helps you work

through some difficult times, you may well need more questions answered, or

perhaps a person to talk to. Many national and local organizations distribute very

useful information in multiple ways: a simple brochure, a phone conversation, or

a Web page. The amount of information can be overwhelming; but with a little

guidance, this sea of information can readily be navigated.

This chapter has been broken up as shown in the Table of Contents on page

197. You will find books and references throughout the chapter. Keep in mind

that the descriptions here are sometimes general. The organization may offer services or information that are not mentioned. Don't hold back from exploring a little. If you find a good resource we didn't mention, or if you are disappointed with one of these, please let us know (see our address at the beginning of section IV).

When contacting an organization, be clear about the needs you have. It is appropriate and reasonable that you ask questions and request written materials or references where applicable. Look through this chapter and highlight a few resources you think will be helpful. Organizations are listed because of their aim to educate and support people during this often difficult period of time. Contact these groups and see what they can do for you. Many of the national organizations listed have local chapters in most parts of the country. There are also many local organizations that are not affiliates of national organizations and are not listed here. So take a look in your phone book. You may be surprised by the amount of information that you will find there. Also, talk with your doctor, nurse, social worker, and religious leader. Your local library is another excellent resource. Librarians can assist you in finding the resources that are right for you. Many libraries have audio or talking books, large print materials, and Braille resources available. Not only will they be able to help you find other good reference materials and listings of local information and support groups, but they may help you with the Internet if this is new to you.

Dead

This is where I died
This is where I hide
This is my only place
This is like a vase

It is like a vase,
A person case,
Holding a flower
Until its last hour.

NICHOLAS GUY LYNN

Child of 7, undergoing chemotherapy (when asked to explain, the author printed "It's like a vase because a coffin holds a person like a vase holds a flower.")

Some of these resources will be more helpful than others. One of the best Internet sites we have found is *Growth House* (http://www.growthhouse.org). This Web site has a very comprehensive collection of information, including such topics as hospice and home care, palliative care and pain management, death with dignity, depression, anxiety, and grief. The search capabilities of Growth House are gradually giving you access to all the Web resources with just one stop.

Locally compiled Resource Guides can be quite helpful in locating local organizations. Unfortunately, the guides themselves are sometimes difficult to locate. These guides often list many of your local agencies that will be able to help you deal with issues such as nutrition, legal services, recreation, homecare, and other supportive services. It is suggested that you contact your local Office on Aging or check the yellow pages under headings such as Senior Services, Health Care Management, or Home Health Services.

I. Issue-Specific

A. Advance Directives, Treatment Decisions, and Law

Choice in Dying, Inc.
1035 30th Street, NW
Washington, DC 20016
202-338-9790
800-989-WILL (9455)
Internet Address: http://www.choices.org
Choice in Dying provides advance directive forms, counsels patients and families, trains professionals, advocates for improved laws, and offers a range of publications and services, all aimed to improve patients' control over their choices. You can get any state's current laws on medical decision-making over the Internet or through the toll-free phone number listed above. Choice in Dying also offers booklets on various end-of-life issues, including "Advance Directives."

Medic Alert (Bracelet information)
800-825-3785
If a medical emergency should arise, a call to the Medic Alert's 24-hour Emergency Response Center transmits your vital medical facts, or your "Do Not Resuscitate" order, to the responding paramedics.

Lawyer Referral and Information Service
Local Bar Association
Check your local phone book for the listing.

National Academy of Elder Law Attorneys
1604 North Country Club Road
Tucson, AZ 85716-3102
520-881-4005
Consumers calling the Academy can obtain a free copy of the Questions and Answers When Looking for an Elder Law Attorney *pamphlet covering issues such as where to find an attorney, what questions to ask, discussing fees, and more. To receive a copy, send a self-addressed stamped envelope (legal size). NAELA does not provide referrals, but consumers can purchase the Experience Registry for $25.*

AARP. *Shape Your Health Care Future with Health Care Advance Directives*
To order, call 800-424-2277 (cost $2.00) or write to:
AARP-AD
PO Box 51040
Washington, DC 20091

HARWELL, AMY. *Ready to Live, Prepared to Die — A Provocative Guide to the Rest of Your Life.* Wheaton, IL: Harold Shaw Publications, 1995.

LYNN, JOANNE (ED). *By No Extraordinary Means: The Choice to Forgo Life-Sustaining Food and Water.* Bloomington, IN: Indiana University Press, 1989.

PEARLMAN R, STARKS H, CAIN K, COLE W, ROSENGREN D, AND PATRICK D. *Your Life Your Choices: Planning for Future Medical Decisions: How to Prepare a Personalized Living Will.*
For information call 206-764-2308.

B. Bereavement

COMPASSIONATE FRIENDS, NATIONAL HEADQUARTERS
PO Box 3696
Oak Brook, IL 60522-3696
630-990-0010
Internet Address: http://www.compassionatefriends.org
Offers bereavement support to families that have experienced the death of a child. The National Headquarters can direct you to one of the over 550 volunteer-run chapters around the country, and have printed materials available for distribution.

GRIEFNET
Internet Address: http://www.rivendell.org
Internet site offering information and support via Internet or e-mail.

WEBSTER'S DEATH, DYING & GRIEF GUIDE
Internet Address: http://www.katsden.com/death/index.html
Internet site with many helpful links. Topics include grief, aging, caregiving, eulogies, funerals, depression, hospice, homecare, palliative care, children, and a list of other Web sites.

BERTMAN, SANDRA L. *Facing Death: Images, Insights and Interventions*. New York: Taylor & Francis, 1991.

Collection of short fiction, traditional and contemporary art, and popular culture to stimulate dialogue and understanding of chronic and terminal illness, enable grieving and provide consolation regardless of age or background. Particularly useful for family and caregivers.

GLADU E, BOUVARD MG, AND BERTMAN SL. *The Path Through Grief: A Compassionate Guide*. New York: Prometheus Books, 1998.

C. Caregiving

ALZHEIMER'S CAREGIVING STRATEGIES (CD-ROM).

Provides basic information on Alzheimer's disease; a tool to assess the relative severity, or stage, of dementia; and stage-specific strategies for day-to-day dementia care. For cost and ordering information, call 888-824-3020 or write:
HealthCare Interactive
PO Box 19646
Minneapolis, MN 55419

ELDERCARE LOCATOR
800-677-1116
Internet Address: http://www.aoa.dhhs.gov
Use the Eldercare Locator to find the Area Agency on Aging for the location of your choice. The telephone book will also list, in the White Pages or Blue Pages, a number of resources for your area.

FAMILY CAREGIVERS ALLIANCE
425 Bush Street, Suite 500
San Francisco, CA 94108
415-434-3388
E-mail Address: info@caregiver.org
Internet Address: http://www.caregiver.org
Support organization for caregivers of adults with Alzheimer's disease, stroke, traumatic brain injury, Parkinson's disease, ALS, and related brain disorders.

NATIONAL FEDERATION OF INTERFAITH VOLUNTEER CAREGIVERS
Internet Address: http://www.nfivc.org
The mission of this group is to promote diversity and interfaith initiatives for volunteer caregiving in local communities.

BEEDLE J. *The Carebook: A Workbook for Caregiver Peace of Mind.*
This workbook focuses on caregiving needs for the person with Alzheimer's disease or other debilitating illnesses. This book will keep all the information on the person you are caring for in one spot and contains helpful caregiver hints. For more information call 503-760-5750, or write to:
"The Carebook"
6622 SE 108th
Portland, OR 97266

CARTER R, GOLANT SK. *Helping Yourself Help Others: A Book for Caregivers. New York: Times Books, 1996.*

D. Care Management, Resource and Benefit Coordination

Check the yellow pages of your phone book to find a local care management office.

ALLIANCE FOR AGING RESEARCH. *Health Care Options Under Medicare: The Choice Is Yours.* To order your free guide, write to:
Alliance for Aging Research
2021 K Street, NW Suite 305
Washington, DC 20006-1003
202-293-2856

CHILDREN OF AGING PARENTS
1609 Woodbourne Road, Suite 302A
Levittown, PA 19057-1511
215-945-6900
800-227-7294
Services include contacts and phone numbers for information and referral on caregiving issues, housing, and respite care. Access to support groups and educational materials are also available.

DEPARTMENT OF VETERANS AFFAIRS
Office of Public Affairs
Washington, DC 20420
202-273-5700
Internet Address: http//www.va.gov
Provides a wide range of services for eligible veterans.

EMERGENCY RESPONSE SYSTEMS
There are a number of emergency response services available from various companies. Some private care managers provide this service, and there are companies that specialize in this service. For a listing of companies in your area, check your local yellow pages or contact Children of Aging Parents: 800-227-7294.

FSC (FAMILY SUPPORT CENTER) FOR MILITARY PERSONNEL
See your Base Bulletin or the Kaiserslautern American Newspaper

NATIONAL ASSOCIATION OF PROFESSIONAL GERIATRIC CARE MANAGERS
1604 North Country Club Road
Tucson, AZ 85716
520-881-8008
This organization provides a pamphlet describing what care management is and what to look for when hiring a Care Manager. A national referral directory of member Care Managers is also available for $15.

RESOURCE CONNECTORS, LTD. *The Healthcare Notebook*
This notebook can be individualized to address special needs. It contains all the needed information on the person receiving care and includes tools for working with community resources, health care providers, sample "Advance Directives" tools and "Physician Orders for Life-Sustaining Treatment." For further information call 503-228-7023 or 360-750-7321 or write:
"The Healthcare Notebook"
Resource Connectors, Ltd.
5520 SW Macadam, Suite 270
Portland, OR 97201

THE UNITED WAY OF AMERICA
701 North Fairfax Street
Alexandria, VA 22314-2045
703-836-7100
Internet Address: http://www.unitedway.org
The organization provides lists of local United Way organizations across the country, and provides a national database and access to local chapters that have comprehensive information and referral.

E. Children

AMERICAN SIDS (SUDDEN INFANT DEATH SYNDROME) INSTITUTE
6065 Roswell Road, Suite 876
Atlanta, GA 30328
Voice Mail: 404-843-1030
E-mail: prevent@sids.org
Internet Address: http://www.sids.org
Dedicated to the prevention of Sudden Infant Death Syndrome and the promotion of infant health through research, clinical services, family support, and professional and community education.

BRAIN TUMOR FOUNDATION FOR CHILDREN, INC.
2231 Perimeter Park Drive, Suite 9
Atlanta, GA 30341
770-458-5554
This organization provides family support, educational programs, a speakers' bureau, and a telephone network.

CANDLELIGHTERS CHILDHOOD CANCER FOUNDATION
7910 Woodmont Avenue, Suite 460
Bethesda, MD 20814
301-657-8401
800-366-2223
This organization provides help to children and their parents through a network of peer-support groups, a newsletter, counseling, speakers' bureau, pain management, and access to information and educational materials.

GUNTHER, JOHN. *Death Be Not Proud; A Memoir.* New York: Buccaneer, 1997.

RAWLINGS, MARJORIE KINNAN. *The Yearling.* Atheneum, 1985.

SCHAEFER, DAN AND LYONS, CHRISTINE. *How Do We Tell the Children?: A Step-By-Step Guide for Helping Children Two to Teen Cope When Someone Dies.* New York: Newmarket Press, 1993.

SEGAL, LORE AND MARSHALL, JAMES. *All the Way Home.* Farrar, Straus & Giroux, 1988.

VARLEY, SUSAN. *Badger's Parting Gifts.* Lothrop, Lee & Shepard, 1984.

VREDEVELT, PAM W. *Empty Arms: Emotional Support for Those Who Have Suffered Miscarriage or Stillbirth.* Questar Publishing, 1995.

F. Counseling and Support

AMERICAN ASSOCIATION FOR GERIATRIC PSYCHIATRY
7910 Woodmont Avenue
Suite 1350
Bethesda, MD 20814
301-654-7850
E-mail Address: aagpgpa@aol.com
Internet Address: http://www.aagpgpa.org
The organization provides referrals for geriatric psychiatrists and written materials for patients, families, and caregivers.

AMERICAN PSYCHOLOGICAL ASSOCIATION
750 First Street, NE
Washington, DC 20002-4242
202-336-5700
TDD: 202-336-6123
Internet Address: http://www.apa.org
The Association has state chapters that offer referral services, investigate complaints, and can provide public education materials.

NATIONAL MENTAL HEALTH ASSOCIATION
1021 Prince Street
Alexandria, VA 22314-2971
703-684-7722
800-969-6642
Toll-free (information read aloud or faxed): 888-836-6070
The Association is dedicated to improving the mental health of all individuals and provides a variety of public education materials.

KÜBLER-ROSS, ELISABETH. *On Death and Dying.* New York:
Macmillan Publishing Co., 1969.
One of the most famous psychological studies of our time, this classic grew out of one of the author's interdisciplinary seminars on death. Sample interviews and conversations provide a better understanding of the effects that imminent death has on patients and their families.

G. Funerals and Memorials

FUNERAL & MEMORIAL SOCIETIES OF AMERICA
P.O. Box 10
Hinesburg, VT 05461
800-765-0107
Internet Address: http://www.funerals.org/famsa

A non-profit organization with 120 local chapters around the country. Call the 800 number to find the chapter closest to you. The organization maintains a funeral price survey as well as materials on a wide range of funeral services available.

FUNERALNET
Internet Address: http://www.funeralnet.com

Offers comprehensive funeral home directories for the U.S. and Canada as well as information on funerals, cremations, cemeteries, and other related subjects. A special section for all retired and active U.S. military personnel covers the services you are entitled to receive.

H. Hospice and Home Health Services

HOSPICE EDUCATION INSTITUTE
190 Westbrook Road
Essex, CT 06426
860-767-1620
E-mail Address: hospiceall@aol.com
Web page Address: http://www.hospiceworld.org

Services include toll-free information and referral, educational materials and seminars, advice, and assistance.

HOSPICE FOUNDATION OF AMERICA (HFA)
2001 S. St. NW, Suite 300
Washington, DC 20009
202-638-5419
E-mail Address: hfa@hospicefoundation.org
Internet Address: http://www.hospicefoundation.org

HFA not only provides general information about hospice, but also will aid you in locating a hospice near you, refer you to related organizations, and share hospice stories and resources that it has collected.

NATIONAL ASSOCIATION OF HOME CARE
228 7th St., SE
Washington, DC 20003
202-547-7424
Internet Address: http://www.nahc.org
   This organization can provide information on available resources (most will be member organizations) and materials about homecare services.

NATIONAL HOSPICE ORGANIZATION (NHO)
Internet Address: http://www.nho.org
   NHO is dedicated to promoting and maintaining quality care for terminally ill persons and their families, and to making hospice an integral part of the U.S. health care system. The Internet site will help you find a hospice.
The NHO Store
200 State Road
South Deerfield, MA 01373-0200
800-646-6460
   The NHO Store offers both professional and consumer-oriented materials.

I. Organ Donation

UNITED NETWORK FOR ORGAN SHARING (UNOS)
888-894-6361
Internet Address: http://www.unos.org
   Through the UNOS Organ Center, organ donors are matched to waiting recipients, 24 hours a day, 365 days a year.

J. Pain and Symptom Management

AMERICAN CHRONIC PAIN ASSOCIATION
PO Box 850
Rocklin, CA 95677-0850
916-632-0922
   This is a membership-based organization that provides support for those suffering from chronic pain, has over 800 local chapters, and provides written educational materials.

MAYDAY PAIN RESOURCE CENTER
  City of Hope National Medical Center
  1500 Duarte Road
  Duarte, CA 91010
  626-359-8111 ext. 3829
  E-mail Address: maydaypain@smtplink.coh.org
    The consumer may want to recommend this center to his or her health care provider. It is a resource for health professionals that covers information about pain management.

NATIONAL CHRONIC PAIN OUTREACH ASSOCIATION
  7979 Old Georgetown Road, Suite 100
  Bethesda, MD 20814-2429
  301-652-4948
    Serves as a clearinghouse of information related to chronic pain and provides written materials.

PHARMINFO NET
  Internet Address: http://www.pharminfo.com
    The Pharmaceutical Information Network is provided by VirSci Corporation, a company not associated with any pharmaceutical company. A broad range of information and educational materials is available.

There are Indigent Drug Programs available through a number of drug companies. In order to access these programs, your physician must apply to these programs on your behalf. Certain states have Pharmaceutical Assistance Programs, which are operated by state governments. To get a listing of the companies and states with these programs, contact Cancer Care, Inc. (p. 210), for a copy of *A Helping Hand: The Resource Guide for People with Cancer.*

K. Spiritual Concerns and Complementary Care

AMERICAN SELF-HELP CLEARINGHOUSE
  St. Clare's Health Services
  25 Pocono Road
  Denville, NJ 07834-2995
  973-625-9565
  TDD 973-625-9053
    Services include a national directory of over 4,000 local self-help groups.

CENTER FOR ATTITUDINAL HEALING
33 Buchanan Drive
Sausalito, CA 94965
415-331-6161
E-mail Address: cah@well.com
Internet Address: http://www.healingcenter.org
This agency provides an AIDS hotline for kids, counseling, support groups, referrals, and a speakers' bureau.

NATIONAL SELF-HELP CLEARINGHOUSE
Graduate School and University of the City of New York
25 West 43rd Street Room 620
New York, NY 10036
212-642-2929
Provides information and referral services and assistance with self-help groups and community support systems.

BORNAT, JOANNA (ED.). *Reminiscence Reviewed: Evaluations, Achievements, Perspectives (Rethinking Aging).* Bristol, PA: Open University Press, 1994.
Medical, health care, and social workers reflect on their use of reminiscence and recall as part of the care of older people. May be of interest to anyone who cares for the elderly.

KUSHNER, HAROLD. *When Bad Things Happen to Good People.* New York: Schocken Books, 1981.
Harold Kushner, a Jewish rabbi facing his own child's fatal illness, deftly guides us through the inadequacies of the traditional answers to the problem of evil, then provides a uniquely practical and compassionate answer that has appealed to millions of readers across all religious creeds.

REMEN, M.D., NAOMI RACHEL. *Kitchen Table Wisdom — Stories That Heal.* New York: Riverhead Books, 1996.
Remen, a physician, therapist, professor of medicine, and long-term survivor of chronic illness, is also a down-home storyteller. Every story guides us like a life compass, showing us what's good and lasting about ourselves as well as humanity.

SATTERLY, LAMONT R. AND BOYLE, MICHAEL J. (ILLUSTRATOR). *If I Should Wake Before I Die — Healing Words for Dying People.* Search Foundation, 1997.

II. Diseases

Increasing your understanding of the condition or disease you face provides a greater sense of control and sense of direction. Though it may seem that there are only a few organizations listed, keep in mind that each of these organizations may simply be a starting point. Along with the information these groups distribute, they can also introduce you to the network of other organizations, both local and national, that may be even more useful.

A. Alzheimer's and Other Dementias

ALZHEIMER'S ASSOCIATION
919 N. Michigan Ave. Suite 1000
Chicago, IL 60611
800-272-3900
TDD: 312-335-8882
Internet Address: http://www.alz.org
A national voluntary organization that focuses on education, information and referral, and support to people with Alzheimer's disease, their families, and caregivers. Many local chapters with excellent access to support groups and special services.

ALZHEIMER'S DISEASE EDUCATION & REFERRAL CENTER
P.O. Box 8250
Silver Spring, MD 20907-8250
800-438-4380
E-mail Address: adear@alzheimers.org
The Center provides information about the disease and related issues for patients, their families, and the general public.

MACE, NANCY L. AND RABINS, PETER V. *The 36-Hour Day/ A Guide to Caring for Persons With Alzheimer's Disease, Related Dementing Illnesses and Memory Loss in Later Years.* Warner Books, 1994.
Combining practical advice with specific examples, this is a newly revised, updated, and comprehensive edition, and is a helpful guide for people dealing with these care issues.

B. Cancer

AMERICAN BRAIN TUMOR ASSOCIATION
2720 River Road, Suite 146
Des Plaines, IL 60018
800-886-2282
847-827-9910
This national organization assists people with brain tumors and provides a listing of support groups, a pen-pal program, newsletter, and information on treatment facilities.

AMERICAN CANCER SOCIETY
1599 Clifton Rd., N.E.
Atlanta, GA 30329
404-320-3333
800-227-2345
Internet Address: http://www.cancer.org
ACS is a national voluntary organization that focuses on research, education, advocacy, and service. Patient and community services are available but vary with the chapter.

CANCER CARE, INC.
1180 Avenue of the Americas, 2nd Floor
New York, NY 10036
212-221-3300 (National Office)
800-813-HOPE (4673)
E-mail Address: info@cancercare.org
Internet Address: http://www.cancercareinc.org
This is a national organization that serves people with cancer and their families through counseling, support groups, and educational programs. Help line and various materials available for cancer patients.

CANCER INFORMATION SERVICE
Johns Hopkins Oncology Center
550 Broadway, Suite 300
Baltimore, MD, 21205
800-422-6237
This program is part of the National Cancer Institute and provides people with cancer, their families, and health professionals current information. Their regional offices refer people to services and resources such as FDA-accredited mammography facilities and licensed genetic counselors.

CHEMOTHERAPY FOUNDATION
183 Madison Avenue, Suite 403
New York, NY 10016
212-213-9292
This organization is dedicated to educating both professionals and the public regarding chemotherapy. A variety of pamphlets are available as well as a semi-annual newsletter.

NATIONAL CANCER INSTITUTE
Cancer Information Services
P.O. Box 24128
Baltimore, MD 21227
800-422-6237
Internet Address: http: //www.nci.nih.gov
The Institute provides patient information through its Web site and a toll-free number.

C. Chronic Heart or Lung Disease

AMERICAN ASSOCIATION OF CARDIOVASCULAR AND PULMONARY REHABILITATION
7611 Elmwood Ave., Suite 201
Middleton, WI 53562
608-831-6989
E-mail Address: aacvpr@tmahq.com
Internet Address: http://www.aacvpr.org
This organization provides many products, audiovisual materials, and publications for the general public.

AMERICAN HEART ASSOCIATION
National Center
7272 Greenville Ave.
Dallas, TX 75231-4596
214-373-6300
800-242-8721
Internet Address: http://www.amhrt.org
This national voluntary organization provides information and referral, public education programs, and events, as well as written materials.

Lung Disease Support Assistance
American Lung Association
1600 Race Street
Denver, CO 80206
303-388-4327
FAX: 303-377-1102
Supportive assistance designed for persons with or interested in learning more about lung disease.

D. Diabetes

American Diabetic Association
1660 Duke Street
Alexandria, VA 22314
703-549-1500
800-232-3472
Internet Address: http://www.diabetes.org
This organization, with its local chapters, provides educational materials, support services, information, and referral aimed at improving the lives of persons with diabetes.

E. Frail Elderly

Meals on Wheels Council, Inc.
A volunteer program that provides one hot meal and a light supper once each day, five days a week, to the homebound. Weekend delivery is available in some locations. Fees vary; contact your local agency (check the listing in your local yellow pages) for more information or for meals to serve the frail elderly.

National Institute on Aging
Information
P.O. Box 8507
Gaithersburg, MD 20898-8057
800-222-2225
In addition to research, NIA is dedicated to education, training, information, and referral. A broad range of written materials is available, as well as information on special activities and media presentations.

VOLUNTEERS OF AMERICA
National Office
110 South Union Street
Alexandria, VA 22314-3324
800-899-0089
E-mail Address: voa@voa.org
Internet Address: http://www.voa.org
   A community-based organization that offers a variety of client services for those most in need.

F. HIV/AIDS

HIV-AIDS TREATMENT INFORMATION SERVICE
P.O. Box 6303
Rockville, MD 20849
800-448-0440
Internet Address: http://www.hivatis.org
   Information resource on federally approved treatments for HIV infection. Distributes treatment-related publications.

NATIONAL ASSOCIATION OF PEOPLE WITH AIDS
1413 K St., NW
Washington, DC 20005-3442
202-898-0414
Internet Address: http://www.napwa.org
   This organization serves as a national information and resource base.

THE BODY: A MULTIMEDIA AIDS & HIV INFORMATION RESOURCE
Internet Address: http://www.thebody.com
   An Internet site that allows you to connect with others, find where to get help, and obtain useful information about HIV and AIDS.

G. Kidney Failure

NATIONAL KIDNEY FOUNDATION
30 East 33rd St.
New York, NY 10016
Internet Address: http://www.kidney.org
   Among its many goals, the Foundation strives to improve the health and well-being of individuals affected by kidney diseases and to educate the public.

National Kidney & Urologic Diseases Information
Clearinghouse
3 Information Way
Bethesda, MD 20892-3580
301-654-4415
E-mail Address: nkuic@aeroe.com
Internet Address: http://www.niddk.nih.gov
   The Clearinghouse provides information about diseases of the kidney and urologic system.

H. Liver Failure

American Liver Foundation
   1425 Pompton Avenue
   Cedar Grove, NJ 07009
   800-465-4837
   Internet Address: http://www.liverfoundation.org
   At a small cost, pamphlets and information can be mailed to you. Their Web site has free information as well as links to other sites with liver information.

I. Neuromuscular Disease

The Amyotrophic Lateral Sclerosis Association (Lou
   Gehrig's Disease)
   21021 Ventura Boulevard, Suite 321
   Woodland Hills, CA 91364
   818-340-7500
   800-782-4747
   Internet Address: http://www.alsa.org
   A national voluntary organization focused on patient support, education, and information dissemination.

The Muscular Dystrophy Association
   National Headquarters
   3300 East Sunrise Drive
   Tucson, AZ 85718-3208
   520-529-2000
   800-572-1717
   Internet Address: http://www.mdausa.org
   The Association provides support services, an information hotline, and educational materials.

THE NATIONAL MULTIPLE SCLEROSIS SOCIETY
733 Third Ave., 6th floor
New York, NY 10017-3288
212-986-3240
800-344-4867
Internet Address: http://www.nmss.org
   The organization provides information and referral, counseling and self-help groups, special activities and programs, and written materials.

J. Parkinson's Disease

AMERICAN PARKINSON'S DISEASE ASSOCIATION
1250 Hylan Boulevard, Suite 4B
Staten Island, NY 10305-1946
800-223-APDA
Internet Address: http://www.apdaparkinson.com
   A voluntary organization that provides patient education, support services, and written materials.

UNITED PARKINSON FOUNDATION
833 West Washington Boulevard
Chicago, IL 60607
312-733-1893
E-mail Address: upf_itf@msn.com
   An international organization that provides extensive information and referral service, patient and family education materials and programs, and support services.

DUVOISIN, ROGER C. *Parkinson's Disease: A Guide for Patient and Family.* New York: Raven Press, 1996.

K. Stroke

NATIONAL STROKE ASSOCIATION
96 Inverness Dr. East
Suite I
Englewood, CO 80111-5015
800-STROKES (800-787-6537)
Internet Address: http://www.stroke.org
   This national organization is dedicated to prevention, treatment, research, and rehabilitation, and provides a variety of services for stroke survivors and their families.

STROKE CONNECTION OF THE AMERICAN HEART ASSOCIATION
7272 Greenville Avenue
Dallas, TX 75231
800-553-6321
E-mail Address: strokaha@amhrt.org
Internet Address: http://www.amhrt.org

   Offers information packages ranging from prevention to caregiving. Also maintains a list of 1,300 stroke support groups around the country for referral to stroke survivors, their families, caregivers, and interested professionals. Also publishes Stroke Connection *magazine, a forum for stroke survivors and their families to share information about coping with stroke.*

III. GENERAL INFORMATION AND RESOURCES FOR REFORM

AMERICAN ASSOCIATION OF RETIRED PERSONS (AARP)
601 E Street, NW
Washington, DC 20049
202-434-2277
800-424-2277
E-mail Address: member@aarp.org
Internet Address: http://www.aarp.org

   AARP is a consumer organization that provides a number of services and information with a focus on improving the quality of life for older persons. Services include counseling groups, advocacy, educational materials, information, and assistance to the homebound.

AMERICANS FOR BETTER CARE OF THE DYING
4125 Albemarle St., NW
Washington, DC 20016
202-895-9487
Internet Address: http://www.abcd-caring.com

   A non-profit charity dedicated to social, professional, and policy reform, and to education aimed at improving services for patients with serious illness and their families.

ASSISTED LIVING FEDERATION OF AMERICA
   10300 Eaton Place, Suite 400
   Fairfax, VA 22030
   703-691-8100
   This organization can provide a listing of member-assisted living organizations.

CENTER TO IMPROVE CARE OF THE DYING AT RAND
   1200 S. Hayes St.
   Arlington, VA 22202-5050
   703-413-1100
   E-mail Address: CICO@rand.org
   Internet Address: www.medicaring.org
   A unique interdisiplinary team of committed individuals engaged in research, advocacy, and education activities to improve the care of the dying.

COMPASSION IN DYING
   6312 SW Capital Hwy
   Suite 415
   Portland, OR 97201
   Voice mail: 503-221-9556
   E-mail Address: info@compassionindying.org
   Internet Address: http://www.CompassionInDying.org
   Compassion in Dying and its affiliates offer information and emotional support for all end-of-life options, including intensive pain management, comfort or hospice care, and humane, effective aid-in-dying for those who are in the final stages of illness and whose suffering has become intolerable.

GROWTH HOUSE
   Internet Address: http://www.growthhouse.org
   An award-winning Web site providing resources on life-threatening illnesses and end-of-life issues ranging from hospice care and pain management to grief and bereavement. Their own online search engine offers quick access to a comprehensive collection of information and issue-specific internet links. Also available are a chat room and an online bookstore.

HEALTHFINDER
Internet Address: http://www.healthfinder.gov/
A health and human services information Web site. Can guide you to online publications, clearinghouses, databases, other Web sites, and support and self-help groups. Government agencies and not-for-profit organizations that have been found to provide reliable information are also listed in this Web site.

LAST ACTS
Internet Address: http://lastacts.rwjf.org
A call-to-action campaign designed to improve care at the end of life. The goal is to bring end-of-life issues out into the open and to help individuals and organizations pursue the search for better ways to care for the dying.

THE END OF LIFE — EXPLORING DEATH IN AMERICA
National Public Radio (NPR)
Internet Address:
http://www.npr.org/programs/death/readings/essays/gartan.html

PROJECT ON DEATH IN AMERICA
Internet Address: http://www.soros.org/death.html
Seeks to understand and transform the culture and experience of dying and bereavement in the U.S. through support for initiatives in research, education, the arts, and public policy.

ALBOM, MITCH. *Tuesdays with Morrie: An Old Man, a Young Man, and the Last Great Lesson.* New York: Doubleday, 1997.

BYOCK, IRA. *Dying Well: A Prospect for Growth at the End of Life.* New York: Riverhead Books, 1997.
None of us gets out of here alive, but reading this book will lessen your fear of the ultimate end and give you some guidance about enjoying your life to the fullest right up until your final moment.

DOKA, KENNETH J. *Living With Life-Threatening Illness: A Guide for Patients, Their Families, and Caregivers.* Lexington Books, April 1993.

MILLER, JAMES E. *When You Know You're Dying — Twelve Thoughts to Guide You Through the Days Ahead.* Willowgreen Publishing, 1997.

NULAND, SHERWIN B. *How We Die: Reflections on Life's Final Chapter.* New York: Alfred A. Knopf, 1994.

The author has used his experience and knowledge to explore the meaning of death. His approach is straightforward and personalized. Included are the author's insights and recommendations.

QUILL, M.D., TIMOTHY. *A Midwife Through the Dying Process.* John Hopkins University Press, November 1, 1996.

Dr. Timothy Quill examines the partnership and the complex end-of-life issues that surround physician-assisted death, demonstrating the tension inherent between the fight for life and the mandate to relieve suffering.

THE TASK-FORCE TO IMPROVE THE CARE OF TERMINALLY-ILL OREGONIANS. *The Oregon Death with Dignity Act: A Guidebook for Health Care Providers.* Portland OR: OHSU Center for Ethics in Health Care, 1998. For an order form, write to:
OHSU Center for Ethics in Health Care
3181 SW Sam Jackson Park Road
Portland, OR 97201

SEAKWOOD, JOHN (PRODUCER/DIRECTOR).
Walk Me to the Water: three people in their time of dying. (Video.)

An award-winning program that portrays the special needs and insights of the dying and their families. For additional information contact:
"Walk Me to the Water"
100 Bird Road
PO Box 55
Lebanon, NY 12125
518-794-8081

IV. PERSONAL RESOURCES

If you find something worth sharing with others, please do so. If you would like to send us the resources you have found, or things we have included that weren't as helpful as you had hoped, please e-mail your comments (cicd@gwu.edu) or mail them to:
The Center to Improve Care of the Dying
2175 K. Street, NW
Suite 820
Washington, DC 20037

∾ Acknowledgments ∾

INTRODUCTION

1. Eighty-two-year-old blind woman with heart and lung failure.

1, 3. Photo by Doug Barber. (301) 855-2295. Web address: http://members.aol.com/barberfoto/photos.htm.

2. William Carlos Williams, from *Collected Poems 1939-1962*, Volume II. Copyright 1944 by William Carlos Williams. Reprinted by permission of New Directions Publishing Corp.

4. Walt Whitman, from *Whitman: Leaves of Grass*. New York: First Vintage Books, 1992.

CHAPTER 1

5. Benjamin Spock and Michael B. Rothenberg. *Dr. Spock's Baby and Child Care*. New York: Simon and Schuster Inc., 1992.

5, 14. Photo by Joan Harrold (Hospice of Northern Virginia).

6. Reprinted by permission of Louisiana State University from *In All This Rain*, by John Stone. Copyright © 1980 by John Stone.

7. Adapted from *Dying Well: The Prospect for Growth at the End of Life*, by Ira Byock. New York: Riverhead Books, 1997.

8. Photo by Barry Lynn.

9. Patient with a serious illness. See above, p. 5, 14.

10. Hospice patient who died one hour later. Richard J. Smith, MD (Hampden, ME).

12. Used with permission by On Lok Senior Health Services, San Francisco, CA.

13. Sharon Olds, "Grandmother Love Poem," from: *The Dead and the Living*. New York: Random House, 1985. Used with permission.

CHAPTER 2

15, 25. Zen hospital director, Frank Ostaseski, with hospice resident. Photo by Russell Curtis (1996). Used with permission.

15. Norma.

16. Thomas Mann. *The Magic Mountain.* New York: Alfred A. Knopf, Inc., 1955.

17. Photo by Debora Hunter (Southern Methodist University), with the cooperation of the Visiting Nurse Association in Dallas, TX and Evanston, IL. Used with permission.

19. Photo by Rob Crandall (Arlington, VA). Used with permission.

20. "Mother and Daughter." Photo by Sandra Bertman. Palliative Care Project, UMMC/Ward St. Studio, Newton, MA. Used with permission.

22. Alan Marks, as quoted in The Washington Post, "The Life of the Party: Dying Stockbroker Alan Marks Is Guest of honor at His Wake." February 16, 1998:D1.

24. Mitch Albom. *Tuesdays with Morrie: An Old Man, a Young Man, and Life's Greatest Lesson.* New York: Doubleday, 1997.

26. Rebecca Brown. *The Gifts of the Body.* New York: Harper Perennial Library, 1995.

CHAPTER 3

27, 37. See above, p. 1,3.

27. Steven A. Schmidt. When You Come Into My Room. *Journal of the American Medical Association* 1996; 276:512. Copyright: 1996, American Medical Association. Used with permission.

28. Used with permission of Gara LaMarche, Director of the U.S. Programs of the Open Society Institute, New York, NY.

29. "Illness and Healing," from Robert Pope's *Illness and Healing.* Hantsport, Nova Scotia: Lancelot Press, 1991. Used with permission of the Robert Pope Foundation.

31. From *The Country Road,* by James Laughlin, Zoland Books, Cambridge, Massachusetts. Copyright 1994 by James Laughlin. Used with permission.

31. Used with permission of Rabbi Kenneth L. Cohen, Bethesda, MD.

33. Mother Julian of Norwich, in *Dying: A Book of Comfort*, Pat McNees, editor. New York: Doubleday Direct, 1996.

34. Reverend Patrick McCoy, Director of Chaplaincy, Dartmouth-Hitchcock Medical Center, Lebanon, NH. Dr. Thomas Smith, Executive Director, National Institute for Healthcare Research, Rockville, MD.

35. Ellen Glascow. *Barren Ground*. New York: Harcourt Brace, 1985.

37. See above, p. 1, 3.

38. Anonymous. Beth Baker, "The Faith Factor." *Common Boundary Magazine*, July/August 1997, p. 20-26.

CHAPTER 4

39, 46. "Meredith Rose helps her great-grandmother Mary walk across the yard." Photo by Janice Lynch Schuster.

39. Robert J. Samuelson, "Death With Common Sense." *Washington Post*, Wednesday, July 19, 1995; pg. A21.

40. Daughter of a Cancer Patient, from Video Vignette Trigger Tapes. See above, p. 20.

42. Photo used with permission from the video, "Walk Me to the Water," an award winning program that portrays the special needs and insights of the dying and their families. For additional information, contact "Walk Me to the Water," 100 Bird Road, PO Box 55, New Lebanon, NY 12125. (518-794-8081).

43. Wallace Stegner. *Crossing to Safety*. New York: Random House; 1987.

44. Photo by Joanne Lynn at the Washington Home.

45. Rosalynn Carter & Susan K. Golant. *Helping Yourself Help Others: A Book for Caregivers*. New York: Times Books, 1996.

CHAPTER 5

47, 54. Photo by Thomas Treuter, used with permission from Hospice of Michigan.

47. Robert Stinson, from *The Long Dying of Baby Andrew* by Robert & Peggy Stinson. Boston: Little, Brown and Company, 1983.

48. See above, p. 44.

49. A family member.

51. Photo courtesy of the Program of Medical Humanities, UMASS Medical Center, Worcester, MA. Used with permission.

52. Sherwin B. Nuland. *How We Die: Reflections on Life's Final Chapter*. New York: Alfred A. Knopf, Inc., 1994.

53. See above, p. 12.

CHAPTER 6

57. Photo courtesy of the DANA Project, Bertman Archives, Ward Street Studio, Newton, MA.

57. Photo courtesy of the DANA Project. See above, p. 20.

58. Excerpt from W. H. Auden, "The Art of Healing," from *W.H. Auden: Collected Poems*. New York: Random House; © 1969 by W.H. Auden. Used with permission.

59. Photo by Mary Fisher, taken from *Angels in Our Midst*, published by Moyer Bell. Used with permission.

60. National Institute on Aging. *Talking with your Doctor: A Guide for Older People*. December 1994.

64. Photo courtesy of the Bertman Archives. See above, p. 20.

65. See above, p. 59.

66. See above, p. 17.

69. Photo by Sandra L. Bertman, from *Facing Death: Images, Insights, and Interventions*. Bristol, PA: Taylor & Francis 1991.

70. "Patient and Doctor." See above, p. 64.

CHAPTER 7

71, 77. See above, p. 44.

71. William Carlos Williams. *Collected Poems, 1909-1939. Vol. I.* Copyright 1938 by New Directions Pub. Corp. Reprinted by permission of New Directions Publ. Corp.

72. A. Jacox, D.B. Carr, R. Payne, et al. *Management of Cancer Pain. Clinical Practice Guideline* No. 9. AHCPR Publication No. 94-0592. Rockville, MD. Agency for Health Care Policy and Research, U.S. Department of Health and Human Services, Public Health Service, March 1994.

76. Reynolds Price. *A Whole New Life: An Illness and a Healing*. New York: Atheneum, 1994.

78. Paul Wilkes, "Dying Well Is the Best Revenge." *The New York Times Magazine*, July 6, 1997; pp. 32-38.

80. See above, p. 44.

81. Charles Frazier. *Cold Mountain*. New York: Atlantic Monthly Press, 1997.

83. Archie Cochran. One Man's Medicine: An Autobiography of Professor Archie Cochran. *British Medical Journal*, 1989.

84. Photo by George Gryzenia, used with permission of Hospice of Michigan.

Chapter 8

85, 91. Photo by Joanne Lynn.

85. L.M. Liegner. St. Christopher's Hospice 1974: Care of the Dying Patient. *JAMA* 1975; 234:1047-1048. Copyright 1975, American Medical Association. Used with permission.

86. Peter Siegenthaler (ed). *Emily Dickinson: Collected Poems*. Philadelphia: Courage Books, 1991.

87. See above, p. 69.

89. Tim Brookes. *Catching my Breath: An Asthmatic Explores His Illness*. New York: Vintage Books, 1995.

92. See above, p. 1, 3.

Chapter 9

93, 97. See above, p. 44.

93. Dody Shall, 7 year breast cancer survivor, Texas. Taken from Shirley M. Gullo's *Silver Linings: The Other Side of Cancer*. Pittsburgh, PA: Oncology Nursing Press, Inc., 1997.

96. See above, p. 86.

99. James Dickey, from *The Eye-Beaters, Blood, Victory, Madness, Buckhead*. New York: Doubleday, 1970. Used with permission.

100. Photo courtesy of Margaret Campbell, Detroit, MI.

101. William Shakespeare, *King Richard II*; Act ii Sc. 1.

103. See above, p. 17.

104. See above, p. 17.

106. S. Haywood, from Mark Rosenberg's *Patients: The Experience of Illness*. See above, p. 93, 97.

107. See above, p. 100.

108. See above, p. 64.

109. Nathaniel Hawthorne. *The American Notebooks*. Claude M. Simpson, (ed), Ohio State University Press, 1972.

110. R. Bergin. *Anthony Perkins: A Haunted Life*. London: Little Brown & Co., 1995.

111. See above, p. 17.

113. Photo courtesy of T. J. Keay, MD, MA-Th. Photograph by Anita S. Frankenberg.

114. James and Hilde Lindemann Nelson. *Alzheimer's: Answers to Hard Questions for Families*. New York: Doubleday, 1996.

115. Photo by Michael Geissinger. Used with permission.

117. Thomas Jefferson, from a letter to John Adams, July 5, 1814.

CHAPTER 10

119, 126. Photo by Anna Kaufman Moon. Used with permission.

119. Jane Kenyon, "Otherwise" from *Otherwise: New and Selected Poems*. St. Paul: Graywolf Press, 1996. Used with permission.

120. "Resident." Photo by Sandra Bertman. Used with permission of Riverside Health Care Center, Missoula, MT.

122. Vermont Ethics Network. *Taking Steps: To Plan for Critical Health Care Decisions*. Montpelier, VT: Leahy Press, 1995.

123. "Sparrow." See above, p. 29.

124. Photos courtesy of Medic Alert.

127. See above, p. 17.

CHAPTER 11

129, 132. See above, p. 44.

129. Raymond Carver, from *Where Water Comes Together With Other Water*. New York: Random House; 1986. Reprinted by permission of International Creative Management, Inc.

130. Michael Vitez. *Final Choices: Seeking the Good Death*. Philadelphia: Camino Books, Inc. 1998.

135. Peggy Stinson. See above, p. 47.

136. William Shakespeare, *Julius Caesar*.

138. "David N. Borkum: The Dignity is the Choice." Used with permission. See above, p. 20.

CHAPTER 12

139, 148. Photo by David Terbush.

139. Rand Richards Cooper. The Dignity of Helplessness. *Commonweal* 1996; 123:12-14.

141. Helen Chen, "Reflections in the Dusk." Translated by her husband, Myles Chen. Used with permission.

142. Photo by Janet Heald Forlini.

143. See above, p. 129.

144. See above, p. 51.

147. Joanne Lynn. "Travels in the Valley of the Shadow." *Empathy and Practice of Medicine*. (Howard Curnen, Enid Peschel and Deborah St. James, eds). New Haven: Yale University Press, 1993.

CHAPTER 13

149, 160. See above, p. 69

149. See above, p. 86.

150. Sarah L. Delany with Amy Hill Hearth. *On My Own at 107: Reflections on Life Without Bessie*. New York: HarperCollins Publishers, 1997. Used with permission from HarperCollins Publishers.

152. "The Death of a Good Old Man," from *The Grave* by Robert Blair. Used with permission of the Clendening History of Medicine Library, Department of History and Philosophy of Medicine, University of Kansas School of Medicine.

153. Alice Walker, *Good Night, Willie Lee, I'll See You in the Morning*. Orlando, FL: Harcourt Brace & Company, 1984. Used with permission.

154. See above, p 150.

157. "Helping Children Cope." Project on Loss and Grief/Charitable Trust, See above, p. 20.

158. See above, p. 64.

159. See above, p. 86.

CHAPTER 14

161, 169. See above, p. 47, 54.

161. See above, p. 135.

162. See above, p. 59.

163. Henry David Thoreau, from a letter to Ralph Waldo Emerson, March 11, 1842, in Harding and Bode's *The Correspondence of Henry David Thoreau*. New York: New York University Press, 1958.

165. Photo by Richard J. Smith, MD.

166. Photo by Brenda Eng, from Sandra Bertman (ed). *Grief and the Healing Arts: Creativity as Therapy*. Courtesy of Baywood Publishing Co., Amityville, NY, 1998.

167. Photo by Chuck Kidd. Barre Rd. Gilbertville, MA. UMASS Medical Center, Program of Medical Humanities.

168. Dr. Seuss. *Horton Hears a Who*. New York: Random House, 1956.

170. "Children, Families, and Death." Project/Charitable Trust. See above, p. 20.

CHAPTER 15

171, 178. Photo by Brad Markel. Used with permission of Liaison Agency, Inc: New York, NY.

171. Madeleine L'Engle. *A Severed Wasp*. New York: Farrar, Straus, Giroux, 1982.

172. Dr. Billy Graham. Prayer Service, Oklahoma City. In: *Requiem for the Heartland: The Oklahoma City Bombing*. San Francisco: Collins Publishers, 1995.

173. Photo by Steve Liss. Used with permission of Liaison Agency, Inc: New York, NY.

175. Photo by Paul Mosely. Used with permission of Star-Telegram: Fort Worth, TX.

CHAPTER 16

179, 192. See above, p. 44.

179. C. S. Lewis, *A Grief Observed*. San Francisco: Harper & Row, Publishers, 1961.

182. Anton Chekhov. *Misery*. Copyright 1972 by Macmillan Company.

183. Photo by Carl Cordonnier; Lille, France. Used with permission.

184. Leo Tolstoy. *The Death of Ivan Ilyich*. New York: Bantam Books, 1987.

184. "In loving memory of John Gordon Hamilton, 'Gordie'," written by Gordon Hamilton for his funeral mass.

188. Photo courtesy of Kathy Vargas: *San Antonio AIDS Foundation: Sharon and Robert Rupp in Their Garden, 1995*. Used with permission.

189. Courtesy of Alan D. Wolfelt, Ph.D., of The Center for Loss and Life Transitions.

190. See above, p. 86.

191. "Louisa." See above, p. 64.

193. Grace Paley, "On Mother's Day," from *Grace Paley: New and Collected Poems*. Gardiner, ME: Tilbury House Publishers, 1992. Used with permission.

194. "The Sweater." Written by Donna Peratino, in memory of her father.

CHAPTER 17

195, 197. See above, p. 1, 3.

195. See above, p. 24.

196. "Dead," by Nicholas Guy Lynn (unpublished).

Index